This book is due for return by the last date shown
above. To avoid paying fines please
renew or return promptly.

**www.portsmouth.gov.uk**

PETER ZIMONJIC

# Into the Darkness

An Account of 7/7

**VINTAGE BOOKS**

London

Published by Vintage 2008

2 4 6 8 10 9 7 5 3 1

Copyright © Peter Zimonjic 2008

Peter Zimonjic has asserted his right under the Copyright, Designs and Patents Act 1988 to be identified as the author of this work

This book is a work of non-fiction. In some limited cases names of people have been changed to protect the privacy of others. The author has stated to the publisher that, except in such minor respects not affecting the substantial accuracy of the work, the contents of this book are true.

First published in Great Britain by Vintage

Vintage
Random House, 20 Vauxhall Bridge Road,
London SW1V 2SA

www.vintage-books.co.uk

Addresses for companies within The Random House Group Limited
can be found at:
www.randomhouse.co.uk/offices.htm

The Random House Group Limited Reg. No. 954009

A CIP catalogue record for this book
is available from the British Library

ISBN 9780099506065

The Random House Group Limited supports The Forest Stewardship Council
(FSC), the leading international forest certification organisation. All our titles
that are printed on Greenpeace approved FSC certified paper carry the FSC
logo. Our paper procurement policy can be found at
www.rbooks.co.uk/environment

Typeset by Palimpsest Book Production Limited,
Grangemouth, Stirlingshire

Printed in the UK by CPI Bookmarque, Croydon, CR0 4TD

FOR DONNA, ANJA AND JAKOB

# Location of bomb sites: London, 7 July 2005

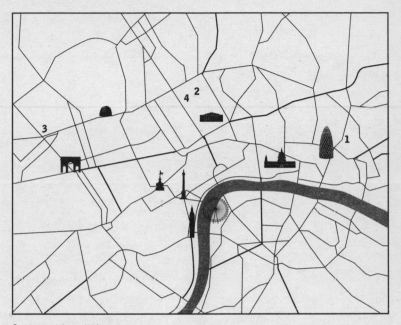

1: Liverpool Street/Aldgate
2: King's Cross/Russell Square
3: Edgware Road
4: Upper Woburn Place/Tavistock Square

# Thursday 7 July 2005, London

It was well before 6.00 a.m. and most of London was still in bed. The roads were quiet. Parliament Square was empty and the rising sun was just beginning to shimmer on the Thames. The city's underground, however, was already buzzing with activity. Postal workers, night cleaners, nurses and doctors packed the carriages of the underground network as if it was the middle of the morning rush hour. It's a face of the tube most never see.

It was probably the same 160 years ago when the first underground steam trains starting running beneath London's streets from Paddington to Farringdon. The late-night shift workers and tradesmen kept the seats warm for the businessmen who would flood the underground a few hours later. Now, as then, the early morning faces were the same every day, on every train, in every carriage. Like Ray Whitehurst, most passengers even took the same seats.

On 7 July 2005 Ray woke early and caught the 5.24 Victoria Line service from Stockwell in south London. He sat in his usual seat in the second carriage from the front and took the train to Oxford Circus where he changed on to the Bakerloo Line bound for Edgware Road.

Ray was an Edgware Road tube driver. He had been reporting there every morning for the past six years to be booked on for his shift. He was due to start at six that morning but he got in a quarter of an hour early so that he could have a cup of tea in the staff canteen while he waited for the service manager based at Edgware Road to assign him his train. He liked to chat to some of the other tube drivers before setting out for the day.

Ray is a gruff looking Londoner with a dark complexion that gives him an almost Mediterranean appearance. When he speaks, however, any doubts about his origins are instantly dispelled. His accent is as south London as they come.

That day his shift was meant to be a short one. He had to do three anti-clockwise loops of the Circle Line before switching to a Hammersmith and City Line train. Then he had one trip to Hammersmith and back to Edgware Road before knocking off for the day. Each loop took about fifty-five minutes. He expected to finish in plenty of time to pick up his car from the garage, where it was being serviced, by half past three.

Ray was making good time. His first loop had none of the usual delays that cause commuters to complain about the service. The Circle Line is often slow or delayed: the blame lies with its design. The Circle Line shares its northern tracks with the Hammersmith and City Line and its southern with the District Line. Every time a train from one of those two lines enters or leaves the network the Circle Line has to stop at a junction to let them pass. When a Circle Line train stops every train behind it has to stop as well. On a circular system, this means that every train on the line has to stop.

When the schedule is running on time London Underground keeps the Circle Line moving by merging trains from the other lines onto the tracks in-between Circle Line trains, in the same way a car merges with traffic on the motorway. When the schedule is out of sync, trains from the Hammersmith and City and District Lines force Circle Line trains to stop at junctions to let other trains enter the network. On the morning of 7 July, the schedule was gelling and Ray passed the time in the dark of the driver's cab listening to the good-natured bantering on the radio of controllers from the District and Circle Lines; they were mainly joking about each other's use of the railway. A friendly rivalry exists between staff members of each line. In that respect not much has changed since competing private companies first built the lines in the 1800s.

Unlike the Piccadilly Line through King's Cross station, which was running late that morning, Ray was early. This meant his train wasn't crowded; if anything, it was lighter than usual. On his second loop of the Circle Line he sailed around, picking up passengers at King's Cross, dropping more off at Baker Street and then running light again into Edgware Road.

He was two minutes early for his third loop. The signal was red. He stayed at the platform to wait for the green light on the tracks ahead of him. This was to be his last lap of the line before stopping for a late breakfast.

As Ray was preparing to pull out, an Asian man in a long brown overcoat came running down the steps.

'Hang on,' the man called out. 'Is this one going to High Street Kensington?'

'Yes,' Ray replied.

'Can you just wait till I get in? I'm in a rush,' the man asked.

'Go on then,' Ray said back, keeping the doors open long enough for him to jump into the second carriage. As he did so a woman in black with long pink hair jumped out of the same carriage and made her way up the platform. In that instant the fates of both of them had been exchanged.

The doors to the carriages closed. The signal flashed green. Ray pulled away from the platform and into the tunnel towards Paddington where he expected to double his load

3

of passengers. He stuck to the speed restriction of fifteen miles per hour but then started ramping it up as he reached the junction where the tracks split below Praed Street. There was a train coming the other way. He nodded to the other driver as they passed. Just as he did so, he heard from behind him what sounded like a car door being slammed violently shut.

The carriage lifted up in the air high enough to cause Ray to bounce back awkwardly in his seat. Thick black smoke surged past the windows on both sides of the driver's cab as if it had been shot out of a gun. It temporarily blocked out the dim tunnel lighting and the glow coming from inside the carriages of the train on the other track. Then Ray's train stopped so suddenly that the force of it threw him out of his seat, causing him to wrench his back as he slammed against the windscreen of the cab.

It was pitch black. Ray struggled to his feet. He could hear screams from behind him but he couldn't tell if they were coming from inside the train or out in the tunnel. After a minute or so they died down. Then came the banging. Someone was hammering on the door of his cab from inside the first of his six carriages. He tried to open the door. Something was blocking it. He could only push it three inches open, enough to show that one of the service hatches in the floor had been blown from its fittings before landing back on the hole, wedging itself against the door of the cab.

A passenger inside the carriage pushed Ray's door shut, muttering something about clearing it away. A moment later the same man pulled open the door from the other side. He was wearing glasses and carrying a shoulder bag. Ray looked past him. It was dark in the car. No one was more than a silhouette. The only light came from the train on the next track. It seemed unaffected. Ray couldn't work that out. He looked down into the carriage of his train.

Some of the passengers at the first set of doors were trying to smash their way out of the carriage. A man was holding on to the rail above his head swinging wildly with both feet at one of the windows, trying to break it. About a dozen passengers had congregated around Ray's door.

'Wait a minute,' Ray said. 'There's a lot more smoke out in the tunnel. If the windows break it will flood in. Everyone stay calm. I am doing the best I can.'

The man who had helped with the hatch and the door stepped forward. He was about fifty, balding, wearing a shirt and tie. He told Ray he worked for National Rail and would be willing to lend a hand if he needed one.

'Have you been able to contact anyone?' the man asked.

'I've tried the radio but it's dead. All the electrics in the cab have given up the ghost,' Ray said. 'The mobile doesn't seem to be working either.'

The Circle Line was, in the most literal sense, the first underground railway in the world. It was built using a construction method called the 'cut and cover'. It involved digging a trench down 15 metres through the street, laying a railway track at the bottom and then creating a tunnel by covering the top of the trench over with steel beams and brick to form a roof. This meant the sub-surface lines, like the Circle, were very close to the surface. They had to be. The original trains running on what was then called the London Metropolitan Railway were powered by steam. Building so close to the surface allowed the engineers to leave a number of open-air sections to the street above to let the steam dissipate.

More than 150 years later those openings have since been covered over with glass but they still let mobile telephone signals in to over 70 per cent of the line. Unfortunately for Ray, he was in one of the dark spots: neither of his two phones would work.

'I can't raise line control on my radio or my phone,' Ray told the passengers from the doorway of his cab. 'I am going to have to walk down the line to the signal phone and call from there. Everyone stay where you are. The traction current could still be on.'

Ray didn't like the idea of leaving his train. He viewed his passengers as a ship's captain would his crew. He wanted to stay until the last one was out, but getting word to ground level meant he had to leave them, for the moment at least. The distance up the track wasn't too great, perhaps only two carriage lengths. The signal phone would patch him into the signalman's booth at Edgware Road.

Leaving the passengers, Ray walked down the dark tunnel. When he reached the signal phone he turned around to look at his train. Carriage doors and metal panelling littered the tracks on either side of the train. The roof of the second carriage had been blown upwards and part of it was embedded in the tunnel ceiling. On either side passengers lay on the track. The smell of burning metal thickened the air.

Ray could now see that the train on the neighbouring track was, somehow, undamaged. Beyond both trains he could see sunlight pouring down on to the platform through the glass roof at Edgware Road station. It was shift change. There were probably thirty staff in the canteen or station office. Ray could see a number of figures in London Underground-issue high-visibility vests running down the station steps and into the tunnel. Help was on its way.

As he realised the full horror of the situation, Ray's hands began to shake. He picked up the phone, wondering what to do next, and pressed the call button. There were injured on the track and inside the train. 'What the hell am I going to do,' he wondered. 'Where do I start?' Ray could hear the phone ringing in his ear. He checked his watch. It was 8.55 a.m.

'Hello,' the signalman said.

'I'm down here at the Praed Street junction. There has been an explosion on my train. I think it was a bomb,' Ray said.

'Whoa, whoa, whoa, just a minute, driver, I've got a duty manager next to me. Let me put him on,' the signalman replied, passing the receiver to Trevor Rodgers.

That morning, Trevor Rodgers was in the duty manager's office on the second floor at Edgware Road station. His job was to schedule trains in and out of Edgware Road, making sure that every train had a driver. He was also an instructor. He wasn't working that day but had come in to renew his teaching certificate. That meant he was going to get out of the office for once and spend the day driving trains.

He was reading through some paperwork when there was a crack so loud that it could be heard throughout the station offices. The floor shook beneath Trevor's feet. At first he thought a truck had dumped its load outside the station. It wouldn't have been the first time. He ran down to the despatch desk to check.

The duty manager saw Trevor and said: 'It feels like a possible explosion in the tunnel.'

Trevor grabbed his high visibility vest, hat and radio and made for the station concourse. Black smoke was gushing up the steps to the station exit. Drivers were filing out of the canteen and rushing into the tunnel. Trevor immediately radioed the duty operations manager at line control based at Baker Street. The line controller was responsible for the Circle and Hammersmith and City Lines.

'This is Trevor Rodgers down at Edgware Road. We've had a loud bang in the tunnel and there is smoke flooding up the platforms. Can you tell me anything?' he said.

'Hello, Trevor. We think it might have been a power surge.

Traction current in the whole area has been lost. Tracker Net is down. We're blind. We've just had the same thing happen at Liverpool Street,' the line controller reported.

Tracker Net is London Underground's electronic eye. Sensors on trains and in the tunnels project a map of each line fitted with electronic eyes up on to a series of plasma screens in each line control centre and at the Network Operations Centre at St James's Park. At a glance a controller can tell where every train is on any given line. Without Tracker Net the only way line control can get this information is by radio or by a cumbersome search of the hand-written logs. It was going to get confusing.

Trevor knew the signalman might need to move trains past a red signal to clear any trains stuck further up the tunnels. This could only be done if a duty manager of trains, such as Trevor, was present. He knew where he had to be.

'The best place for me is in the signal cabin,' Trevor told the line controller. 'I'll head over there now and call you when I know more.'

He walked across the station. Drivers from the canteen flooded down the steps past him to the platforms. He pressed on to the signal cabin and swung open the door.

The signal cabin is a relic from the early days of railway engineering. It contains a series of levers which are used to change lights and points on the line. Trevor had hardly walked in the door before the phone started ringing. It was Ray, stuck at the Praed Street junction. The signalman handed the phone to Trevor who recognised Ray's voice straight-away.

'There has been an explosion on my train,' Ray said. 'The doors have been blown off, people are fully out of the train. There are people on the track. There is lots of smoke. You've got to come down here and help me.'

8

'Are you sure there was an explosion, Ray? We've got reports from line control that it was a power surge. It's the same at Liverpool Street apparently,' Trevor answered back.

'It is *not* a power surge. I can tell you that for sure. There are people on the track down here,' Ray said.

'Are you telling me that you are doing an emergency de-trainment?' Trevor wanted to know.

'It's too late for an emergency de-trainment,' Ray said. 'There are pieces of people all over the track. Passengers are jumping off the train. The doors have been blown off. I am going to send those that can walk back towards Edgware Road. I need to confirm that traction current is off and you won't put it back on again.'

Trevor confirmed the tracks were no longer live between Ray's train and Edgware Road and would remain that way. There was no way to tell if the power was still live towards Paddington, however, so Trevor told Ray not to let anyone wander that way down the tunnel.

'Just do the best you can down there. Emergency services are on their way. Hold on as long as possible,' Trevor said.

'I will but I need help,' Ray said.

'Was the explosion track side or train side?' Trevor asked. If it was track side it meant the cause of the explosion was probably electrical and therefore tied up in the hundreds of cables that line the tunnel wall.

'It was definitely train side. I felt the train lift,' Ray replied before hanging up the phone.

Trevor handed the signalman back his phone and put in another call to line control on his radio. It was now 8.57 a.m. Trevor explained to the duty manager the scene Ray had just described and was told there was now confirmation from Liverpool Street that a similar explosion had ripped apart a train there as well. There was a power-generating station near the Aldgate/Liverpool Street area and it was thought that was the cause of the blast. Something similar had happened seven months earlier. Trevor left the signal cabin and walked out into the tunnel to help the drivers evacuate passengers to the station.

Back in the tunnel Ray walked down the tracks to his train, climbing up the wooden steps he had earlier placed at the front door of the cabin. He knew from the damage to the train that he couldn't evacuate the passengers through the broken car, nor could he walk down the train to tell people in the four cars behind the explosion what was happening. He had to hope the PA was working. He picked it up and gave it a try. He was in luck.

'Will everyone in the first and second carriages walk to the front of the train if they are able to do so,' he said. 'Passengers in the last four carriages please walk to the back of the train where London Underground staff are waiting to assist you. Those who are unable to walk, someone will be with you shortly. Emergency services have been contacted and are fully aware of the situation.'

The announcement was heard everywhere but in the second carriage, where the speakers had been destroyed by the blast. Even if they had been working it is doubtful whether anyone would have been able to hear Ray's announcement. Almost everyone in the blast zone had had their hearing damaged when Mohammad Sidique Khan blew himself up. Besides, those who had survived the initial blast had other things to worry about. They were fighting for their lives.

## Edgware Road: feet away from the explosion

In the darkness of the second carriage at Edgware Road, Jason Rennie, a building project manager, stood in wonder. He had been only feet away from the bomb when it went off. Jason was South African, well built, fit and in his mid-thirties, but none of that could be credited with saving him. It was only chance that triumphed over fate that morning.

It was twenty to seven when Jason's wife dropped him off at Cockfosters tube station. The car journey was routine, and although it lasted barely five minutes it gave them time to chat before he took the Piccadilly Line into work. They spoke about trying to start a family. It was something they looked forward to in the way that young married couples do.

Jason kissed his wife, got out of the car and walked into the station. He bought a ticket through to Reading, via Paddington, and made his way to a packed platform. There were delays on the Piccadilly Line that morning and when the train arrived it quickly jammed with passengers. He pushed his way on and tried not to think about how uncomfortable he was. Piccadilly Line carriages are some of the smallest on the underground. Their long tubular shape makes it hard for anyone of significant height to stand anywhere but the middle of the carriage. When the trains are as packed as they were that morning those standing just inside the doors, as Jason was, are forced to stoop towards the centre of the car.

It was too crowded to read or to play video games on his

mobile so Jason just hunched inwards and waited for his time in the carriage to end. At King's Cross he got off his train just as suicide bomber Jermaine Lindsay was about to step on. They might have crossed paths on the long, packed escalators, or they might have missed each other altogether; it's impossible to tell. No one notices anyone in the morning crush of tube travel.

Either way, when Jason left the Piccadilly Line he was pleased to be heading for the Circle Line; 'It's always less crowded,' he told himself. On a normal day he'd have stayed in the sardine can of the Piccadilly Line all the way to his firm's offices in South Kensington, but today he was on site in Reading where he was supervising the refurbishment of a hotel.

The Circle and District Line platforms at King's Cross were moderately crowded compared to the Piccadilly Line. There were only about a dozen people ready to jump on each carriage when the train arrived. Mohammad Sidique Khan stood only a few feet away from Jason wearing a white baseball cap and carrying a rucksack over his shoulder. He was waiting to get on the same carriage of the same train.

Jason had swapped one bomber for another.

A few feet back along the platform a young Italian stood in a long brown coat reading a novel. She was going to get on the second carriage. She did so every morning but when the train pulled up, a small crowd gathered at the last door to the carriage so she hopped on at the front of the third to avoid the hassle. A man in his twenties in a tan leather coat was part of the crowd that put her off. She would later learn he was autistic. He couldn't help it but his piercing gaze and unusual manner scared several people enough to stop them getting into the second carriage with him. Not Jason. He didn't notice anyone.

Jason and Khan stepped forward together through the

second set of doors and into the middle of the car. Walking a few steps back and across the grey ribbed rubber floor of the carriage Jason turned and took up position in a doorway on the opposite side of the car. He leaned against the glass partition with his right shoulder. He started to play golf on his mobile. It was how he liked to pass the time under-ground, by distracting himself.

Khan decided to sit down about twenty feet diagonally across from Jason, towards the front of the carriage. Apparently he wanted to die sitting down.

The train rolled heavy through to Baker Street where there was an exchange of passengers. Several people got into Jason's carriage including a middle-aged man reading from a script and a woman in black with long pink hair that hung down her back. Jason didn't notice either of them. A few minutes later they arrived at Edgware Road where the train stopped to wait at the platform.

There is natural light at Edgware Road station. It comes through the transparent roofing covering the platforms that were left open to let the steam trains breathe when the railway was built in 1863. Sudden bursts of sunlight at various points along the line shake people from their stupor. On this occa-sion the carriage doors were open long enough for Jason to notice he wasn't moving any more. 'How am I doing for time?' he asked himself, looking at his watch: 'Ten to nine. I'm going to be a little late.'

A middle-aged Asian man wearing a brown overcoat ran down the station stairs and jumped into the carriage near him just as the doors were closing, shouting to the driver as he did so. A woman with long pink hair suddenly changed her mind and decided to hop out at the last minute. She needed to make a quick stop at Marks & Spencer to pick up dinner on her way into work. Jason didn't look up. The doors shut and the train rolled out of the sunlight and into the tunnel. It was only one stop to Paddington. He was almost there.

As the train passed beneath the brick arches of the tunnel, the natural light disappeared and a gust of wind swept down the carriage. It knocked the mobile phone right out of Jason's hand. Or so he thought. It was actually a piece of shrapnel chasing the explosion. It seared itself into his exposed forearm. A great burst of white light, accompanied by a metallic crashing, overloaded Jason's senses. When the flash passed he found himself standing in the dark looking at the floor of the carriage, from where the screen of his mobile phone glowed up at him. 'That's my phone,' he thought.

He lurched forward to pick it up and was overcome by dizziness. He started to tip uncontrollably to his left, then forced himself to grip the rail in his right hand to steady himself. Pain shot through his arm. His back slammed into the carriage doors behind him. He rested for a moment, bent in half, still on his feet but only just.

'Stand up, fuck, stand up,' he told himself. 'Check if you're okay, see if you have everything.' His thoughts instinctive: his mind issuing orders he felt compelled to obey. Touching his arms through the sleeves of his white shirt he moved his hands up to his face, then down to his stomach and legs. Everything seemed to be in place. 'I'm okay, everything is still here,' he told himself.

As he drew a deep breath, the smell of burning metal speared into his nose. 'This is a bomb,' he thought. His assessment wasn't based on careful examination of the facts; it was simply instinct. It was that smell; so familiar.

Back in South Africa Jason had spent over a year in the army completing his national service. He'd been fortunate in that his government had decided not to send him to Angola; otherwise, he would have gone to war. Despite seeing no action he had been within fifty metres of exploding artillery shells and as close as four to five metres away from grenades in training. The experience left him with certain points of reference: smells, sounds, air pressure changes, all of which told him that what was happening now was somehow familiar.

As Jason stood in the dark he could hear screams of terror all around him. They were slowly growing louder. The voices were always there but Jason could only now start to hear them. His eardrums were perforated in the blast. Everything sounded as if he had his fingers in his ears.

'We have to get out of here, we have to get off this train,' a young woman standing directly in front of him yelled in panic. She was with another woman; both were in their early thirties and were on their way to the office. They were screaming, loud and terrified. Jason tried to make them out in the dark when a tall City gent carrying a leather satchell and an umbrella pushed past on his way towards the rear of the carriage. When he'd gone Jason stepped forward and grabbed both of the women by their arms.

'Calm down, you're okay, calm down,' he shouted. They were in such a state of hysteria they could be bleeding their guts out and never know it, Jason thought. 'Take it easy and check to see if you are okay or if you have been injured.' Everything had gone black and he could barely make out their faces in the dark. He didn't need to see them to know they were terrified and confused.

The women looked at Jason as if he was some kind of nut. He had no idea how loud his voice was. Dazed and shouting in the darkness he was afraid he wasn't the slightest bit calming. Yet the women followed his instructions, their cries subsiding as they did so. They appeared to have all their fingers and toes. He felt relieved. Then came a voice.

'Help me, please help me.'

The voice was shallow, male, coming from the front end of the carriage. Jason couldn't see where from exactly. Pushing the young women towards a rail so that they could steady themselves, he said: 'Look, I am going to see who is calling for help. Stand here and hold on to each other. You are going to be okay.'

Then, stumbling across the glass-strewn floor, ignoring people sitting quietly in his way, Jason moved through the smoke, towards the whimper in the dark. At the first set of doors to Jason's right there was a man about the same age as him. The doors were open; perhaps they had been blown off. It was too dark to discern.

The man was wearing suit trousers that were in shreds. He was trying desperately to force open the sliding doors of the train on the next track in an effort to escape. Jason looked over towards it. The lights were on in the adjacent train. People were walking about inside. He could see them in their clean and tidy suits and skirts. It didn't look as if they knew what was going on. It was strange, such a contrast of realities. Jason thought about stopping to help the man open the doors but he couldn't ignore the voice in front of him.

The cries for help crept up from floor level as he moved closer. Stooping over to see whose voice it was, and waving the smoke away with his hands, he was afraid of what he would find. Then, there in the floor, was a man. How could that be? He was in a crater blown out of the bottom of the carriage. Only his body from the chest up was visible. The rest hung below the train. Looking up at Jason, with his hands on the edge of the hole, the man tried to push himself out, his eyes pleading to Jason as he did so. He was wedged in among the twisted steel poking up out of the floor.

'Help me, help me please,' he said again, his voice rapidly weakening.

Jason stepped forward and took the man's hands to try and pull him out. As he did, he lost almost all the strength in his right arm and had to stop. He held his hand up and could see that his wrist was pouring blood. It was the hand in which he had been holding his mobile seconds before the blast, the one that caught the shrapnel.

Jason looked around for help. A few feet away a middle-aged Asian man stood peering out of the second set of carriage doors towards Edgware Road. It was the man who had jumped into the train just moments before it left the station. The doors he was leaning out of appeared to have been blown off their runners and into the tunnel. 'Can you give me a hand over here?' Jason asked, nodding towards the man in the hole. 'I can't free him on my own, my arm's knackered.'

The Asian man was cut across his forehead and blood was streaming down his face but he moved over to help, taking the man's left arm while Jason used his good hand to grab the man's right.

A look passed between them.

The man in the hole gripped their hands at the same time. They heaved upwards while he tried to push himself out with his legs.

'He doesn't look that badly injured,' Jason thought. 'Apart from the fact that his shirt has been blown off there is barely a mark on him from the waist up. We might be able to get him out of here.' But just as he was thinking things were getting better, Jason realised they were about to get much worse.

Leaning over the man as he pulled on his arm he could see down into the hole and the tracks below. The man's legs were not moving with the rest of his body; it looked as if they had been hacked to bits.

The man whimpered.

Jason and the man helping let him slump back into the hole where he came to rest as if he had fallen there backwards. 'We need to wait for some kind of professional help,' Jason thought. It was a decision based on his army medical training and was probably right, but it made him sick all the same. He wanted to do something useful. He wanted to help the man. In the end it wouldn't matter. There was nothing anyone could do for him. There was only a faint hope, and even then, only if the paramedics arrived in the next few minutes.

The Asian man lowered himself out through the doors, stepped into the tunnel and, without saying a word, disappeared. He left as someone else came into view a few feet away. He came out of shadows that enveloped them all. Jason thought he looked about fifty; that might just have been the grey hair, he couldn't tell. He was wearing a brown blazer and carrying a leather satchel. 'Can you stay with him,' Jason asked the new arrival, pointing at the man in the hole. 'He needs someone to keep an eye on him.'

'Yes,' the man replied, 'yes, I can.'

Jason stood back to think. 'What now? What kind of fucking mess is this?' He backed away from the man in the hole. On his second or third step he nearly fell over someone sitting on the floor behind him. He turned around. He could see the back of a middle-aged man sitting with his legs straight out towards the rear of the train. He was propped up on one arm and seemed calm and composed. At first Jason thought he was probably fine: 'Are you okay down there, mate?' he asked.

There was no answer.

'Are you okay?' Jason asked again.

To David Gardner, Jason's voice sounded Australian. It shouldn't have. David was also a South African ex-pat and if there was one accent he should have recognised in the dark he thought it would have been South African. But, then again, David barely knew he was alive. All he could hear until Jason started talking to him were a few lines of Shakespeare running through his head.

David was directing and starring in a production of *Julius Caesar* at his local church in Hampstead. He had the script in his hand when the bomb went off. That's why the lines were there. The play was opening on 14 July and he had spent the night before doing a run through, first at the church and then at his local pub, the Flask. After a good rehearsal, and hearing that London was to host the Olympic Games in 2012 (the announcement had been made the previous day) he stayed out late drinking and talking into the night.

The next morning David sat in the bay window of his flat, both legs under the dining table, and ate a bowl of muesli with his cup of tea. He looked out at the tree-lined street while Angela, his wife, was slipping on a black trouser suit. When the clock struck half past seven David and his son Matthew stood at their bedroom window facing the road outside, as they did every day, and waved goodbye to Angela as she strolled down Well Walk to work.

Matthew then charged around like any two-year-old, watching Noddy on television, while David dressed in his navy-blue suit, white shirt and green tie with a motif of golf balls. As he knotted his tie he thought of his brother, Dr Richard Gardner, living in Sydney. The tie had been a present from him. The night before Richard had called his brother at the Flask promising he would be in London to see the Games in 2012, just as David had come to Sydney in 2000. They are close. The golf balls reminded them both of their father, a keen golfer. David was as well but had recently taken to marathon running and was putting in some pretty good times for a man in his mid-forties. He had a good build for long-distance running: just under six foot and medium across the shoulders.

At 8.00 a.m. he grabbed a copy of the script to his play, a carrier bag full of other relevant material, and bundled Matthew out of the door towards the nursery on his way to catch the tube. Employed in the accounts department at Associated Newspapers, he was heading to High Street Kensington. But first it was to the nursery with Matthew. Hand in hand they walked through the nursery doors and David took off his son's jacket, hanging it on a hook under the boy's name on the wall.

Once outside on his own it was time to light a cigar for the walk to the station. Out came a small Hamlet and the script to his play, and before long David was power walking. He went down Thurlow Road, passed his mother's house, and bumped into a friend. 'Morning, David,' Fritz called. David was momentarily distracted. 'Hi, Fritz,' he replied, not even slowing up. Head down again, he marched past Hampstead station and on towards Finchley Road, one stop to Baker Street overground, thereby avoiding the hell of the Northern Line's dodgy trains.

Using his weekly travel card at the barrier, he boarded one of the two front carriages for the short trip to Baker Street where he would catch the Circle Line. David wasn't the sort of person who got on to the train at the same place every day. He stood wherever he felt like and paid no attention to his surroundings. That morning he felt tired and hung over and so he stood in the first place he found on the platform. That just happened to be where the second carriage stopped. When Ray Whitehurst pulled his train up David stepped on and took a seat next to the door.

On the other side of the doorway, to David's left, sat Mohammad Sidique Khan.

David didn't notice the suicide bomber any more than he noticed the two American girls sitting to his right, or the university professor from Bristol further back in the carriage. He didn't notice the hulking young man between himself and Khan, the Australian woman with long blonde hair, the autistic lad at the other end of the carriage, the builders from Manchester or the Asian man who had jumped on the train just as they left Edgware Road. And he certainly didn't notice Jason Rennie, as absorbed in computer golf as David was in Shakespeare.

David was preoccupied with his script, awaiting Caesar's betrayal, when there was loud pop to his left.

The bomb had gone off.

The carriage filled with a rush of wind and fire. David flew through the air, up towards the roof on a cushion of flames. He spun in the air, slamming into the window behind him.

'When I land will I still be alive?' he wondered.

A split second later his body crashed into the carriage floor. He landed in a sitting position in front of the seat he had occupied only moments earlier, the lines from Shakespeare still running through his head.

'Am I in one piece?' he wondered. 'Do I have everything? Am I still me?' He started feeling himself all over, face, chest, arms – all there. Then he felt down to his left leg and knew something was wrong. He could feel soft, chewy flesh. There was no sensation. David knew instinctively that what he was touching was all that was left of his leg. 'I'm just an ordinary guy,' he thought. 'I'm not a politician or an army officer. I'm nobody important and yet I've been bombed. How can that be?

'Will I ever run a marathon again?

'Will my wife still love me?'

David was burning up with what felt like a fever, his skin still scorched from the fireball. His mind started to buzz: 'The play is in a week's time, will I be all right for opening night?' He even remembered the nights the play was scheduled to run, reciting the dates over and over in his head until the thought of his son, Matthew, overwhelmed him.

He hunched over his leg for a better look. There was something resting on his thigh. An arm. It wasn't his. Its owner wasn't alive. David moved it off and dropped it on to the floor. It was still attached to the man lying in the shadows to his left. His hearing started inching back. He could make out voices in the dark but not what they were saying. Except one.

'Hey mate, are you okay?' Jason asked again.

'It's that Australian accent again,' thought David, raising his left hand towards the voice without turning around. His arm had been gashed open. As he held it up a piece of skin flapped loose. Motioning towards his thigh, he said: 'I think it's my leg.'

Jason looked over David's shoulder and could see both his legs stretched out towards the rear of the train. His left foot was cocked over to the right in a way that seemed unnatural. It was difficult to see clearly in the dark yet there were obvious gashes running down David's leg. Jason's army training had taught him that leg injuries were serious. The femoral artery runs through the thigh: if that is ruptured a man can bleed to death in twenty minutes.

The wound was too large to bandage and it was too dark to see. This left only one option: a tourniquet. Jason took his shirt off. His right arm was now almost useless and he needed David's help to tear the cloth. They made a long strip using the sleeves and part of the back. But fearing it wasn't enough, Jason took off David's shirt as well, ripping it the same way.

'Sorry, but I am going to have to lift your leg to do this,' Jason said There was no response from David.

Then, kneeling over and sliding one hand under David's damaged leg, Jason and the injured man endeavoured to wrap the makeshift tourniquet around his thigh twice before tying it off. Using a remaining scrap, they bandaged the flapping wound on David's arm and then the shrapnel wound on Jason's. When they had finished, Jason noticed something warm running down his face.

'What's that?' he thought, feeling just above his right eye. Blood. The top of Jason's head had caught a bit of flying debris. He saw the collar of his shirt lying on the floor and wrapped it around his forehead like a laurel wreath.

'Who are you?' David asked.

'My name is Jason,' he replied.

'My name is David.'

There was not much else to say. Jason's head was spinning and so was David's. The fact that they had managed to find one another in the dark and perform basic first aid together was an amazing feat but one they were in no mind to laud. They still had a long way to go.

Jason stood up and looked around him. The smoke that filled the carriage moments before had now gone. There was plenty of ventilation. The sliding doors on both sides of the train had been blown off and most of the windows around where Khan had been sitting were similarly shattered. There was a crater in the floor the diameter of a pillar box and another in the ceiling to match. No smoke could stay in a place like that.

The improved visibility meant that Jason could see up towards the place he had been standing when the bomb went off. The light was poor but the train on the opposite track was still bright. It let in just enough light to illuminate the scene. A few feet away from the hole in the floor he could make out what looked like a torso hanging out of the carriage. There was a body on the floor next to David. The scene was one of utter devastation.

The cheap upholstery of the seats was covered in a thick and sticky mixture of oil and blood, as were the plastic advertisements hanging overhead. Thousands of pieces of broken safety glass littered every surface. The walls looked scorched, as if someone had taken a blow torch and burned them beyond recognition.

'How could I possibly have survived something like this?' he wondered. 'All this damage. All these people, hurt, dead, destroyed. What was it that saved me and not them?' Just then he caught sight of light reflecting off the glass he'd been leaning against earlier. Somehow it had saved him. Holding his right hand in front of him, and trying to clench it into a fist, it was obvious now why he was alive.

'I'm feeling a bit dizzy,' David whimpered. 'I think I need to lie down.' Jason had almost forgot about him, but snapped back to reality the moment he heard David's voice. This was no time to let his mind drift. The former second lieutenant knew he had to get David to lie down if he was to have any chance of stopping the bleeding. With broken glass all over the floor, this was no place for a shirtless man.

Jason saw a leather folder on the ground and put it against David's back to protect him. He then lowered him on to his back, holding his head gently. 'Help should be coming soon,' Jason thought. 'We've been here for at least five minutes. They must know something serious has happened. Wait, are those voices? People?'

A man in glasses approached from the back of the carriage

and stopped to look at the man trapped in the hole in the carriage floor. He checked to see if he was all right. He put something behind the man's head. Next he felt his neck, but it was quickly apparent the newcomer couldn't help from where he was, so he jumped out of the door of the carriage and disappeared under the train to get a closer look.

The next person to appear was tall, wearing a suit. 'He looks so clean. He can't have been in here when the bomb went off,' Jason thought. Someone was yelling at him for help. It was the grey-haired man with the satchel whom Jason had told to look after the man in the hole moments before.

'Help this man,' he was screaming, 'help this man.' 'He is pleading for the guy in the hole. He is desperate for him to live,' Jason thought. 'We all are.'

Jason stayed where he was and watched as the tall man in the suit eased the screaming man out of the side of the train. For a second Jason closed his eyes. When he opened them he could see that the rescuer was now kneeling down, looking over David's leg. They were talking to each other quietly. Jason thought he could detect an American, maybe a Canadian, accent. He stood up and walked forward.

'I tied a tourniquet around his leg with my shirt,' he said.

## Edgware Road: five minutes after the explosion

The accent was strange. I couldn't quite place it but it seemed to be almost South African. Perhaps it was the sharpness of the syllables in the pronunciation of the word 'tour-ni-quet'. Perhaps I was just guessing. The man talking to me had no shirt. Not over his chest anyhow. The collar had been tied around his head. It looked like something Julius Caesar might have worn.

'What is your name?' I asked.

'Jason,' he said, the accent now more distinct.

'What is your last name, Jason?' I asked.

'Rennie. Jason Rennie.'

Not that last names really mattered in a place like this; it was just the kind of question a reporter asks. Looking back, I am surprised I didn't ask him to spell it for me. I suppose it was the part of me searching for something normal in a situation that was anything but.

How did I come to be here? I was puzzled. Only half an hour earlier I had been wondering what to wear to work.

I woke up early that morning having slept badly. Not because I was worried; no matter how worried I am, sleep always finds me. My night was restless because my wife was eight months pregnant and *she* was sleeping badly. Not unexpectedly I was in a daze as I showered and confused as I dressed.

I wanted to wear my red checked shirt. It is the most comfortable one I have. I like being comfortable. I had worn it earlier in the week and even though I knew I could get away with wearing it once more, I also knew I should wear my new blue one. It was clean and neatly pressed. Still, I hated my new blue shirt. It was too big. I felt like a bin bag with a collar every time I slipped it on.

My wife laughed at my indecision: 'You and your clothes, man,' she said. It was a regular thing; me and my clothes. I'm six foot six. Finding stuff to fit has been a lifelong pain in the ass. I don't like wearing shirts unless they are spotless, perfectly pressed, and fit, well, perfectly. Therein lay my dilemma. My cosy shirt needed a wash and press and my frumpy shirt was clean and wrinkle-free. There was only time to choose, not to wash or press. I was going to be uncomfortable and it irritated me. I didn't know it was the last time I would wear that shirt.

'Are you coming with me or not?' Donna snapped, growing weary of watching my sleep-deprived mind struggle with this mundane task. She wanted to know if I was going to take the train into work with her. Normally this wasn't an issue. She starts work at nine just opposite the Old Bailey. I wasn't due in the newsroom till ten-ish over at Canary Wharf, which means our routes were not parallel. Of course, today was different.

Although I had only been in London for two years I had been doing reasonably well for myself. I came to England knowing no one in the newspaper business and managed to find work as a reporter for the *Sunday Telegraph*, a big paper for a colonial dreamer like me. I was way down the pecking order, of course, which meant I was assigned crappy jobs and meaningless tasks, but I was learning a great deal about newspapering, so I sucked it up.

One of the upsides was working closely with some of Britain's finest journalists. The seventh of July was a case in point. I had spent the weeks leading up to that day working with a reporter friend of mine named Daniel Foggo. We were trying to expose a corrupt police officer. To the British public who ignore newspaper bylines Daniel is an unknown hack but to any print journalist in the UK he is a legend in the making. I loved working with him not only because I learned so much about the craft but because he was my friend and I don't have too many of those in London. That day Daniel wanted me to go to Farringdon to pull some documents for our story. I decided to leave home an hour early so that I could get the records I needed and be at work ready to go by the time Daniel rolled in at his usual half past ten.

Leaving the house early meant I was able to travel in with Donna, which is why she was rushing me over my sartorial deliberations. She didn't want to be late. I could have skipped the pleasure of her company – and probably would have – but today, Thursday, was Donna's penultimate day at work before she left on maternity leave. It was my last chance to take the train in with her for a while and I wanted to make sure she got in safely.

We left our flat and walked, hand in hand, the 200 metres to Hanwell station in the western suburbs of London. Hanwell is always busy in the morning peak. The trains running through the station had recently been cut from four an hour to two. Seats were far from guaranteed.

We timed our arrival well. The train was just arriving as we reached the platform at the top of the stairs. We somehow managed to find two seats opposite each other. I was hoping she would remain on the train all the way to Paddington and then take the Circle Line around to Farringdon with me. The Old Bailey was a relatively short walk from there.

'Stay on the train. It's your second to last day. We can have a chat about stuff and grab a coffee at Paddington or something,' I said, trying my best to convince her not to jump on board the Central Line at Ealing Broadway.

'I'll have to stand all the way to Farringdon,' she complained. 'I'm getting off at Ealing so I can grab a seat. I'm too massive to stand, look at me,' she said.

She was swelling, and not just around the belly. The heat that summer had caused her legs to swell from the knees to the toes. She was right about getting a seat. She would be uncomfortable standing. Chances are she wouldn't get a seat if she took the Circle Line. Ealing was the start of the Central Line. She'd be sure to get a seat there. I let it drop. We passed the rest of the trip flirting. We'd been together ten years, we still loved each other and now we had a kid on the way. Life was good for us. The train stopped at Ealing and just like that she was gone.

At Paddington I considered buying a paper. Normally I would have picked up a couple but for no particular reason decided not to. It should have been an insignificant decision but, on 7 July, insignificant decisions became life-changing. Stopping would have delayed me just long enough to miss the tube, which means I would have missed the bomb, which means I would have missed everything.

Making my way down the steps in front of the fast-food outlets on the concourse at Paddington, I grabbed a copy of *Metro*, put my weekly travel card through the barrier, and marched down the long tunnel towards the Circle and District Lines. At the platform I turned left and walked along a bit. I could see the eastbound train coming. It was a relief. Sometimes you could wait twenty minutes for the tube at Paddington and when it arrived the train, and the platform, would be packed to the rafters. Today, however, both were relatively empty.

*

A young woman wearing designer glasses and a black trouser suit waved to a similarly clad woman on the opposite platform as I arrived. It was an informal and friendly gesture not often seen in the morning rush hour. Although she was only a few feet away from me I didn't notice her, buried as I was in that morning's *Metro*. I was reading about the Olympics. However, a dark-haired teacher in his early fifties standing nearby did notice them.

Tim Coulson was not a regular London commuter. He had caught the train in from Reading that morning to help launch a qualification course for teachers wishing to enter his field of adult education. He was dressed casually in dark grey trousers. A waterproof nylon jacket hung off his slight frame. From behind his glasses Tim thought the girl waving to her friend was a nice antidote to the impersonal nature of the underground. It made him smile.

In truth Tim was himself that same remedy. He had arrived at Paddington at 8.25, almost a full half-hour before he found himself standing next to me on the platform. When his train pulled in from Reading he ambled over to the Costa Coffee near platform one and bought himself a medium filter coffee, white, no sugar. He had just enough time to brag to his wife, who was still on her way into work, so he pulled out his mobile.

'Hi, Judy, it's me, I've got a coffee, plenty of time and I am standing here drinking it quite comfortably in Paddington station,' he said cheekily.

'For God's sake, haven't you got anything better to do? Go to work,' Judy shot back.

Their marriage is a loving one, its chemistry as defined by affection as it is by a mutual sense of humour. They stayed on the phone for a moment joking and chatting as Tim walked around people-watching. He liked to observe people because, quite simply, he liked them. Tim was one of those rare personalities who can make everyone feel as though they've known him for years even if they've only just met.

That morning he was heading to Farringdon, same as me, where he would walk to his appointment for 9.30. When he got to the Circle Line platform a train was pulling in. It was only going one stop before terminating at Edgware Road so he stood there and waited for the next one. As he waited I arrived with my *Metro* and walked past him. The young women waved to each other across the railway lines.

Equally engrossed in the Olympics was Ben Thwaites, except that Ben was reading about them in a proper newspaper rather than a free handout, as I was. He bought a copy of *The Times* that morning at the newsagents in the small rural station of Crowthorne in Berkshire where he caught a train to Reading before changing on to the west coast line for Paddington.

He had a tidy appearance. His dark hair was full but cut short. He wore glasses, a dark suit, shirt, tie and carried a shoulder bag. Ben was thirty, a year younger than me, and lacked my pudge. Every morning he walked for about half an hour across Crowthorne to the station. It took him past the posh boys' school of Wellington College, through village fields and down country lanes. Radio Five Live kept him company on his headphones. The talk that morning was all about London winning the Olympics the day before. He could hardly wait to buy a paper and read more.

Ben arrived at the station and bought his paper. He turned straight to the sports section for the Olympics coverage, and, as with me, his paper absorbed him, cutting him off from everything else going on around him for the rest of his journey. When he got to the Circle Line platform at Paddington he too turned left out of the tunnel but stopped a carriage's length short of Tim and me.

A few feet away from Ben were an Asian woman and her daughter. The little girl looked barely twelve years old. They were chatting to each other. Ben didn't pick up on them. Neither did Tim or I but they were noticed by Steve Huckelsby, a man in his early forties who was almost as interested in people-watching as Tim.

Steve saw mother and daughter talking and thought how odd it seemed for them to be in a tube station at that time of the morning. You tended not to get families on the tube during the morning rush hour. Although Steve lived in Leamington Spa, he travelled into London every day where he worked as the Secretary of International Affairs for the Methodist Church. He was a regular on the tube and noticed when things were different.

Steve was also a father. He had two boys of a similar age to the young girl with her mother and perhaps that, too, is why he picked them out. He hadn't seen his own kids that morning. Waking just before 6.00 a.m. he had slipped out of the door while his family were still tucked up in their beds and hopped on his bike for the ten-minute ride to Leamington Spa station.

It was early when he left and there was a slight chill in the air. Steve put on his green waterproof, black jeans and a white shirt. Over his shoulders he carried a small rucksack. His dark clothes emphasised his grey hair and white skin which, although lighter than most people's, didn't leave him looking pale. Steve had the appearance of a doctor, clean, healthy and fit, if perhaps lacking a bit of sunlight.

The woman and her young daughter were engrossed in conversation. It looked as if they weren't sure that the train they were about to catch was the right one. After further conversation they decided they were in the wrong place and turned to walk back towards the exit. They disappeared from the platform just as the Circle Line bound for Farringdon rattled out of the dark tunnel. They would miss this journey.

Steve and Ben entered the third carriage from the front with a number of other people. Ben walked in through one of the middle doors and stood in the centre, holding on to a rail. Steve went in the forwardmost of the four sets of sliding doors and leaned his back against them once they'd closed behind him. In the two seats opposite Steve sat a man reading the *Guardian* and a woman in her forties, with blonde hair. She was wearing a long white coat. Leaning against the doors opposite Steve was a young woman reading through a stack of A4 papers. It was a typical morning: people reading, dozing, fiddling with their mobiles.

As the train pulled up I looked at the time on my mobile: 8.48. Not that it mattered. I wasn't due into the office for an hour yet and starting times were pretty relaxed. I just liked to know the time. Tim and I stepped into the middle of the second carriage from the front, one up from Ben and Steve. We were only a few metres apart. The train was not crowded but all the seats were taken. I leaned against one of the glass partitions and let the doors close behind me. I opened up the *Metro* again and closed off the world around me.

The train left and the darkness of the tunnel swallowed us up carriage by carriage. Another train approaching through the tunnel from Edgware Road shook us slightly as it passed. I looked up briefly. The lights from its carriages flashed in the dark.

One carriage back Ben couldn't see the train pass. He was looking at his watch. He always set it a couple of minutes fast. He had a habit of being late for the train and the added minutes helped him stay on time. It was 8.52 a.m. There would be enough time for him to make his meeting at King's Cross, he thought, if, that is, there were no delays.

A loud crack reverberated down the tunnel in both directions. From where I was standing it sounded like the same sharp clang of metal on metal as when two cars collide at an intersection. Ben thought someone had thrown gravel at the windows. Both trains slammed to a halt and everyone was thrown forwards. The train on the opposite track came to a halt outside our window.

A rush of air and smoke surged over the platform at Edgware Road, knocking over a woman dressed all in black with long pink hair who was making her way up the steps. Those around her also went down. Dark clouds washed over them as they scrambled their way up to the station exits. The bang could be heard right through the drivers' canteen, the ticket booths and up to the station manager's office overlooking the street above.

'We've hit another train in the tunnel,' I thought. 'Just as they passed one must have clipped the other. I read about this happening a couple of years ago. These old trains are useless.' I was agitated. I would be late now. Smoke started to seep in through the doors behind me. I could see it oozing along the floor. It smelled like burning plastic. It hit the back of my throat hard. Worry that the fire would consume us alive overcame any lingering fears about being delayed. Images of wooden escalators flashed into my mind.

As children in the suburbs of Toronto in November 1987 we were pulled into the library of our middle school several days after the King's Cross fire. I had no idea where King's

Cross was but I understood fire. People had died. A discarded match on a wooden escalator had started it. The lesson was clear: we should never play with matches. It was a harsh way to teach kids a lesson but I never forgot it. All I could think about now was fire and how it spread. Would we burn too? Would people panic and run? Would I be trampled? I had to stay calm.

A Hispanic woman in her forties started to fret. 'I don't normally take this train. Normally I cycle,' she said. 'I only took the train today because I thought it was going to be chilly but it wasn't. I wish I had taken my bike. I wish I wasn't here.' She was rubbing her hands together desperately and shifting from one foot to another.

Tim was standing right next to her. He put a hand on her shoulder and leaned into her face gently. In a warm voice he said quietly: 'Try and relax. We don't know what it is that has just happened but I am sure things will work out.' Tim looked over to a row of seats and made eye contact with a man who stood up to give the woman a place to sit down. She moved over and took a seat.

As Tim was doing this I looked around for some kind of explanation. I could see a family of blond foreigners further down the carriage. They looked as if they were from Scandinavia or Finland. Probably on holiday. The two children's faces were masks of terror. The little girl was about eight. She was crying and trying to sit on the floor but her mother was pulling her up with both hands. It's horrible to see frightened children. I felt sorry for them. Closer to me a short, pudgy man in a suit started to bang on the windows behind. He was in the early stages of panic. He might infect the others. I was terrified of being caught up in a panic. I had to calm him down.

'Everybody stay calm,' I said, loud enough for the entire

carriage to hear me. 'There was a collision. We clipped a passing train. London Underground knows what is going on. This kind of thing has happened before. We have to stay still and wait for word from the staff. Everything will be okay.' It was bullshit, of course. I had no idea what I was talking about. We might be about to burn to death for all I knew. I said what I said because I had taken a number of lengthy first aid courses a few years back and one of the things I remember is that when they are panicking people will stay calm if someone tells them, in an authoritative voice, to do so, even if that person is making everything up.

People around me seemed comforted, but the pudgy guy was setting the crowd off again by trying to open the sliding doors behind me. 'We need to get out of here,' he said, grasping wildly. 'The train could be on fire.' I told him to stay still. I told him there was no fire and that the tracks were live with electric current. I repeated that to the people around me. I was afraid that if the pudgy guy kept panicking the crowd would start to doubt what I'd said. Then I had a lucky break. A middle-aged woman in a shell suit sporting a peroxide blonde haircut spoke up.

'He's right,' she said in a harsh London accent. 'I work on the railways, not for London Underground, but for National Rail. I know how these systems work and there's a signal that lets line control know when a train comes to a stop. They will be on to this. We just have to be patient.' A look passed between us acknowledging what we were trying to do. Had she taken the same first aid course as I had?

People began to quieten and now, for the first time, we could all hear the screams across the tunnel from the train on the neighbouring track. They were horrible: shrieks of pain and fear. 'It probably sounds worse than it is,' I thought. I imagined a number of people had probably been thrown about and broken bones when the train screeched to a halt; maybe someone was having an anxiety attack, nothing more. At least that was what I hoped. Still, it made everyone think: how bad was it over there that people were screaming like that?

Silence filled the carriage.

We wondered.

'Does anyone know first aid? We need some help down here. Is there anyone medically trained?' The voice came through the interconnecting doors from the carriage behind. The view into it was obscured by an unused driver's cabin that separated our carriage from Ben's and Steve's. There is one in the middle of every Circle Line train. A woman had opened the door and was yelling from inside, 'We need some help down here.'

When the explosion shook the tunnel Ben's immediate feeling was the same as mine: there'd been a collision. But when he saw the train on the opposite track he changed his mind. 'A concrete or steel beam must have fallen off the ceiling in the tunnel,' he reasoned. 'Both trains must have hit it. That's what stopped us.' Ben didn't know anything about underground tunnels. He just needed an answer that made sense and the idea of a falling beam seemed to fit.

The sudden jolt as the train stopped, combined with the bang, convinced Steve that it was a collision. Tim, Ben, Steve and I were not even close to guessing the cause of the bang. In those initial moments the word bomb never entered our minds. For some inexplicable reason we all developed our own theories and accepted them as fact.

Perhaps we didn't want to believe it was a bomb no matter how obvious the signs were.

When his carriage began to fill with smoke, Steve thought there must be a fire. He looked in both directions down the train. Despite the unused driver's cabin partly blocking the view Steve was standing right next to the interconnecting doors and could see through the window into my carriage. He was hoping for some sign of where the fire might be coming from, behind or in front. There were no clues. 'Something serious is going on here,' he thought. Finding out exactly what would have to wait. The smoke was getting thicker.

A few feet away Ben could hear a woman crying softly: 'Oh God, oh God, no.' Her cries were unsettling as they continued unabated. They belonged to an attractive young girl. Ben could see that the girl's boyfriend was holding her close, trying to calm her down. Ben took off his bag and his MP3 player and put them down on an empty seat with his copy of *The Times*. 'Is everyone okay?' he asked no one in particular. There was no answer, not even from the girl; everyone seemed confused. Ben stood there, unsure what to do next.

A man pushed his way towards the doors Steve had been leaning against when the bomb went off. Steve watched as he tried to pull them open. They wouldn't budge more than a few inches. 'Is the air out there any better than it is in here?' Steve asked the man who was now sticking his face into the crack, breathing the tunnel air deeply. 'Yes it is,' he replied, 'a little.'

'Let's try and keep the doors open then,' Steve suggested. They wedged a bag into the gap and left it there.

Steve could hear voices from within the unused driver's cabin and stepped over to stick his head in. He saw two women and a man crouching as low as they could on the floor. It was the man who had been reading the *Guardian* opposite him earlier and the woman in the long white coat. They had been joined by another woman and all three were talking together in low voices.

The man reading the *Guardian* was called John. A Kiwi, he was a professor at the University of York. John was in London that day to do research at University College London library on an urban planning project. When smoke started filling the carriage he began to panic. He was asthmatic and whether there was fire or not was irrelevant; if the smoke got any thicker, it would be enough to bring on an attack.

A few minutes earlier, when Steve and the other man began jamming a bag in the sliding door opposite to where John was sitting, he tried to stop them: 'No, don't do that,' he said, 'if there is a fire out there that is the worst thing you can do.' Steve and his helper either ignored John or didn't hear him. Either way John convinced the women sitting next to him that the best thing they could do was to crawl into the unused driver's cabin, staying as low as possible. There, he hoped, they could escape the smoke.

The only person at Ben and Steve's end of the carriage who neither moved, said anything nor appeared even the slightest bit fazed after the initial explosion was a young woman named Rhian Jones who had flown in from Edinburgh that morning. She was leaning with her back against the set of doors opposite the set jammed open by Steve. Behind her, in the darkness, stood the train stalled on the other track. She couldn't see it. At first she thought only about being late.

When the train came to a halt she barely moved, wedged as she was into the corner between the sliding doors and the glass partition. She was busy preparing for a meeting with colleagues from the London headquarters of the Royal Bank of Scotland. As people moved around her she watched. The severity of the situation had yet to sink in. She could only think of how late she was and so kept thumbing through her stack of A4 papers nervously. After a few minutes she thought she could feel a knocking at the glass window on the door behind her.

She ignored it.

There it was again.

She turned around. The doors started to edge open a millimetre at a time. She looked at the crack appearing between them and could see bloody fingers emerging from outside the train. A hand was thrust through the opening. It frightened her. She tried to grab it. It was too slippery. It disappeared back out through the doors. 'Did that really happen?' she thought.

She pressed her face against the glass and cupped her hands around her eyes to look out of the window. She was trying to see the owner of the fingers, of the hand. It was so dark. She strained to see.

SMACK.

A bloody hand slammed against the glass from outside the train, leaving a streak of red down the window. Rhian shot back. She could see something else moving in the dark now. 'Is that a face?' she asked herself, leaning forward for a better look. 'It *is* a face. It's soaked in blood. Oh, my God,' she thought.

A man from the other train pressed his forehead against the glass. He was frantic. He was trying to escape whatever was going on out there. He tried to force his arm through the doors again. 'This is like something out of a horror film,' Rhian thought. The face was framed in black but she could see the whites of the man's eyes. Beyond it she could see twisted metal. The other train looked mangled. 'There's been a bomb,' she thought, no longer in any doubt. 'There's been a bomb.'

'Help me, I need help,' Rhian yelled at the top of her voice. Her plea turned everyone's head in the carriage. 'Help.'

Her cry made the blood curdle. Ben stepped forward. He could see someone had forced his leg and arm through the sliding doors from outside the train. The trousers the bloody man was wearing were in tatters, leaving his skin exposed right up to his hip. Any thought of a falling beam having caused the trains to stop now evaporated. 'This was a bomb,' Ben thought. Stepping forward, Ben could see through the crack in the doors and caught a glimpse of the damage that lay beyond.

As the man tried to force his way into Ben's carriage he left bloody handprints up and down the inside of the sliding doors. 'Do we really want him to come into our carriage?' Ben thought. 'He could bring whatever did that to him over here. It might kill us.' It was an irrational thought. One based on panic. Ben was beginning to lose his sense of calm. He could hear screams coming from inside the bombed carriage opposite. He was frightened.

Steve, standing a few feet away, saw the bloody man at the same time as Ben did. It was obvious he was in a bad way. Up to this point Steve had assumed his carriage was the worst affected, that it was himself and those around him he should be worried about. When fire did not follow the initial rush of smoke he, and those in his carriage, began to calm down. The appearance of the bloody man changed all that. The full horror of the situation was beginning to reveal itself.

'Help, help get me through this door,' the bloody man

yelled, trying to jam his head into a crack in the doors that was still far too narrow to allow him to do so. 'We are dying in here; help us.'

Ben and Steve rushed forward to help. As they did so, Rhian stepped back. She knew she wasn't strong enough to open the doors. She saw the unused driver's cabin to her left and stepped inside it. She opened the door on the other side, which led into the second carriage where Tim and I were trying to calm people down with the help of the woman with peroxide blonde hair in the shell suit.

Rhian saw the blond family and the terrified children. She called out, 'Does anyone know first aid? We need some help down here. Is there anyone medically trained?' she yelled. 'We need some help.'

I stood there for a moment wondering whether or not I should answer Rhian's call. I did know first aid. I had taken a two-week wilderness first aid course but that was seven years ago. 'Would I be of any use now? Would I do more harm than good?' I wondered.

It was a dilemma. My feet wanted to step forward but my mind was holding them back. I needed a push to get me going. That's when I saw Tim. He was already walking forward to help. He had an air of calm about him, as if he was taking a walk in the park. I assumed, for some reason, that he was some kind of doctor. 'Maybe I can't do much myself,' I thought, 'but I can assist that doctor guy. I'm going.'

We walked to the end of the carriage together. I looked at the blond family again. They sounded as if they were speaking a Slavic language. The two children were hugging their parents and crying – they were so scared. I wanted to stop and offer some kind of help or comfort but I knew

I was needed elsewhere. Besides, if they were Russian I couldn't speak their language. Stepping through the interconnecting doors into the carriage behind, I could see a man trying to force his way on to our train from the one on the neighbouring track. He was soaked in blood. Adrenaline surged through me. I stepped forward with Tim to try and help.

Rhian stood back and watched as Steve, Tim and I tried to force the sliding doors wide enough to allow the bloody man to wriggle through and onto our train from his. The doors would not budge so Tim and I both dropped to the floor and, bracing our feet against the glass partition on either side of the doorway, each pulled on a sliding door in an attempt to gain leverage. Still nothing. 'Can we get some help here?' I asked. A tall Spanish-looking guy came over to join the three of us already at work. 'You grab up high and we'll pull down here.' It didn't look like he spoke English but he understood my intention. On the count of three we pulled as hard as we could. Nothing happened. Those doors would not budge.

Ben could see the trouble we were having and rushed into the driver's cabin, coming back with a large red fire extinguisher. He tapped me on the shoulder.

'Will this help?' he asked.

'It might,' I said, taking it from him and sticking it between the doors to try to force it open somehow.

Ben could see the fire extinguisher was all but useless and returned to the driver's cabin for something more practical. He saw a panel in the door. On the latch was a plastic ring, the kind that hotel guests have to break before they can use the mini bar. On it was a warning: 'The unlawful opening of this panel will result in a £50 fine.'

Ben's pragmatic British nature caused him to pause for a

moment. 'Do I really want to break this tab?' he thought. 'I could get into trouble.' It was silly, and seconds later he felt an idiot for even considering the consequences of snapping some stupid plastic tab when there was so much at stake just a few feet away. A man was bleeding. He might even be dying. Behind the panel were a number of tools that looked as if they might be used for track maintenance. He took out what appeared to be a giant circuit breaker. It had a positive sign at one end and a negative one at the other. It looked as if it fitted across a railway track. He handed it to me.

'That looks like it could hold an electric charge,' I said to him. 'I am a bit wary of bending it in the doors. Is there anything else in there I could use?'

Ben couldn't understand my reasoning. 'How can someone get a shock from a tool that isn't even plugged in?' he wondered, turning back into the driver's cabin.

I handed the circuit breaker to the Spanish guy standing next to me. Ben was back quickly. This time he had a long wooden pole. At the end was a U-shaped ice scraper that could fit over a railway track.

'Thanks,' I said, trying to figure out how the hell I was going to use either of these tools to lever open the doors.

The bloody man was still trying to force his way in and I was afraid he was going to hurt himself. 'Go back inside your carriage and sit on that seat,' I said, pointing to an empty one just inside the sliding doors of his carriage. 'We are coming; you have to stay still.' Either he wasn't listening, or he couldn't hear me. He stepped back on board his train. It was only a foot away from ours. He started to stumble around in the dark. 'Just sit down,' Tim shouted to him through the crack in the doors. 'We are going to get you out of there.'

It was useless. There was no way the doors could be

opened by force. The only way to open them was to flip up the adjacent seats and release the air from the door-pressure mechanism holding them shut. Of course, we didn't know that, or anything else about how trains work. For us there was only one option. I turned to Tim.

'If I smash this window and go over there to try and help him, will you come with me?' I asked.

'Yes I will,' Tim replied.

'Okay then,' I said, pulling my arm back, preparing to smash the window open with the ice scraper.

'Hang on,' Tim said, grabbing my arm. 'We had better move these people out of the way so they don't get covered in flying glass.'

'Right,' I replied, feeling a little silly for not having thought of that myself.

'Everybody, we are going to smash the glass so we can go over to the next train and help. Everyone stand back,' Tim instructed.

Most of the people in the carriage moved back. Ben stepped into the driver's cabin. There, in the doorway, he noticed for the first time the Russian family and their crying children. He wanted to help them but knew there was nothing he could do. It made him feel powerless. 'We are smashing the glass to get into the other carriage,' he called into the second carriage. There was no response.

Steve overheard Tim and I talking about breaking the glass. 'If anyone goes across I am going with them', he said to himself. Steve stood by closely. The Spanish guy was still holding the circuit breaker. I motioned to him what we were going to do. On the count of three we lunged forward, spearing the windowpane. It shattered with ease.

The window was small. Its lower frame stood at about chest height for a normal man. I used the ice scraper to clear away the remaining fragments so that we wouldn't cut ourselves on the way through. I'd intended to go across first but Tim was already through the window before I had a chance.

I went next.

## Edgware Road: second carriage

I used Ben's shoulder to steady myself as I climbed in through the window. It was dark inside the train and I couldn't see the floor where I was expecting to land. I was worried that my suit or my shoulder bag would snag on the bits of glass still in the window frame, throw me off balance, and send me toppling down on to the track below. I knew it was possible. Tim had made it. I would too. I landed and almost slipped on the floor. It was covered in broken glass and blood.

I moved to the side and could hear the Spanish guy and Steve following me into the darkness. Tim had turned right and was ahead of me, moving forward up the bombed carriage. I followed him, ignoring people sitting quietly at my feet until I was standing in the middle of the carriage. I could see Tim talking to a man who looked as if he had fallen through a hole in the carriage floor. He touched the man's face and neck and then said something to him before turning to his left and jumping out of the carriage doors on to the tracks below. He was on his way under the train to help the man from there.

The doors had been blown off at both sides. There was a hole in the ceiling to match the one in the floor. A man was screaming at me, desperate.

'Help him, help this man,' he kept repeating.

I looked in the direction the screaming man was pointing, at the crater in the floor and the man trapped inside it.

The man on the floor had no shirt. His head was cocked back and blood streaked his face. He looked about fifty. He seemed almost lifeless. The screaming man continued to call for help. I had never heard anyone make that sort of sound before. It was a strange combination of shrieking and speech. Fear and panic had totally consumed him; now there was nothing left but the mind of someone who had seen the face of hell and watched it steal away all sense of reason. He scared me more than anything else that day. I knew that if I didn't retain a grip on my faculties I would end up just like him. Lost in madness in this dark and horrible place.

'You need to sit down,' I said to the screaming man. 'I am a first aid attendant and you need to let me do my job.'

I took him by the arm and moved him over to the side of the carriage doors to help him into the tunnel. Perhaps it wasn't the best place for him but I needed him out of the way if I was going to be of any use. He could barely balance himself and was about to step out of the train oblivious of the four-foot drop to the tracks below.

I moved him to a sitting position and helped him slide out of the train. He turned to his left and disappeared for the moment. Now, apparently alone, I turned back to the man in the floor. I could see hands reaching for him from below the train. Tim's. I stepped forward to see if I could help but suddenly the man seemed to relax and fall through the floor into Tim's arms. I jerked to a stop. There was something odd about the way he had fallen.

I was shaken, scared and unsure of what to do. I stumbled backwards, my head spinning. I trod on the arm of someone behind me on the floor. Turning around, I could see a man. His shirt was missing. 'It's my leg,' the man said calmly. 'There is something wrong with my leg.'

I knelt down to look him over. He was about fifty. His hair was burned into a matted clump. Someone had tied a bandage around his left arm. 'My name is Peter,' I said. 'I am a first aid attendant, I am here to help you. What's your name?'

'David,' he said.

'What's your last name, David?' I asked.

My first aid course had taught me a few tricks about how to speak to victims. The first was that it is always best to tell the person you are about to treat that you are a first aid attendant. It calms them down. The second is that repeating a victim's name is crucial. A person's name is the most familiar sound they could hear. It calms them down, too.

'David Gardner, my name is David Gardner,' he said, in an accent that sounded South African. I looked him over. Something had been tied to his thigh.

'I tied a tourniquet around his leg with my shirt,' someone said. The voice was coming from the shadows just a few feet behind me. I could barely see its owner. He walked forward. A man in his mid-thirties. He, too, was missing his shirt. The collar looked as if it had been tied around his forehead as a bandage. He stumbled out of the gloom and stood over me.

'What is your name?' I asked.

'Jason,' he said.

'What is your last name?'

'Rennie, Jason Rennie.'

'Are you okay? You look hurt.'

'It's my hand, and my head, but I'm okay,' he replied.

I turned back to David. I wanted to get a better look at the leg wound to see if a tourniquet was really the only option. My first aid course had taught me that a tourniquet should almost never be used because it cuts off the blood supply to the lower limb. It almost always leads to amputation. I got down on my knees next to David and told him I was going to look over his wound. He didn't reply.

It was too dark to see. All that was visible was the strip of shirt Jason had tied around David's leg. To get a better look I was going to have to remove it so as to be able to assess the damage. I didn't want to do that. In that light it was impossible to make any kind of proper evaluation. Something was telling me I didn't need to. The way David's left foot was cocked over towards his right was unnatural. I had never seen anything like it before. It worried me. I stopped cold.

'You are going to be okay, David,' I said. 'I will stay here with you until help arrives. Just stay awake.'

I pivoted on the balls of my feet, looking for something to make David more comfortable. That is when I saw the man lying on the other side of the aisle only a couple of feet across from David. I could only see his back. His face was wedged into the corner where the seats met the floor. He wasn't moving. He wasn't talking. His name, I would later learn, was Colin Morley.

The first thing you learn when you take a first aid course is to head for the quiet victims first. The ones screaming are at least breathing. Colin wasn't making a sound and I was worried. 'Is he dead?' I wondered. 'I have to check.' The ABCs of my course ran through my head like a wild horse. 'Check his Airway. Make sure it isn't blocked. Check to see if he is Breathing. Make sure his heart is Circulating blood. Move. Now. Move now.'

Colin Morley shouldn't have been on that floor. He never took the Circle Line to work. In fact, he almost never took the tube at all. Usually he worked from home or drove to his company's offices in Milton Keynes. That morning the father of three was on his way to High Street Kensington for a meeting in which he was going to try to convince another large company of the benefits of switching to ethical business practices. It was what he did.

He was up that morning just past six. His wife, Ros, was not home. She was taking a multi-day course in lithography near Sudbury in Suffolk and decided to stay the night in a bed and breakfast to avoid a long drive in the morning. The only person home in their Woodside Park house except Colin was their youngest son, Jake, but he was still asleep when his father woke.

Colin took good care of himself. He was of medium build and looked fit. When he woke up in the morning the first thing he did was meditate for a good half-hour in the quiet of his bedroom before showering and dressing. He always had a healthy breakfast of fresh fruit and avoided coffee or tea. Caffeine wasn't good for the body.

After checking his e-mails and updating his various internet groups, he walked back into the kitchen where Jake was sitting at the table eating his breakfast. Colin came up behind him and playfully crunched up Jake's shoulders. They chatted and joked. Jake never turned around to see what his father was wearing that morning. He didn't need to; Jake knew he would see his dad later in the day.

Colin said goodbye to his son and left the house for Woodside Park station. It was a five-minute walk. There were problems on the Northern Line that morning and Colin's trip into King's Cross was delayed. When he eventually got into the city he made his way to the platform for the Circle and District Lines and took up position between a South

African named Jason and a suicide bomber named Mohammad Sidique Khan.

When the train arrived they walked together into the second carriage. Colin stood in the middle of the carriage facing an Asian man in his early thirties who was holding a rucksack on his lap with both arms. The train rumbled through a number of stations until it left Edgware Road and into the dark tunnel.

Colin wasn't moving. I put my fingers alongside his neck to feel for a pulse but I wasn't getting anything. That didn't surprise me. I was always really bad at taking pulses during my wilderness first aid course. I was no better now.

'I have to turn him over on to his back,' I thought. I knew that in order to do that I would need help. One person should always hold the head of the victim to protect the neck as the body is rotated. Otherwise the cervical spine in the neck could snap and leave the injured person paralysed.

'Can you give me a hand here?' I asked a man standing a few feet back in the carriage.

'Yes,' he said, stepping forward. He was about forty and wearing a grey suit not unlike my own.

I held Colin's neck and told my helper to rotate Colin's hips over at the count of three. When we tried nothing happened. Colin moved a bit but was heavy and limp. It was as if he'd been glued there. 'He can't be dead,' I thought. 'There has to be a chance to save him.' I told my helper to try again.

I was about to try a third time when the man in the suit put his hand on my shoulder. 'He's dead. You're wasting your time here. Leave him,' he said, walking away into the darkness of the carriage. I never saw him again.

Secretly, there was a part of me that wanted someone to

tell me that Colin had died even if they didn't know what they were talking about. I was afraid of what he might look like if I was, somehow, able to turn him over. I was afraid of what his face might have become, that I would see something I would never be able to un-see.

Police would later tell Ros Morley that Colin had taken the full force of the explosion in the face and chest. They said he died instantly. His family would never get to identify the body. Police advised against it. I would always wonder if they were wrong, and if, somehow, had I persisted that morning, I could have brought him back.

I felt terribly weak and cowardly letting him slump back on to the floor of that carriage. I had never seen a dead body before. Minutes ago I had been reading a newspaper. I thought I was jumping into this carriage to help someone with a few flesh wounds. Now I was kneeling over a man I had never met forcing myself to accept his death. How did all this happen so fast? How could everything change so dramatically? My head was spinning. I stood up to gather myself. I took a step towards the crater in the floor. I needed a second to catch my breath.

I looked to my right where the doors had been torn away. Two legs, blown off at the thigh, were sticking out from a pile of debris. They hung partly out of the door. No blood was seeping from the stumps. I took a half-step towards them thinking I should uncover the body, tie off the legs with tourniquets and try to resuscitate the victim. I didn't. Those legs had no life in them just as Colin had no life in him. I turned my head away and towards the back of the carriage.

On the other side of the crater a woman was lying on her back across the carriage. Her clothes had been partly blown away. I couldn't help but think she looked so calm there. She was obviously dead. A man kneeling on the floor next

53

to her was checking her over. He was Steve Huckelsby. He had come through the window with us.

After a moment Steve straddled the woman and started CPR – cardiopulmonary resuscitation. On each chest compression her body rippled with unnatural movement. She was dead. She had to be. I looked at Steve and thought how desperate he must be trying to bring back what was already gone. But I couldn't help but feel there was something noble about his effort.

Jason watched Steve as well and felt almost the same sense of hopelessness as I did. Two young women on the other train were calling to Steve through a crack in their carriage doors. They were giving him instructions.

There were people, dead people, all around us. Those still alive were seriously injured. We needed help and we needed it now. 'Where the fuck are the ambulance crews, the firemen?' I thought, rushing back to the window we had jumped through moments before. Ben was standing on the other side looking into our carriage.

'Look at all the damage,' he said. 'It's all been destroyed in there.'

'Keep it down,' I replied. 'We don't need to tell everyone what is going on over here. We'll start a panic.'

'Right, of course,' Ben said, looking to his right and left to gauge whether or not anyone had heard him.

'Look. We have four dead and four dying in here. You look quite together,' I said, even though he didn't. 'Go and tell someone we need help in here or more people are going to die. Do you understand?' There was desperation in my voice. I was trying my best to hide it but Ben could hear the strain. Immediately after I had spoken I regretted making it sound as if people's lives were in his hands. I just didn't know what else to say. I was scared.

'Yes, I do, I understand,' he replied. 'Do you need anything? Water?'

'Yeah, sure, some water would be good,' I replied.

Ben turned away into his carriage. When he left I could see people sitting on the carriage floor in his almost fully lit car. They were talking to each other. They seemed really relaxed. I envied them. The light was preventing them from seeing what was unfolding only a few feet away in the bombed carriage. Unless you stuck your head in through the broken window, as Ben had done, all you could see was darkness through the windows. It was the view you get when looking out of the window of your home at night: black. We, on the other hand, in the darkness, could see clearly.

I wished we were all in the light together.

## Edgware Road: second carriage, ten minutes later

Tim stood and watched as a Spanish-speaking man and a tall Canadian in a grey suit smashed the window of his train. It shattered like crystal. Tim thought the glass should have been harder to break than that.

Tim helped to clear away the remaining fragments of glass stuck in the frame before climbing up and wedging himself into the window frame. He was determined to go first. I offered him a hand but he refused and quickly jumped into the darkened train on the other track. Tim moved smoothly for a man his age carrying his disability. He had lost his left eye to cancer years before. He now wore glasses.

When he landed in the bombed train he stood there for a second to let his vision adjust to the lighting. The smell of burning metal was stronger now than it had been on the other train. It was almost completely dark, the only light coming from the train he had just left. It was shining over his shoulders. Twisted metal lay scattered everywhere and everyone was hidden in shadow.

'It's almost normal over there,' he thought, looking back from where he'd come. 'The doors are gone. The windows are broken. Something horrible has happened here. Are those screams getting louder?'

Tim took a step towards the man who, moments earlier, had tried to force his way on to his train. He was cut above his eye but there appeared to be no major injury to worry about so Tim told him to sit on one of the benches and put his head back. He was incidental to the larger scene now. Tim turned to his right and began to walk forward up the train. Someone called out from the dark: 'Watch where you are stepping, there are people down there.'

Stepping over those crouched on the floor of the carriage Tim saw to his left a man, David Gardner, on his back. His shirt was torn from his body and his face was black with soot. 'Something is wrong with his leg,' Tim thought. He was going to stop and help but before he could do so a man jutting out of the carriage floor a few feet in front caught Tim's eye. The sight was horrible and desperate. Tim was compelled to move forward.

The man with the satchel was standing over the man in the floor. He was shouting in a panic, 'Stay with us, mate, stay with us.' It was a desperate plea and one which didn't appear to be making much difference. Tim knelt down. He picked up a paperback lying on the floor and placed it behind the man's head. Tim's first aid course had taught him that if he could keep the head upright it would increase the flow of blood to the brain and help the victim stay conscious.

Tim leaned over the man in the hole and stared into his eyes before looking over the rest of his body. His shirt was missing: 'Fuck,' thought Tim. 'What could have blown his shirt off like that? What happened here?' Tim now believed there had been an explosion but still refused to consider that it might have been a bomb. He thought that an electrical fire had caused one of the engines under the train to explode.

'Hello, my name is Tim. I know first aid and I am here to help you. Can you hear me?' he asked.

There was no response and Tim knew that was a bad sign.

He put both hands around the man's neck to feel for a pulse. There was one, but it was very slow, nearly impossible to feel. Adrenaline mixed with panic began coursing through Tim's veins: 'I have to keep this guy alive. He can't die. He can't die,' Tim was pleading with himself.

'Your pulse is weak,' Tim said. 'I am going to check you over to see what else is wrong. I'm moving away to climb outside the carriage and move under the train. I'm not leaving you. Stay with me.' Tim slid along the floor to where the doors had been blown off. He sat on the edge of the carriage and eased himself on to the tracks before moving under the train where the rest of the man's body was trapped.

Crouching under the train Tim could see that one of man's legs was tangled in the twisted steel hanging beneath the carriage. If he could free his leg, Tim thought, he might have a chance of helping him. Starting at his calf, Tim felt up his leg. Just past the thigh Tim began to realise that his efforts would be to no avail. The man's leg was not attached to the rest of his body.

'Does anyone need any water,' a voice asked.

'I do,' replied Tim, taking a plastic bottle from someone passing along the tunnel wall.

Tim knew there was not much hope for the man but he wanted to see if he could induce a gag reflex by pouring water into his mouth. If the man gagged, Tim reasoned, there might be some hope for him. Pouring water into the bottle cap Tim reached up through the carriage floor to the man's face and dribbled it into his open mouth. There was no reaction. Tim tried again but again there was no response.

Tim looked into the man's eyes, wondering what he should do next, when the man's body suddenly relaxed and fell. Death had taken him. He dropped downwards through the crater on to the track below. Tim caught him as best he could in his arms. When the man came to rest his eyes were open. They looked straight through Tim's face.

Kneeling there, holding this stranger in his arms, Tim was suddenly struck with the full horror of what he was witnessing. Just half an hour earlier he had been joking with his wife on the phone. A few minutes before he had been standing in a tube carriage in a world so normal he would barely remember it. Now he was holding the body of a man he had never met. All around were blood and destruction and screams of terror. Tim had only just arrived to help. Emergency service workers would take another hour to get there. How much worse could it get?

In a way like no other, Tim's first few minutes in the bombed carriage at Edgware Road exemplified the sacrifice people in Britain made to help one another that day. He had answered a simple call for help and was now faced with a horror no one should have to endure in a thousand lifetimes. In that moment, he became a changed man. Part of him died with the man in the floor, a part of him he would never get back. It was a sacrifice made out of goodwill and honour. It was more than anyone should have to give.

Looking down into the man's empty eyes Tim was filled with fear and overwhelmed with despair. The situation he now found himself in was surging out of control. He could hear people screaming around him.

'You shouldn't be looking on the world any more,' Tim thought. Then he put a hand over the man's face and closed his eyes.

Tim then said a prayer:
'I hope that if you believe in God
and even if you don't
that you have a safe journey

into the next world;
your time in this one
is complete.'

As he said those words, Tim began to cry. He laid the dead man on the tracks and sat back. He wanted time to consider what had just happened but there wasn't any. A scream coming from the direction of Edgware Road shook him from his stupor. He stood up and walked towards the cry in the darkness. It was all he could think of doing.

Walking alongside the carriage in towards Edgware Road, Tim could see a woman lying on the tunnel floor outside the very next set of carriage doors. Her head was pointing towards him and her legs were stretched the other way, towards Edgware Road station, which could be seen in the distance. She had blonde hair. She was wearing a black skirt and fishnet tights. One of her shoes was missing. She was screaming in pain.

'My name is Tim. I know first aid. I need to check you over to see if there is anything I can do for you,' he said, kneeling down.

'My name is Alison,' the woman replied. 'My leg is hurting horribly.'

Tim could see that Alison's left eye was badly swollen. Her eyeball was quickly turning purple, and swelling. He checked her body over and worked out that her right leg was broken in more than one place. There was also something wrong with the kneecap on the same leg.

Alison had been blown out of the doors when Khan detonated his bomb. She had bounced against the wall of the tunnel and landed in a heap next to the track as the train continued to move in the dark. She was alone for the first few minutes in the tunnel and when Tim arrived she had no intention of letting him go. Grabbing him by the hand she said: 'Stay with me. Please don't leave me, Tim.'

'I'll stay with you. I won't leave your side until I am told otherwise,' Tim said. 'It is not safe for you to stay here. People are trying to push past. Let me try and move you on to the edge of the carriage just there.'

With the help of another man passing Tim managed to pick Alison up off the tunnel floor and put her down on the edge of the carriage above. Once she was there the helper disappeared down the tunnel to join the queue of other people trying to escape. Tim resumed looking over Alison's injuries. He was acutely aware there was little he could do to help except to make her feel she was not alone.

'What has gone on here, do you think?' she asked Tim.

'I don't know. I think the engine exploded, but don't worry. They must know we are here. The emergency services will have been contacted. They will soon find us,' Tim replied.

When people started jumping through the broken window Steve Huckelsby stepped forward to join the queue. The first to go was Tim. The next was me, the tall man in the suit with the Canadian accent who had been trying to force open the doors moments before. Then a tall, dark guy who Steve thought sounded and looked Mediterranean.

Steve was next. He needed some help and Ben was willing to give it. Together they steadied Steve into the broken window frame and he lowered himself into the darkness. He found himself at one end of the carriage. To his left people were leaving the bombed carriage via the interconnecting doors into the carriage behind. To his right Steve could see there were wounded who needed help.

Following Tim and me forward into the train, Steve passed

by a number of the injured. To his left someone was lying on the floor. The tall guy in the suit was helping him. He moved forward but was stopped in his tracks. There was a huge crater in the floor of the carriage blocking his way.

He looked through the hole and could see a man below lying on the tracks. Tim was holding him, talking to him. Steve considered stopping to help but then thought again. He desperately wanted to help someone but who? Everyone seemed to be looked after. That is when he heard a voice coming from the other side of the crater at the front of the carriage: 'We need some first aid down here.'

Steve strained to see ahead of him. The people on the other side of the crater appeared to be alone. He needed to help them, but how could he get there? Metal and debris surrounded the hole. It was too dark to see where he was stepping. Trying to jump over could end badly. He might slip and impale himself on the twisted spears of metal sticking out of the floor. He didn't want to add himself to the injured.

Steve looked around for another way across. To his right he could see something hanging out of the carriage into the tunnel where the doors had been blown away. At first he didn't recognise it as human. When he looked more closely he could see a pair of legs jutting out from under a pile of twisted metal. They had been torn off at the thigh. They were not bleeding. The torso they belonged to was not moving.

'We need some help down here,' the voice cried out again. It was coming from a well-built man in shirt and trousers. At his feet a woman was crouching next to the body of a victim. She, too, was calling for help: 'She's stopped breathing. What do I do?'

Steve needed to move. He looked at the ceiling. A hole had been blown in the roof but the overhead handles appeared to be sound. He gave them a tug. They were solid. Then, as he had done so many times with his children on the monkey bars in the park, he swung across the crater, hand over hand, landing on the other side on both feet.

The man who had called for Steve's help took a few steps backwards and stood in the interconnecting doors leading to the front carriage. Steve could see that he was middle-aged, slightly overweight with a round face. His close-cropped hair made him look almost bald. Steve stared the man in the eye and saw what he thought was a look of expectation. 'He thinks I am some kind of doctor,' Steve thought. 'He's expecting me to deliver the goods.'

The very thought unsettled Steve. On the floor in front of him was a woman lying on her back. She wasn't moving and most of her clothes had been blown away. Kneeling next to her was another woman with a badly injured leg. Her name was Elizabeth Owen. She was a lawyer in her early forties who had been just a few seats up from the bomber when the explosion killed everyone around her. She was now trying to revive the woman lying on her back.

'She was breathing but then she stopped,' Elizabeth explained, moving away to give Steve enough room to step into the breach. 'She's not breathing now. I don't know what to do.'

Steve looked down at them both and then behind them to the front of the carriage. Before the seats to his left lay the body of a young man. His left leg was missing below the knee. No blood was seeping from the wound. Above him sat a woman. She was wedged into the corner seat. She wasn't moving either. Next to her was a young man with what appeared to be a bad injury to one of his legs. He was in noticeable pain.

The realisation that so much was expected of him by the

man who had called for help alarmed Steve. His entire first aid knowledge came from a one-day course he had taken at work and that had been more than a year ago. At his feet the young woman whose clothes had been blown away lay motionless, her head near the open carriage doors. She had strikingly beautiful hair. It was long and brown and curled around her shoulders like water. Her head was lying in a pool of blood. There appeared to be no life in her but Steve wanted a closer look.

Kneeling down, he put his fingers to her nose as Elizabeth had done moments before. The woman wasn't breathing. There was no pulse either. He sighed. As he did so he heard the voices of two girls calling over to him. Steve looked up to see where they came from. It was two girls who were still on the other train. They were yelling instructions to Steve through a crack in the door of their train. He wasn't alone, then.

'Lift her head up,' one of them said.

Steve did so and then tried to give the woman mouth-to-mouth resuscitation, two breaths. He went through his ABCs in his head. Chest compressions had to be next. He tried to line his hands up on her torso but was in an awkward position.

'Further down,' the girls called across again. 'You need to move your hands further down.'

Steve nodded. He was grateful for the help. He had a pretty good idea what he was doing but it was nice not to feel alone. The man who had called to him in the first place was just standing there, saying nothing. Steve straddled the woman and, placing one hand over the other, pressed down firmly fifteen times in succession on her chest.

'Check her pulse again,' the girls called.

Steve felt her neck and then around to the back of her

head. There was a large wound that must have caused the pool of blood. She was dead. He was sure of it. No one could survive a wound like that. He wanted to stop CPR but felt he couldn't. The girls were watching him. He didn't want them to see him quit without a fight.

He gave her fifteen more chest compressions and then tried to give her further mouth-to-mouth resuscitation. He felt her wrist again. Nothing. Fifteen more chest compressions and another three breaths. Still nothing. He kept going, encouraged by the girls on the other train. Straddling the woman once more Steve did another fifteen compressions before returning to her mouth. Then he stopped. It was no use.

'That's it,' he thought. 'With the amount of blood she's lost there is no way I can sustain circulation.' He felt her nostrils once more just to make sure. It was the hardest thing he had ever had to bear. He was shocked. He had so much wanted her to live. As he stood up there was a chorus of cries from the girls in the next train. They burst into tears. For them it was the realisation of death.

Steve had known for minutes that his efforts were useless. He wanted to turn back to the others around him who were injured and try to help them. It was the girls who had kept him going through his fruitless ABC routine. He didn't want to let them down, or himself. Steve said nothing as he turned away. He had no words.

The man who had called him over, who had been watching the whole thing, said: 'Does she have a pulse?'

'No, she doesn't,' Steve replied.

A look passed between the two men that said everything they were loath to verbalise. Steve turned back to the man with the leg injury and the woman sitting next to him who wasn't moving. Perhaps he could help them.

*

It was about nine o'clock; barely ten minutes had passed since the explosion. So much had happened and so many needed help. We were desperate. The expectation was the same for all of us: help could only be a few minutes away. The paramedics and fire brigade could only be metres from us, ready to descend.

Is that them now?

Every sound down the tunnel was a false hope.

The first ambulance to arrive at street level at Edgware Road would not be there for another ten minutes, the first fire engine not for ten minutes after that, a full thirty minutes after the bomb had exploded. This only put help at the station entrance, not anywhere near the crater in the middle of the second carriage.

What the hell was keeping them?

Everyone was doing their best but there was confusion, with London Ambulance, with the London Fire Brigade, with the police and with London Underground. In the minutes after the explosion between Edgware Road and Paddington the Network Operations Centre for the tube network was receiving calls from station managers across the city suggesting that as many as eight bombs had gone off at once.

The confusion made it difficult for staff to work out exactly what had happened, that there had in fact been three simultaneous explosions and not eight: one at Edgware Road, the other between Aldgate and Liverpool Street and a third on the Piccadilly Line between Russell Square and King's Cross. The first to be identified as a serious incident was Aldgate, and, for the time being, that was where the blood was flowing.

## London Underground Control Centres at St James's Park and Earl's Court: 8.49 a.m.

The London Underground almost never runs smoothly. Most commuters put this down to lazy, uninterested staff who can hardly be bothered to turn up for their shifts, let alone work hard when they do. I used to think this way, too. Few people understand the personality of the world's first underground train network. The truth is vastly different from the widely held, and pessimistic, belief that trains are late and cancelled simply because the underground staff can't be bothered.

Far from being complacent, the staff who work for London Underground are a committed and determined bunch. They work hard to keep an antiquated system operating, one which has no business trying to cope with the huge amount of commuter traffic it manages each day. Rather than viewing their jobs as simply a pay cheque, most London Underground staff are keen railway enthusiasts who are truly attached to this subterranean network of trains. The staff, in fact, might be the only people who do really like the tube.

Like most of what makes London the quirky, often in-efficient, city it is today, the London Underground is a product of history, of decisions taken by people with competing interests more than a century and a half ago. When it was built there was no grand vision of a network of a dozen underground lines all linking up. It began, simply, with an idea for one line and one line only. The idea was to create an inner railway, a circle of track, that would perform two functions: to link all the overground rail terminals that had emerged around the circumference of the city and to provide a much-needed transportation link for people working in a congested city.

But being the first meant breaking new ground, and breaking new ground often means snapping a few shovels. Mistakes were made. When cities like New York and Paris opened their own underground rail networks four decades after London led the way, these cities had the British experience, and blunders, to learn from.

Apart from linking London's railway stations, the idea of running underground trains across London was conceived to solve the city's growing congestion problem, and, of course, to make as much money as possible in the process. By the mid-1800s London's streets were in chaos. The population of Greater London had more than doubled, growing from one million in 1800 to 2.5 million in 1850. Every day a quarter of a million commuters were coming into the city to work. London was prospering, turning itself into one of the world's richest cities. Holding back that growth was the lack of a transport infrastructure.

The main mode of transport within the city was the horse and cart. The affluent and growing upper classes could afford their own horses and carriages, but the increase in traffic clogged and polluted the roads. One estimate claims that every year London's streets had to cope with three million tons of horse manure, much of which was pushed into the poor parts of the city where the stench grew uncontrolled.

The working classes who lived outside the centre of London had to walk for hours each day just to get to work or move into the city and cram themselves into London's filthy inner-city slums. This could only go on for so long.

London was bottlenecked at every turn; there wasn't enough transport or housing to accommodate the growing city. London needed a railway that would allow people to live further outside the city's core to help relieve the pressures on inner-city housing.

The idea of the tube, then known as the London Metropolitan Railway, was born. Its aim was to reduce traffic congestion by running trains underground from Paddington station, in the west, to Farringdon, in the east. The idea of running trains under a city was the first of its kind and fostered a revolution in the way railways would later be built in cities around the world. Some of the funding for the Metropolitan Railway came from overground railways seeking to increase profits by using the new underground tracks to ship freight between London terminals. The City of London stumped up some money as well but the rest of the capital was put in by private shareholders, all of whom were expecting a return on their investment.

When the first line opened in 1863 it was a huge success, ideologically and commercially. It made money, more money, in fact, than most other railways in the country at the time. It also reduced congestion. Other entrepreneurs wanted a slice of this. A different private company, with another group of investors, backed the Metropolitan District Railway to compete. It ran along the southern edge of the city. The two railways became fierce rivals and that put off the completion of what would become the Circle Line until 1884, when the last stretch of track to join the two railways, between Mansion House and Aldgate, was finally completed.

In the ensuing forty years new technology spawned more competition. Electric trains replaced those powered by steam. Circular tunnels were cut deep underground through the thick layer of clay that serves as the foundation for the city of

London and a glut of underground lines flooded the once congested city with transport links. By 1907 there were trains running on what is now the Circle Line, the District Line, the Northern Line, the Central Line, the Waterloo and City Line, the Bakerloo Line, the Metropolitan Line, the Hammersmith and City and the East London Line. Virtually all of them were competing for customers and all had shareholders to please.

The very idea that competing private companies could own London's tube lines may seem insane, but that is how it was. Nothing was designed to work together. Where the lines crossed there were almost no shared stations. There were no shared tickets or standard fares. There was no common vision. By 1948 they were all taken over by the British Transport Commission which had the unsavoury job of trying to turn these separate entities into one compatible network.

Today's London Underground is a vast improvement on what it was a hundred years ago but the incompatibility lingers on. Long, meandering corridors and escalators join stations where the lines cross. A number of stations, such as Hammersmith, have in fact *two* stations, forcing passengers to walk above ground, cross a road, and enter another station to continue a journey. The District Line fights with the Circle and Hammersmith and City lines for priority over track usage. Trains have to stop at junctions to let other ones pass, causing delays to both services. Nothing works as well as it could. Is it any surprise, then, that people who don't understand how the system was built blame the staff? The staff are there every day. History, on the other hand, doesn't wear a name tag and a uniform.

Delays on the London Underground are the inescapable reality we encounter when we expect an antique of railway engineering to meet the demands of twenty-first-century commuter traffic in one of the world's most densely populated cities. Running that system on a day-to-day basis takes not only an ability to solve problems but a dedication to one's work that goes beyond a pay cheque. It takes an army of workers, and, leading that army, a general with an iron will and a sharp intellect.

On 7 July that general was Andy Barr. A gruff and pugnacious Scot, Andy had been with London Underground for forty years. He started as a graduate engineer in 1966, the year England hosted, and won, the World Cup. He began shifting rolling stock around the railway yards, moved into maintenance in 1974 and by 2005 had worked his way up to become London Underground's chief troubleshooter. He was the man everyone turned to when things went wrong.

On the morning of 7 July problems with the network started early for Andy. By 6.30 there was already a report of a defective Northern Line train at Clapham South station. Passengers reported to staff that they'd heard a big bang under the train, followed by smoke flooding the platform. The punters thought it was a bomb.

Andy was in the control room at St James's Park, near New Scotland Yard, when the report came in. The Network Operations Centre control room is the size of an average classroom except that the equivalent of the teacher's desk, where Andy stands, is at the back. There are five large plasma screens on the side wall which link up to display an image of Tracker Net, a computer program which projects a schematic of each underground line currently fitted with the system up on to the screens. The image enables Andy to tell which trains are where, and why, at a glance. The half-dozen other desks that fill the room are like something out of NASA's control centre: flashing lights, tiny monitors, computer screens and blinking telephones.

When the call came in from Clapham, Andy told his duty manager, sitting at the desk in front of him, to despatch emergency services. It turned out to be the equivalent of an electrical engine backfiring. It was a regular occurrence but all trains on the line were suspended south of Kennington until the defective train could be removed.

Half an hour later there was another incident on the Piccadilly Line at Holloway Road in north London. Passengers reported smoke flooding the platform on that one, too. Some told station staff they thought it was a bomb. The message was relayed to Andy. He often heard reports like that. People generally assume smoke means explosion. Andy knew differently. Piccadilly trains travel outside for some of the time. Rubbish blown on to the tracks often collects under the train. When the drivers enter the tunnel the engines heat up and the rubbish sometimes ignites.

It is usually nothing more than smoking rubbish. Procedure, however, requires the train to stop and engineers to be sent to the site to sort it out. It means delays. Andy stayed in the back of the control room standing behind his desk and considered how this would affect the rest of the underground system. It was his job to think that way.

Just over an hour later and there was another bang under a train on the same line, this time at Piccadilly Circus. Similar reports came in: bang, smoke, passengers reporting a possible bomb. It turned out to be a burst air hose, which supplied the brakes to one of the carriages. More delays. The Piccadilly Line was down to a snail's pace. The platforms started to pack out. Andy didn't worry. Gary Fitzgerald, the man in charge at the Piccadilly Line, was as diligent as they come.

As a child Gary would stand on the settee in his grand-parents' lounge on Wandsworth Common and look out of the window to watch the trains on the Brighton main line as they passed. He loved trains and he loved his grand-parents. When he was looking out of that window he always felt safe and happy. He was fascinated by how the railways worked, what they did and the people who ran them. That interest was not merely a child's passing fancy, but the beginning of a lifelong affiliation with Britain's railways.

At sixteen Gary left school and went straight to work for the London Underground as a junior trainee. He spent two years sweeping signal cabin floors, assisting the signalmen and taking various courses at the Railway Training Centre in Shepherd's Bush to further his career. By the age of thirty-six he had worked his way up to service manager for the Piccadilly Line. He was in charge of his own railway, and he loved it. If there were problems anywhere, from Heathrow to Cockfosters, he was the man who sorted them out. His passion for trains made him the perfect man for his job. Nothing was a labour, everything was a challenge.

The morning of 7 July he was on the early shift and was in the office at Earl's Court before his 6.30 start time. The control centre for the Piccadilly Line is located at Earl's Court station. The circular control room itself is just above the station entrance right opposite the Earl's Court Exhibition Centre on Warwick Road. Gary's office is further back in the building, near the Earl's Court Road entrance at the other end of the station. To get to the control room he has to walk along a hallway that connects the two wings of the station. One wall of the corridor consists of windows that provide a view over the tracks leading into the station platforms below.

Every morning Gary stops in front of these windows and spends a few minutes watching the trains full of commuters being transported between the stations on his line. Through the windows on the trains he can see the passengers standing in their business attire, reading newspapers or listening to personal stereos. He watches because it makes him smile. 'I did that,' he would tell himself. 'I help get those people to work every day.'

That was Gary, a proud, tall, well-dressed, pipe-smoking man in his mid-thirties who loved his job.

The two earlier incidents on the Piccadilly Line that morning had forced Gary to suspend part of the line and run trains in shorter loops on each part of the trouble spots. It meant trains were running slow and the stations were jamming with people desperate to get to work. Gary hovered at the back of the control room issuing orders to his staff in an effort to get the line back to a normal service.

At a quarter to nine his trains were running again on the entire length of the line but each tube was ten minutes apart rather than the usual two and a half. Satisfied that things would return to normal soon Gary walked back to his office to prepare his 9.00 a.m. report for Andy Barr's team at the Network Operations Centre. He was hardly in front of the computer in his office before the phone rang. It was the control room he had just left.

'We've had a TT operated from Holloway Road to Russell Square westbound,' came the voice down the line.

A 'TT' is London Underground jargon for a tunnel telephone. Running through every underground tunnel is a pair of parallel copper wires. If a driver's cab radio does not work (it often does not), and he needs to talk to line control or a nearby station, he can stop his train anywhere along the line, open his window and attach a phone to the copper wires. When that happens the traction current, which powers the trains in the immediate area, goes down and a signal is sent to the line control centre, in this case to Earl's Court.

With the electricity powering the Piccadilly Line's westbound trains shut down, no other tube trains could enter or leave the affected area until line control turned the current back on, and for that they needed the service manager. Gary was on his way back to the control room. What he didn't know, or didn't consider at that moment, was that a bomb in the tunnel would have exactly the same effect as a TT. But why *would* he know that? No one had ever detonated a bomb in a tube tunnel before whereas drivers activated a tunnel telephone almost every week.

As he walked down the hallway Gary was cursing to himself. He had spent the first two hours of his shift getting the Piccadilly Line back up to a full, if delayed, service and just when things were starting to get better he had another setback that would all but undo his morning's work.

By the time he reached the control room Gary's team had worked out that the location on the line where the traction current had gone off was between King's Cross and Russell Square stations, but they didn't know the reason why. Gary knew that that particular stretch of tunnel was very narrow, with barely a foot to spare on either side of the train. He also knew that, because of the earlier delays, the train would be jam-packed with passengers pressed up against one another so tightly that they couldn't scratch their noses without elbowing someone in the face.

The cramped conditions would make it hot which, in turn, would make the whole train a serious health and safety issue.

'Get that fucking driver on the phone now,' Gary said, swearing uncharacteristically. 'Talk to that driver and find out why my service has gone down.'

Gary took up position on the raised platform at the back of the room. From there he could see the schematic of the Piccadilly Line encircling him and his team on the control room's curved walls. No one could raise the driver of the stalled train and no one at King's Cross or Russell Square had any answers. The frustration was growing.

As Gary's team laboured away word started to come in via the Piccadilly's liaison man with the District Line. There had been a massive power cut and traction current on the Circle Line, most of the District and all of the Hammersmith and City Lines was also down. Compared to what was going on elsewhere, Gary thought he had a relatively easy run of things. He just had one train to sort out. There was no need to call it in to Andy Barr's team at the NOC just yet.

After a few minutes Alyson, Gary's wife, who also works in the control room at Earl's Court, turned to him and said that she had been on to staff at King's Cross who said they were dealing with an incident and could not send anyone down into the tunnel to check the tunnel telephone. Gary picked up the phone and called King's Cross himself.

'Listen,' Gary said to a member of staff at King's Cross. 'You have got to send someone down into the tunnel to check that tunnel telephone. We have a train stalled down there, up to the hilt with passengers. I need to get those people out of there. I need to know if I can turn the traction current back on and I need to know now.'

The staffer on the other end of the phone promised to send someone down as soon as they had got a handle on the massive power failures that were by then affecting the entire station.

Gary ordered the man sitting at the bench in front of him to switch his CCTV monitor to the platforms around the affected area in an attempt to find out what was going on. There are no cameras in the tunnels, only at the platforms, which meant that the only way to find out what was wrong with a particular train was to talk to the driver or send someone along the tracks to look for themselves.

The westbound platform at King's Cross was empty. That didn't seem unusual to Gary. The power failures around the network had forced station staff to evacuate people from the stations and recommend alternative routes. Gary switched to the eastbound Piccadilly platform at the same station. It was empty, too, but something was strange about the image that was hard to see at first.

Monitors on underground platforms are black and white, which makes it hard to detect slight changes in lighting. It was just past 9.00 a.m. The train had been stuck in the tunnel for over ten minutes. Gary kept his eye on the screen and said nothing. After a few seconds he saw what he thought was smoke coming down the platform and leaned in for a closer look. The image was inconclusive so the man at the desk in front of Gary reached over to switch the screen to another camera.

Just as his finger landed on the button a man in a suit entered the frame. He was running down the tunnel, a cloud of smoke close behind him. The man at the desk missed it and so switched the monitor over to another platform.

'What the fuck are you doing?' Gary shouted. 'Turn that fucking back, turn it back fucking now.'

The man flinched, surprised by Gary's sudden outburst, and moved aside as Gary lunged for the button. When the screen came back more people could be seen emerging from the tunnel. The smoke was thicker now. It had to be a fire, Gary thought. It had to be. But of course it wasn't. Gary's train had just been bombed.

His stomach dropped through the floor. He picked up the phone to raise the alarm at the Network Operations Centre.

'We've got to send an ambulance to Russell Square,' Gary said. 'We have seen smoke and people running down the tracks.'

There was a pause on the line. 'We'll put in the call but I have to warn you that we are in the middle of a major incident at Aldgate.'

The call went into the London Fire Brigade at 9.02; two minutes later the London Ambulance Service were called. The idea that it could be a bomb had yet to enter anyone's mind.

While Gary was trying to sort out what he thought was nothing more than a driver who had activated a tunnel telephone, the lines at the Network Operations Centre were jamming with incoming calls reporting power failures all around the network.

Andy Barr was ten minutes away from heading back to his office to write up his nine o'clock report when the first call came in.

It was a member of staff at Liverpool Street. The power had gone down. The escalators were not working and half the station lights were out. The duty manager from the Circle and Hammersmith and City lines control centre at Baker Street called at the same time to say Tracker Net was down. Andy looked up; there were no more visuals of the Circle Line on the plasma screens. To find trains in the tunnels he would now have to rely on the handwritten log-books kept by every line control centre.

Within three minutes ten other tube stations in the area of Liverpool Street had also called Andy Barr's team at St James's Park, reporting similar power failures. The situation was mushrooming. Andy took a deep breath, put down his coffee and sent a message out to all of his line controllers on the internal messaging system. The general was assuming command of the entire underground.

Andy didn't know it yet but his network was under attack. Over the next two hours it would be up to him to organise the safe evacuation of 200,000 people from more than five hundred trains and then, from there, work out how to put the whole system back together again. For that to happen he needed to organise the soldiers in his army.

## Aldgate: 8.49 a.m.

Celia Harrison was sitting in front of her computer in the station manager's office at Aldgate. She was doing paperwork. It was 8.49. She had just made the last entry in the manager's log when there was a loud crack inside the station. The floor beneath her feet shook. The lights went out. Her computer went down and the little flashing red indicators on the fire control panel behind her disappeared.

'We've had another power cut,' she thought, immediately doubting herself. 'That can't be; the floor shook.'

Celia grabbed a hand-held radio and rushed out of her office. The station concourse at Aldgate provides a direct view over the four platforms and into the tunnel beyond. The station ceiling is glass, as it is at Edgware Road, which floods the station with natural light. The difference at Aldgate is that above the tunnels there is a large opening to St Botolph Street. When walking through the ticket barriers it is possible to see the traffic speeding by on the road outside as well as the trains disappearing into the tunnels below. Thick black smoke was gushing out of the tunnel now and up into the station before being sucked out of the opening to St Botolph Street, like a waterfall in reverse.

Celia had seen smoke in her station before but nothing as thick and black as this. She rushed back into her office and put in a call to the Network Operations Centre. Andy

Barr was standing behind his duty manager when the call lit up the phone in front of them.

'This is Celia Harrison at Aldgate. You had better call emergency services,' she said.

'What for, is anybody hurt?' the duty manager asked.

'There was a loud bang, it shook the floor of the station, we've lost all power and there is a dangerous amount of smoke flooding the platforms,' she said.

Andy's team told her they were calling the emergency services. Celia went back out to the concourse where she could see her colleague Steve Eldridge talking to another member of staff. They were standing on the bridge overlooking the tunnel in front of her. Steve and his companion were both tube drivers. They were waiting to pick up their trains when the explosion reverberated through the station.

Steve had spent almost twenty years as a driving instructor before leaving to join the London Underground. He started working in the ticket office, then as a guard before passing his driver's exam. By 7 July he had been driving trains on the Metropolitan Line for almost three years. That morning he finished his first run of the line, returning his train to Aldgate at about 8.30.

After handing over, Steve left the platforms and went into the manager's office to make himself a cup of tea. He then walked across the concourse and stood on the bridge that carries passengers to the four station platforms. He was standing there with a fellow driver when they both heard a loud explosion deep in the tunnel.

'What on earth was that?' Steve said.

'It could have been a compressor or a motor gone up,' his friend answered.

They looked at each other. Steve knew it wasn't a compressor. It was a bomb. It had to be but neither man used the word. The smoke was too thick and black to be anything else. Celia had already called it in and was now standing twenty feet behind Steve as the two drivers tried to work out what to do next. She saw them talking and then rushing down on to one of the platforms.

A train had been pulling away from the station towards Liverpool Street when the power went dead. It had now stalled on the tracks. Steve and another driver manually opened the carriage doors from the outside and helped to evacuate people on to the platform, directing them up to the station exit where Celia was standing with her radio in hand.

Steve and his fellow driver walked down on to the tracks to help the driver of the stalled train. As they arrived he jumped out of his cab and landed on the tracks facing them. For a moment the three of them stood there staring at one another in silence. Their training had told them this day might come.

Steve spoke first: 'We've got to try and do something but we need to be careful. There could be chemicals or another device.'

The other two drivers agreed but there was not much they could do. They had no breathing apparatus, chemical suits or knowledge when it came to diffusing bombs. If they were going to walk the tracks it would be with nothing but the clothes on their backs. They were deciding what to do when the assistant station supervisor shouted down to them.

'Traction current is off,' he said.

It was safe for them to enter the tunnel. The assistant handed them torches and they pointed the beams into the darkness. The three of them were prepared to go, they wanted to go, but their feet were stuck. That is when they saw the passengers. They were stumbling towards Aldgate station through the tunnel. They were all over the place. They had no idea where they were going, where the dangers were. They were in a daze. Some were covered in blood.

Celia could see the first of the walking wounded starting to emerge. One was a young woman with long blonde curly hair. A man had wrapped her arm around his neck to help her walk. She was grabbing her stomach with her free arm, trying to prevent her insides from spilling out on to the floor. Passengers lingering on the platform saw her and started to scream. It was 8.53.

Celia used her radio to call Andy Barr's team at the Network Operations Centre. She told them two employees, Steve and the driver of the stalled train, were going into the tunnel to assist the wounded and to send every available ambulance at once. The remaining staff stayed at the mouth of the tunnel directing people on to the platforms.

The two men coughed as they advanced into the dust and smoke. Visibility was down to a couple of metres; their torch beams were being smothered. The stricken train was only four or five carriage lengths from the platform at Aldgate but Steve couldn't see it until it was right in front of him.

They arrived just as the driver of the bombed train was climbing on to the track. The three of them were about to start talking when a male passenger came running out of the dark. 'We've got to get people off this train,' he said. 'Come. We have to get them off.' He was white, tall, wearing a cream jacket and in his early thirties. There was blood all over his face and on what was left of his clothes.

The man didn't wait for an answer, he just ran back into the tunnel alongside the train. Steve and the other two drivers followed him. Their eyes were starting to adjust to the light and they could now see over a dozen passengers wandering around on the tracks. Steve followed the man who had called for help. The other drivers fanned out to direct the lost passengers towards Aldgate.

When Steve came to the end of the second carriage, his suspicions about a bomb were confirmed. The doors and siding had been blown on to the track and up into the tunnel ceiling. There was a gaping hole in the carriage floor. Three or four people lay stacked on top of each other on the track outside the blown doors.

They looked as if they were dead.

A man lay on the edge of the pile in nothing but his underwear and a sock and shoe on his right foot. His body was charred black. The rest of his clothes had been blown off. None of the bodies were moving.

Ahead, at the front end of the third carriage, a group of passengers were yelling and pounding on the windows. Steve could see people inside trying to prise open the forwardmost set of sliding doors. It was dark in their carriage. He moved over to try and help. The doors weren't going to open no matter how hard they all pulled.

The front side window of the third carriage was broken. It had shattered when the blast ripped through from the second into the third. 'Maybe I can get them out through there,' Steve thought. He called up to the people inside to stay calm, telling them he was going to the driver's cab to get a stepladder. Someone shouted back for him to hurry.

Inside the carriage of the Aldgate train Ian Webb was aware of the exchange between the people in his carriage and the London Underground worker on the tracks but he couldn't make out what they were saying. All he heard was a succession of short, sharp sentences. They sounded animated whatever they were talking about.

Ian was standing in the front of the third carriage. He

never took the tube. He was frightened of enclosed spaces. Once, while trapped underground for over an hour, he had passed out and had to be revived by his fellow passengers. Ever since, Ian had preferred the overground service, where the doors to the carriages open to the outside world rather than the subterranean darkness of the underground. It was strange that this, of all days, would be his first on the tube for three years.

That morning Ian caught the train from Cheshunt station, near Enfield, north of London, into Liverpool Street, as he did every day. From there he usually walked across the City to Blackfriars. That took him a little over twenty minutes. Ian enjoyed the exercise; he had never made the journey to work by tube.

A few days before, he'd bought a new pair of shoes. For the first few days he left them in the office, to break in during the day, and then switched to a more comfortable pair for the walk back to Liverpool Street. The previous night he was in a hurry and left the office in his new shoes by mistake.

On the morning of 7 July Ian put them on with the intention of changing again at work, but by the time he got to Liverpool Street his feet were screaming. He didn't want to take the tube but he didn't want blisters either. So, with the step of a man not quite sure where he was going, Ian made his way across Liverpool Street station to the underground.

Once at the Circle and District Line platforms Ian almost caught the train in the wrong direction before realising his mistake and backtracking to the correct platform. When the train arrived a young woman with blonde curly hair rushed past in front of him, nearly knocking him over. She was wearing combat trousers. He shook his head in exasperation and stepped into the third carriage, looking for a seat to take the weight off his feet. They were all full.

Ian stood at the first set of doors, his back to the driver's cab, and grabbed a vertical bar to steady himself. When the bomb exploded in the next carriage the sound of twisting metal rang through his ears. Ian saw the glow of the explosion out of the corner of his right eye. It was like fire shooting out of a flamethrower, licking down the side of the train. Orange flecks of shimmering glass seemed to hang in the air for several seconds around his head like sinister fairy dust. The temperature turned hot quickly. Ian could feel heat on the back of his neck. The train stopped dead, as if the driver had suddenly dropped an anchor, and Ian fell.

He landed in a heap of fellow passengers on the floor of the carriage. The blast in the next carriage up was right near the end of that car. It blew out the windows into the third carriage, where Ian was, twisting the interconnecting doors unrecognisably. Everyone was covered in glass, their skin blasted raw where it had caught the storm of fire and shrapnel sweeping their carriage.

For a moment everything was dark. Ian didn't know where he was but he knew he wasn't standing up any more. Opening his eyes, he could see he was lying on top of a man in a suit whom he would later learn was visiting London from his native Turkey. Together they helped each other to their feet.

'Sorry for standing on your foot,' Ian said to the Turk, with characteristic British politeness.

'Are you okay?' the Turk asked.

'Yes, what on earth was that?' Ian asked.

'I think it was a bomb,' the Turk answered.

Ian stared back blankly, not knowing what to say. Keen to find an alternative answer, he peered into the second carriage. He could see the blackened mess that it had become and knew his companion was probably right.

Deep in the carriage the beam of a torch was swinging around. From his position in the third carriage, it was too dark for Ian to see anything but the dancing beam of light. It intermittently lit up silhouettes as it swung from one shadow to the next.

Ian stepped forward, drawn in, for a better look.

He got to within a few feet of what was left of the inter-connecting doors to the second carriage and stopped. He could see the orange glow on the floor where the bomb must have been; it was lighting up a wreath of twisted metal. 'Is the train going to catch fire?' he wondered. 'Are we going to burn? Am I on fire?'

A female voice was calling out of the darkness: 'Get this off me, get this off me. Help!'

Ian took the last few steps towards the bombed carriage and leaned in at the window. To his left he could see a man in a suit and a white shirt sitting on a seat. He looked dead; it was something about the colour of his skin. The woman was still screaming. It was coming from floor level. Ian's fear of enclosed spaces took over. He couldn't bring himself to look down.

'I can't see this, I can't be here,' he thought, backing away from the screams. 'I don't want to see this.'

As he moved away, another passenger pushed past him to have a look into the bombed carriage. Ian was panicking now. The smoke was making it difficult to breathe. The day he lost consciousness while stuck in a tunnel came flooding back. He thought it might happen again.

'I don't feel so well,' he said to the Turk.

'You are just shocked,' the Turk said. 'You are going to be okay.'

'No,' said Ian, 'You don't understand. I'm not so good on tubes.'

Ian moved away to an empty corner and crouched down on the floor. It was covered by an inch of broken glass and awash with blood. It was uncomfortable but he wanted somewhere safe from the smoke. He wanted to hide until it was all over. The smell of blood was disgusting; he could taste the iron dripping off his tongue.

The woman from the second carriage was still calling out. Hers wasn't a lone voice. It was joined by several others in the same carriage. They were screaming. People were banging on doors and windows. Ian was afraid. He wanted to go and soothe the desperate cries but he couldn't move. He was frozen. He felt helpless because he knew that it could just as easily have been him in there crying for help, and there would have been no one to help him. He buried his head in his knees and stayed low to the carriage floor.

Ian wasn't the only one afraid. Several others standing around him were also frozen, able to see but unable to move. Fear was rampant in all six carriages of the train. The explosion could be heard all the way to the last car. Passengers in every carriage tried to call for help on their mobiles but no one could get a signal. It was another mobile phone black spot in the tunnel.

The bomb knocked out the public address system as well. When the driver tried to make an announcement the speakers just crackled, making it sound as though sparks were flying along the top of the train all the way to the end. There was no way to communicate with the surface. More than a thousand people were alone, in the dark, and scared.

Emma Brown was blown out of one of the windows in the second carriage when the bomb went off. She landed on the tracks alongside the carriage. She was still conscious and face down when she hit the ground, her head resting on her crossed arms.

'It's cold here,' she thought, shivering. 'Why am I so cold?'

Her body was covered in blood – hers and that of her fellow passengers – but that is not why she was feeling cold. Her stomach had been ripped open. Part of a seat from the train was still inside her gut, chewing up her insides. She was losing blood. She was in shock. Her shivering was a natural reaction to the trauma her body had experienced.

Emma opened her eyes and stood up, unable to feel the open wound in her abdomen. When she got to her feet everything started spinning. She was dizzy, nauseous and confused. She stumbled across the tracks and tried to steady herself on the wall. But when she touched the hot cables running along the tunnel she burned her hands.

'Get a grip, get a grip, get a grip,' she told herself.

'Be calm, watch where you are going.

'Where *are* you going?

'What just happened?

'Where am I?

'Get a grip, get a grip, get a grip.'

'Keep off the track. Hey you, get off the track,' someone yelled at her.

Emma looked up towards the front of the train and could see the blurry outline of the driver leaning out of the side window of his cab. He was shouting down to her. She had lost her glasses. Everything was blurry. 'What's he saying?' she wondered.

'Get off the track,' he repeated, this time loud enough for Emma to hear.

'Fuck off,' she thought, irritated. 'I'm not getting back on that train. Are you fucking joking? How the fuck am I going to get back on that train?'

'She's got to get out of here, she needs help,' another male voice said, this time coming from the carriage in which, seconds earlier, Emma had been a passenger. 'She can't get back on the train.'

The voice belonged to a young man with whom she had shared a quick joke on the tube moments before. They had both gone for the same seat as they were boarding the train at Liverpool Street. The young man had got there first but had offered the seat to Emma. She'd refused his offer and stood near him as the train entered the tunnel towards Aldgate.

Emma shouldn't have had to race for a seat. She was at the platform at half past eight, plenty of time to be one of the first in the carriage. She stood next to the pastries and coffee bar that sold last-minute breakfasts to passengers waiting for the train for almost twenty minutes. She was one of the first people on the platform. It took ages for a Circle Line train to arrive.

When it finally sailed in she heard familiar voices over her shoulder. They belonged to a couple of guys in their early twenties who had been on the same overground train that Emma and her boyfriend, Andy, had taken into Liverpool Street minutes before. All the way into the city the young Asians were slagging off the Olympics, saying what a mess they would turn out to be. Emma and Andy found their negativity annoying. They were 100 per cent behind the games.

Even though Emma waited ages for a Circle Line train to arrive, and was now poised to be one of the first into the carriage, she couldn't bear the thought of having to listen to the jabbering of those morons maundering on about the Olympics for another train journey, especially without Andy to roll her eyes at. So, rather than step aboard, she ran down the platform, towards the bomb in the front of the train, desperate for another carriage.

Ian Webb was about to step into the third carriage with his blistered feet when Emma's curly blonde locks brushed past in front of him. He turned and saw a young girl with glasses in combat trousers and trainers. She looked about twenty-three, slim and attractive. Ian stepped on to the front of the third carriage while Emma just made the rear of the second before the doors closed.

She tried to get one of the last seats but a young man beat her to it. Bit of a cheek to let a girl stand, she joked. The man offered her his seat but Emma was fine where she was. The next thing she remembers she was lying outside on the track.

'She's got to get out of here,' the same young man was saying to the driver hanging out of his window. 'She can't get back on the train.'

Emma tried to walk again but stumbled. She felt someone take her arm and wrap it around his shoulder. It was the young man who had taken the seat, he said his name was Will. He had jumped off the train and rushed over to help Emma.

'Step, just take a step,' he said encouragingly.

The two of them walked arm in arm down the tunnel, through the thick smoke, towards Aldgate. Other passengers were in front and behind them on the tracks. Emma was virtually blind without her glasses and continuing to lose blood.

Will told her where to put her feet, guiding her to safety. When they got to the platform Emma could see the shapes of several London Underground uniforms racing about. She felt relieved. The sight of the uniforms was bliss. It meant that whoever was in them would be able to give her the help she so badly wanted.

Then she heard the screaming.

Two young girls, perhaps in their late teens or early twenties, were standing on the platform looking at Emma. She was a frightening sight. Her clothes were shredded. Her skin was covered in black soot and her hair was burned and matted. Passengers who saw the first of the wounded emerge from the train said they looked like grim cartoon characters.

Emma held her arms up while two people tried to pull her up off the tracks and on to the platform. As they lifted her she screamed in agony. They had to let her back down. Emma's stomach was on fire. She put her hand down to touch herself. Her belly felt weird, as if something was not quite right, as if what she was touching was somehow not hers.

When she brought her hand back up she could see it was covered in her own blood. Her stomach was hanging open. It was the first time she realised just how badly she was injured. She put her arm back down to try and hold her belly together.

Will helped her around to the end of the platform where there was a ramp. She held his hand as the two of them made their way to the station entrance. Other injured passengers were now passing her up the steps and congregating by the ticket barriers. She was the first of the seriously injured to appear. By the time she made it past the gates the first fire engines were only minutes from pulling up outside the station. Emma wanted to go home, to find Andy, to feel safe.

'Just sit down here on the kerb,' Will said. 'Just lie down.'

'I want to go home,' replied Emma. 'I just want to go home.'

'You will go home but I need to look at you first,' Will said back, moving Emma out of the station and to the left where he sat her down on the pavement.

All she could think about was what a mess she looked. Her hair was burned and covered in soot. Her clothes were shredded. Blood was dripping from her ears. Part of a seat was sticking out of her stomach. She should have been dead. Many people back in the second carriage already were, or soon would be. 'How on earth did I survive?' she thought. 'How on earth?'

## Edgware Road: second carriage, fifteen minutes later

Jason Rennie was standing over David Gardner next to the crater in the floor when I returned from the broken window. Jason was gripping the bandage on his wrist and looking absently at David lying on his back. The wound was now bleeding through the dressing on Jason's arm. The job both he and David had done to dress the wound was not quite good enough any more.

Jason turned to me. He wanted to know if there was any sign of paramedics. I told him what I had heard from Ben through the broken window: nothing yet.

David was looking greyer and paler by the minute. There was a man standing on the tracks outside the train talking to him. It was the screaming man with the satchel I'd ushered off the train when I had first arrived in the carriage. He was still deeply panicked but he was talking to David, keeping him awake. It sounded like gibberish but it was having the desired effect.

I stood there for a moment thinking, looking for something to do that would be equally useful. 'People need bandages,' I reasoned. 'I could use my shirt. I could rip it up.' It seemed silly, standing in the middle of so much horror, to think how much time I'd spent deliberating about what shirt to wear that morning now that I was about to tear it to shreds.

The only thing I was wearing that I did care about were

my cufflinks, a gift from my mother-in-law. They were blue and shaped like maple leaves. Across the face of them was the name of my home-town ice hockey team: The Toronto Maple Leafs. I wore them to remind me of home, and the family that had given them to me. I took them off and slid them into my pocket, instantly feeling guilty.

'I can't keep them,' I thought, 'people are dying here and I am thinking about some fucking cufflinks. What's wrong with me?'

I fingered the cufflinks in my pocket for what seemed like several minutes. Over and over again I thought about throwing them away, that somehow keeping them was wrong, petty, selfish. The cufflinks confused me, took me away from where I was, made me think of other things – of home, the Christmas morning in Dorset when I had unwrapped them, family.

My mind was going round in circles. I couldn't decide what to do. I was overwhelmed by fear, excitement and guilt. I was pumped up just being there, because I thought I was helping, but I was overwhelmed by my inability to do something that matched the need of the situation. Why was it not me lying on the floor instead of David, or in that hole in place of the man I'd watched die?

I could have stood there for the rest of the day, dazed, trapped and confused, if Jason hadn't put his hand on my shoulder. 'I need some more bandages for David's arm,' he said. 'He is still bleeding.'

'Of course, of course,' I said dropping the cufflinks back into my pocket and forgetting about them. I took off my suit jacket and folded it into a pillow. I knelt down to David and, with Jason's help, put it behind his head to make him more comfortable. 'I am doing something useful.' I thought, 'I'm helping.'

I unbuttoned my shirt, slipped it off and held it by the tail with both hands. I had seen people rip dresses in the movies. I was sure this was how it was done. Putting both hands together and then yanking them apart briskly, I expected the cotton to tear. It didn't. I felt embarrassed. Everyone could see me. I was bigger than most people. Here I was trying to play the hero and all I was succeeding in doing was making an ass of myself.

After several more attempts I took a short cut and made a tear in the shirt with my teeth. I could see several people sitting on the floor of the carriage at David's feet as I started to make my bandage-sized strips. I was feeling desperately self-conscious and annoyed at myself. I wanted this to end. I wanted to think no one had noticed my failing attempt at being a hero.

'Look, Katie, things are getting better already. How often do you get a strapping man like that to rip his shirt off for you, hey Katie?' It was a male voice coming from the floor, the voice of a man called Andrew Ferguson, and he was trying to calm two American girls who were sitting near David's feet.

He was making me feel better, too.

I looked down into the shadows on the floor of the carriage. Tim, Steve and I had stepped over the American girls without stopping to see how they were when we first entered the carriage. I could see now that they were women, young, perhaps in their early twenties or late teens. They were sitting on broken glass and debris.

They were sisters. Katie and Emily Benton had only been in London for a couple of days. Katie was working in Europe for several months and the pair decided to meet in London to do some sightseeing. Emily had flown over from the girls' home in Tennessee a couple of days before. The previous night they had been to a West End musical. Until that morning they had been having a great time together.

Now they were seriously injured and were being comforted by a man they had never met. Andrew's voice was all they had besides each other. He had been trying to put them at ease by talking about music and some shirt-tearing Canadian who was coming to their aid. But they were in no condition to appreciate the joke.

I kept ripping my shirt into strips and slinging them over my shoulder. I turned back to Jason and handed him a strip so that he could reinforce the dressing on David's arm. He took it, thanked me, and immediately knelt down to re-dress the wound. I crouched down with Jason to watch him work. As Jason tied the knots I noticed the bandage around his own wrist had bled through as well.

Blood was running down Jason's arm. He had been so instinctively helpful after the explosion, so concerned about others before himself, that I had forgotten to check just how seriously injured he was. One of his eardrums had burst, he had cuts and glass all over his face, his wrist was bleeding badly and his leg needed a dressing.

'I think you need a new bandage yourself, Jason,' I said.

Jason finished what he was doing and held up his wrist. He could see that I was right. I rested his hand on my shoulder and then used a piece of my shirt to wrap over the top of the bandage already there, tying it tight enough so as to apply pressure to the wound. I then did the same to the gash on his leg.

'Thanks,' Jason said, moving away dizzily to find a seat and rest. 'I didn't notice how bad it was.'

'Of course,' I replied. 'You had better sit and rest.'

I turned to look towards the rear of the carriage where we had broken the window. I was starting to adjust to the poor lighting by then and could see that Katie and Emily were in a bad way. They were both squatting on the floor. Katie was being supported by Andrew; her sister Emily was hugging her knees and rocking back and forth.

'Do you need some bandages?' I asked Andrew, who continued talking to Katie in a calm and reassuring voice, repeating her name over and over again in an attempt to convince her she was in a safe place, when nothing could have been more untrue.

'Yes, I'll take some,' he said.

I handed Andrew a couple of strips and then looked the girls over myself. It was hard to see their faces under their matted and burned hair. Scanning down their legs I could see they were both dressed in shorts, and that neither of them was wearing shoes. It was summer and they had been walking around the city in flip-flops, fine for the beach but no protection from the blast of a suicide bomb. When the explosion sent pieces of shrapnel careening along the carriage floor the girls' legs were torn to shreds.

I could see the front of Emily's feet. They were little more than mangled lumps of flesh. I had never seen wounds like that before. It was as if the skin had mushroomed outwards into a pillow of fluffy grey tissue. Despite the size of the wounds they were not bleeding. The fire from the bomb had somehow cauterised the exposed skin. While the threat of blood loss was minimised by the way the fireball had singed the exposed flesh, it did nothing to make the wounds look anything but appalling.

I took one of the bigger strips of my shirt and wrapped it around Emily's right foot, tying it tight around her ankle. She barely moved as I worked but, to keep her calm, I continued talking, telling her what I was doing. Her ears were damaged so I had to repeat myself several times. When

I had finished with Emily's foot I moved to her right hand. There was an open gash between her fingers. I only had one strip of shirt left but enough to wrap between her bloody fingers and tie across her palm.

'This is Katie and her sister Emily,' Andrew said to me. 'They are over here from America.'

'Oh,' I said. 'I am Peter, I am from Canada. You are going to be all right, girls. We are here and we are going to stay here.'

'That's right, Katie, do you hear that?' Andrew said. 'We are going to stay right here with you.'

I turned to Andrew, looking for some kind of expression that would indicate how badly injured he thought they were. I could see nothing but the outline of his head in the darkness. Andrew had cropped hair and an athletic build, that I could see, but his features were a mere shadow, his face no more than a hole with a kind voice to make it seem human.

Michael Frost was in the first carriage when the bomb went off. Afterwards he helped Ray, the train driver, evacuate most of the passengers from the front carriage, but, instead of walking with the rest of them down the tunnel, he decided to stay behind with the driver. Michael worked for Network Rail and was qualified to walk the tracks. He didn't want to leave Ray alone with his train and so stayed behind to lend a hand.

When the passengers in the first carriage had left via the exit in the driver's cab, Michael walked back into the second carriage to see if anyone was left. He made it to the rear of the carriage and stepped through the interconnecting doors into the front of the bombed carriage.

From where he stood he could see a tall, bare-chested man trying to rip his shirt, talking in a low voice.

Michael was immediately impressed that someone appeared to be taking charge, to be organising care for the injured. He wished, in that instant, that he too could have done something to help, to take charge and treat the wounded, but the whole situation was too overwhelming for him. He was beginning to think that everyone but him was being brave; he had no idea how scared the tall, bare-chested man was, how jumbled his thoughts were and how he too wished someone would come and save them all.

Michael looked around at his feet and could see two dead people lying on the floor. One was a man who was missing his left leg. He was just inside the interconnecting doors. The other was a woman to his left with long dark curly hair. There was another woman sitting just inside the door to his right who was staring off into space, and two more injured people next to her.

Michael turned around quickly to walk back to the front of the first carriage to tell Ray what was happening on his train just one carriage behind. There were several people still in the rear of the first carriage and Ray would want to know about them too.

Andrew Ferguson found himself crouching on the floor of the second carriage while I ripped my shirt apart at Edgware Road that morning because he'd forgotten the power cable to his laptop. As a roving IT consultant he needed his computer and all its component parts to do his job.

He was on his way to Reading to conduct an evaluation of one of the consultants under his supervision. He had intended to drive to Reading from his home in Brighton and avoid the hassle of taking trains through London, but that was before he realised he'd left his power cable at the office of a client in the City the day before.

Andrew shook his head. If he tried to drive into London to get the cable and then out to Reading it would take him at least three to four hours to get where he was going. There wasn't time for that. The only sensible option was to take the train into town, pick up his cable from the office, and then make his way to Paddington, where he could catch another train to Reading.

When Andrew got to the train station he found a spot to leave his car, slipped his rucksack over his shoulders and made his way to the mobile espresso bar in the car park. He went there whenever he took the train into London. He loved his coffee first thing and enjoyed the early morning banter with the espresso bar's owner, Gary, who was always eager to talk about his sailing boat.

Andrew was one of Gary's friendlier customers. Despite being in his early thirties, his thick hair had turned a light grey. With his friendly tone and smiling face, Andrew came across as someone fatherly, easy to talk to, disarming. After chatting about Gary's boat and his own children, Andrew went into the station. So began the journey that would culminate in his meeting the two young Americans at Edgware Road.

When Andrew got to Victoria station he took the Circle Line to Embankment, collected his cable from his client's office and left for Paddington. The easy thing to do would have been simply to take the Circle Line anticlockwise, going eastbound. This would have meant no changes. But it was early and Andrew wasn't thinking.

He decided on a route that required two changes, the last at Baker Street, where he would pick up the Circle Line again for the short journey to Paddington. When he got to the platform at Baker Street, Andrew stepped into the front of the third carriage and stood next to a small Italian woman

101

in a long brown coat who was reading a novel. She had boarded the train at King's Cross where she narrowly avoided stepping into the second carriage with the bomber.

She was immersed in her reading and didn't notice Andrew until his rucksack started to bump her book as the train rumbled along the tracks. She kept trying to catch Andrew's eye to make him realise what a nuisance he was being, but not once did he turn around. She would have moved, but that end of the carriage was packed and her spot was as good as any. Andrew was facing forward, looking at the front of his carriage, lost in thought, when a loud thud hammered through his eardrums and into the back of his head.

The sound was immediately followed by the train screeching to a halt for what felt like at least twenty seconds. Andrew was thrown forward into the glass partition in front of him. Along both sides of the carriage he could see what he thought was a spray of sparks bouncing off the windows.

The Italian woman in the brown coat saw the light show as well and thought it was a bomb. The sparks were coming from high up rather than from track level. 'What else could it be?' Andrew never considered terrorism, and, despite where he would spend the next hour, he would not realise what had happened until he was sitting at the bar of a hotel, two hours later, having a drink to steady his shattered nerves.

For now people were screaming in Andrew's carriage. He turned around and came face to face with the Italian woman. She was afraid. Andrew could see that clearly.

'Oh my God. Oh my God,' she repeated.

'You're okay,' Andrew said to her, grasping her shoulders. 'Try to stay calm. You're all right. What is your name?'

'Andrea, my name is Andrea,' she replied.

'Andrea, my name is Andrew. Try to stay calm.'

Smoke was now starting to fill the carriage, and, as it did, people standing near Andrew and Andrea became increasingly frantic. Some people were screaming. Others were crying. Two men standing in the doorway near Andrew were trying to force open one of the sliding doors to help clear the smoke that was flooding the carriage but the doors wouldn't budge.

It was then that Andrew noticed the initial screams of panic from within his carriage had stopped. People were still afraid, but their fear had been replaced by concern, or curiosity, or both. There were louder screams, more terrifying screams, coming from the carriage in front of Andrew's.

The voices were painful, desperate. Andrew noticed that everyone around him had stopped to listen. It was the same in my carriage when the bomb first went off. We all stood there wondering how bad it must be to make people shriek like that. But Andrew was closer to the horror than I was; it was only on the other side of the door into the next carriage. He couldn't see in there because, like me, his carriage was divided from the one in front by an unused driver's cabin that didn't have windows on one side.

As he stood listening to the chorus of fear, among the screams came a cry for help that cut through all the others:

'Somebody get me out of here,' the voice shrieked. 'Please get me out of here.

'Someone help me, someone please.

'Someone help.'

It sounded as if it was under the train. That was odd. Most of the screams were coming from the carriage in front of him. Andrew moved towards the door into the unused driver's cabin and looked for a way to prise it open. The screams of agony from under the train were still ringing in his ears.

## Edgware Road: on the tunnel floor between the train and the wall

The scream that rose above all the other screams, the voice ringing in Andrew's ears, belonged to a man lying on the tunnel floor between Edgware Road and Paddington. He'd been blown out of the train when the bomb went off. He was alone. He was in darkness.

At first his sense of uncertainty was not dissimilar to the one you have when waking in a strange bed in a dark room. For a moment you're not sure which way you're lying, or which way the bed is facing. If you lie still long enough you can piece it all together without having to turn on the light. Ultimately you know you are somewhere safe. If you don't know where you are, all you have to do is turn the light on. Mystery solved.

On 7 July there was no light, no place safe from the dark. One minute hundreds of people were reading their newspapers, ignoring the person next to them or listening to music on their headphones. Then, suddenly, the entire world dropped away and they were in shadow. But unlike the darkness of a strange bedroom, the carriages underground were not quiet that day. They were filled with screams of terror and the murderous wrenching of metal train parts ripping and twisting under the heat and force of a deliberate explosion.

Few ever hear screams like the ones heard in the tunnels on 7 July. They were complete in their expression of an emotion experienced to its absolute maximum: fear. People couldn't have been more afraid because they didn't know where they were, if they were alive, if they were whole or if they were about to die. There was nothing to suggest clarity, only horror and fright.

A dim light from the dirty bulbs along the tunnel walls (or perhaps it came from a train on the parallel track) slowly began to establish itself through the clearing smoke. First there were only silhouettes, then barely lit faces. Each of the trapped, each of the bombed, looked around desperately for something they could recognise, something safe they would remember from the light. But the faces now coming into focus were not like the ones they had seen in the illuminated carriage a few moments before. These faces were masked in fear, soaked in blood, and distorted by panic. Each new visible clue was more horrible than the last.

This was terrorism.

At first people felt themselves all over. For those who found they were in one piece there was relief. There were others, though, who regained consciousness only long enough to die, confused and afraid in the dark, and there were still more who were filled with terror as the dread of their predicament became clear.

For Danny Biddle the nightmare came to him with a scream so loud that it reverberated down the tunnel and into the train carriages packed with commuters on their way to work. Danny's scream stopped people in their tracks and made them forget, for only a moment, that whatever was happening to them, however afraid they were, was nothing compared to the terror in the voice of the man screaming for help from somewhere under the train.

The leap from normality to horror was just as sudden for Danny as it had been for everyone else, but the outcome would be far worse. One minute he was concerned about being late for work, the next worrying not if but when he was going to die. If he could only turn back the clock a few hours, to the moment when he had decided to go to work, after all, despite not feeling well, perhaps then it could all still be a dream.

Perhaps it would end like a nightmare always does, perhaps he could wake up and leave the horror behind.

When his alarm had gone off that morning just before five, Danny could barely open his eyes. A migraine had a hold of him and it was squeezing his brain till he felt like being sick. Danny's fiancée told him to stay in bed, to call his boss and take the day off. Danny didn't listen to her advice. Instead he reset the alarm, went back to bed and tried to sleep off the pain.

An hour later he awoke feeling much better; he showered, had breakfast and dressed before leaving to catch the 248 bus down Clockhouse Lane to Romford station. He would be late for work but he wanted to go in regardless. It was in his nature to work hard. When Danny got to Liverpool Street he looked at his watch; he was still behind schedule. He started running for the tube.

Danny was heading for Baker Street to catch the Bakerloo Line to Wembley where he was working as a building site manager. Knowing he was bound to be late he composed a text message on his mobile phone. When he got to Baker Street he planned to leave the station briefly, text work and then return to the underground for the rest of his journey. But Danny was useless at texting.

It took him ages to compose his text to his boss and when he had finished he realised he'd just missed his stop. He was at Edgware Road, two stops past Baker Street. Looking at the map above the seats opposite, Danny could see that the Bakerloo Line also stopped at Paddington, the next station. He could change for the Bakerloo Line there.

When Danny got on the Circle Line at Liverpool Street there were no seats, and so, when he stepped through the doors and into the second carriage, he simply let them close behind him and leaned with his left side up against the partition. When the train stopped at King's Cross he was so busy trying to thumb out his text that he didn't notice Khan, wearing a rucksack and a white baseball cap, stepping into the carriage to take the vacated seat directly to his left on the other side of the glass.

All the way around to Edgware Road both men were preoccupied, Danny with his text messaging and Khan with his plot to murder everyone around him. As the train left Edgware and pulled into the tunnel, Danny put his phone away, and for a moment looked down at Khan sitting in the seat to his left. The two men were only feet apart.

Danny noticed Khan's light-green jacket, the watch on his left wrist, the white baseball cap and the small backpack he was holding on his lap. Danny didn't suspect a thing about the Asian man. Why would he? Khan looked like a guy on his way to work, or out for a day's shopping. Lots of people looked like Khan on the tube. There was no reason to give it a second thought.

Then Khan put his right hand through the top zip of his bag. And that was it.

At first Danny was overwhelmed by a burst of light, as if millions of flash bulbs had suddenly gone off at once. Then came the abrupt change in pressure, as if someone had pumped the carriage full of compressed air. White noise slammed into his eardrums and he felt himself flying backwards, out of the train, and crash hard into the tunnel wall before landing on his back next to the tracks on the gravel-covered ground.

Lying there in the dark, his body angled towards Edgware Road, Danny couldn't see anything at first. Then he made out a train speeding at him over his left shoulder towards Paddington. It was inches from his head. The train looked like a mountain of moving metal. His first thought was that he had somehow fallen out of the doors and been electrocuted. It seemed to make sense.

Except for a flickering light everything was dark. It was coming from his stomach. It was fire. Danny tried to sit up but couldn't move his body so he craned his neck to look across his chest; it seemed fine, but there were flames on his left arm. It was on fire, too. The flames were several inches high and stretched from his fingertips, past his wrist, up to his bicep. He looked at his other arm. It was engulfed in flames as well.

'Fuck, I'm on fire,' he thought, 'fuck, fuck, fuck.'

He could feel the metal strap of the watch on his right wrist searing into his skin like a branding iron. He fumbled it open and threw the watch away. Then he started waving his arms frantically, patting them down with his hands until they stopped burning.

With the flames out he dropped his head behind him and looked back. The lighting along the tunnel wall was only dim but Danny could see the train had been destroyed. There was debris all around him. Ten metres behind him, lying in almost the same position as him, was a woman with blonde hair. Like Danny, she had been blown out of the carriage. She was crying out. He was not alone. She must have fallen out too.

Danny allowed his head to drop again and his eyes to drift upwards to the tunnel roof as he tried to catch his breath. He could see the brickwork in the tunnel ceiling. He could see row upon row of thick cable lining the walls and wondered what it was for. His eyes were adjusting to the darkness. Then, in among the cables, he could see something else.

It was a human leg.

He tried to lift himself to get a better view but he was pinned to the ground. The carriage door he had been leaning on was now lying across his waist like a blanket of steel. He tried to move it with his hands but it was too heavy. He couldn't get any leverage, and he wondered why. His eyes returned to the hanging leg. That's when it occurred to him: 'I can't feel my legs.'

He put his hand down under the door to try and feel for his thigh but there was nothing, no sensation, just mangled flesh and mush. Panic surged. Instinctively he put his right hand up to his forehead, but when his fingers touched his scalp there was immediately something wrong. Danny paused for a moment. There was a gash in his forehead. He felt further and half his hand slid under his scalp. He could feel his fingers on his exposed skull. When he pulled his hand away to look at it he could see the tendons moving under his charred skin.

He was on fire; it looked as if one of his legs was suspended above him, he was pinned to the ground and his head was pouring blood. But worst of all, there was no one there to help. The realisation of what had happened to him sent Danny into a screaming panic that people would be able to hear from the front to the back of the tunnel.

'Somebody get me out of here,' he yelled, 'please get me out of here.

'Someone help me, someone please help me.

'Someone help.'

Andrew Ferguson could only bear to listen to Danny screaming for a moment before feeling compelled to do something to distract himself. His carriage was filling with smoke and it was difficult to breathe. If he could open the door into the unused driver's cabin, which led to the carriage in front of him, he might be able to clear some of the foul air.

He moved towards the driver's cab and tried the door. It was locked. A middle-aged man in a suit was kicking a small pane of glass close to the carriage floor. Behind it lay a handle that could be removed and used to open the door. Force wasn't working. The man delved into his bag and pulled out an adaptor plug. He stabbed it at the emergency glass a few times until the plug broke.

'Here, let me have a go,' Andrew said stepping forward with a shoe in his hand.

Andrew swung the heel of his loafer into the glass and after a couple of tries it broke. He took out the handle, slotted it into the door and pulled it open. The driver's cabin was in darkness. Windows on the other side of it afforded a view into the second carriage. Through the windows Andrew could see several figures moving about in the dark. Then he saw a face. It was pressed against the glass door from inside the second carriage. Andrew stepped in and opened the door.

The face was that of a City gentleman. He was wearing a suit and carrying a black leather satchel with an umbrella through the straps of the handle. He stood taller than Andrew's five foot eight but was less athletic in appearance. His cultivated accent, upright posture and confident attitude gave him the air of someone used to being in a position of authority.

'Did you get the fireball?' he asked Andrew. 'We got a fireball.'

'No, we—' Andrew tried to answer.

'Is everyone in here okay? Did you try to get anyone out?'

'We were just—'

The man cut Andrew off again.

Andrew was beginning to get irked as the man didn't seem to be listening to a word he was saying. He kept on firing out questions and statements at Andrew, without giving him a chance to reply.

'Right,' the man said. 'I am going to go to the back of the train. I will find a way out and then I will send someone back here for you.'

And with that he was gone, storming up the carriage towards Edgware Road, never to be seen by Andrew again. The next to step out of the second carriage was a much younger man, probably early to mid-twenties. He had a dark complexion, was wearing a tan leather jacket and looked as if he needed a shave.

'I'm autistic. Do you know what that means?' the young man asked Andrew. 'I need to get to college. How am I going to get to college? I need to tell my mum where I am. Who is going to tell my mum where I am? I'm autistic, do you know what that means?'

'Yes, I know what autistic means,' Andrew replied, moving the man to one of the free seats just inside the front of the third carriage. 'Come and sit here and I will help you out.'

Andrew could see how frightened the young man was and it brought tears to his eyes. There was no way the young man could understand what had happened to him; all he knew was that he was scared and wanted his mother. It was heartbreaking.

When Jackie Putnam arrived at King's Cross station earlier that morning to catch the Circle Line she made her way on to the platform where she knew the second carriage would stop. She stood there every day. The last two weeks had been hard for Jackie. She had just finalised her divorce. She was stressed and was looking for a hassle-free ride on the tube.

But just as the train pulled up she noticed a young man walk over and stand next to her. He was in his early twenties and was wearing a tan leather jacket. But what Jackie noticed most were his eyes. They were staring intensely at everyone standing near him. He was walking awkwardly and making strange sounds.

Jackie didn't like the idea of sharing a carriage with him. She wasn't up for adventure today. So as the train came to a stop she rushed along the platform and jumped into the first carriage, taking a seat just behind the cabin from where Ray Whitehurst was driving his train.

The man with the intense eyes had no intention of harming her. He was simply autistic and a little confused. But it was his confused behaviour that quite probably spared Jackie's life.

Three or four young women came through next and Andrew turned away from the autistic lad to see if they were all right. All could walk but some of their faces had been burned or lacerated by flying glass. The passengers at Andrew's end of the third carriage helped them into seats as Andrew went into the unused driver's cabin to see if he could find out why everyone coming from the second carriage was covered in soot and blood.

He stepped through the interconnecting doors and peered into the gloom. Then there was a crashing sound. Someone was breaking a window to Andrew's right.

'Vandals,' Andrew thought. 'Someone is trashing the place.'

He stepped through for a better look and could see people

climbing through the window they had just broken. They were coming from the train that had stalled on the parallel track. The first figure was a balding, middle-aged man who Andrew would later learn was a school teacher named Tim Coulson. The next through was a tall guy in a suit. He sounded American. Two more people came through and they all moved forward in the carriage.

Andrew followed them. He didn't understand what was going on. 'Why would someone break a window? Why would they want to cause damage to the train? Why climb in here? This place is a mess,' he said to himself.

Andrew still couldn't tell that anyone was injured.

He walked forward a little more and could see two young women sitting on the floor. Both of them wore shorts and had long, dark hair. One was facing forward, towards a crater in the floor. A man in a suit was supporting her from behind. The other girl was sitting next to the first, hugging her knees and rocking back and forth.

Andrew looked at the girls and could see they were sitting next to a man's feet. Andrew was drawn to them because one of the feet was cocked over in a way that seemed unnatural. Andrew was looking at David Gardner. His eyes moved up David's leg to his chest; then he saw me leaning over him. We were talking in low voices.

At Andrew's feet lay another man, who he would later learn was a university professor from Bristol. He was slightly overweight and his face was covered in blood. He wasn't moving his limbs but Andrew could see from his chest that he was still breathing.

'Does anyone have some water?' a voice called out from the shadows. 'We could do with some water.'

Andrew looked around to see who was calling out but couldn't see anyone.

'Does anyone need anything in there?' another voice asked, this time coming from the broken window where he had just seen people climbing through. Andrew looked through into the train on the parallel track. On the other side was a young man with short-cropped dark hair.

'Water, yes, we do need some water,' Andrew answered instinctively.

When I jumped through the window with Tim and Steve into the bombed carriage Ben stayed behind. He was convinced the three of us were medically trained, perhaps even doctors. He decided, therefore, that there was no reason for him to go over as well, so he stayed put.

Ben was shocked by what he saw. It was as if the whole carriage had been gutted: seats were missing, windows were broken, the floor was twisted and everything was burned, black or in darkness. There was little to remind him that he was looking at what had once been a tube carriage.

He could see there were injured people on the floor being attended to by other passengers. He could see people moving about in the darkness, but not what they were doing; it was too dark for that. He was beginning to wish he had gone in to help himself but not enough actually to climb through the window.

'Does anyone need anything in there?' he shouted. For a second there was no answer, then a voice called out:

'Water, yes, we do need some water.'

Ben turned around and asked everyone within earshot if they had any water for the bombed carriage. He received several bottles and passed them through the window to Andrew. He was handed perhaps a dozen bottles, all of which he passed through.

\*

Andrew handed the first few bottles of water out to the people standing around him. When it kept coming he started to stockpile it in a corner of the carriage. He joked through the window with Ben about how much people were carrying that day and where it might be coming from.

Andrew handed a bottle to Katie and Emily. As he did so the man in the suit who had been sitting behind Katie, comforting her, looked up to Andrew and said: 'Would you mind taking over?'

'Of course,' Andrew replied kneeling down behind Katie and helping to support her weight.

Both of the girls were hurt but Katie was worse off than her sister and would soon struggle to stay conscious.

'I'm Andrew, are you okay? What's your name?' he asked.

'I'm Emily and this is my sister Katie,' Emily said.

Andrew was talking to both of them but Emily was the only one answering. Katie was already too weak to speak. To keep them alert Andrew asked them where they were from and what they were doing in London. They were from Tennessee, they answered, and had only been in London a couple of days.

The conversation continued. Andrew asked them if they liked country and western music, provoking laughter from Emily. It was neither sisters' kind of music. They were deeply religious. Emily was in a choir. Andrew's chatter was working. He was distracting them from their injuries, which he could now see were quite extensive, especially to their feet.

Andrew looked towards the front of the carriage as he talked with the girls. He could see David Gardner on the floor in front of him. Andrew saw the awkward angle of David's foot and scanned up his leg. It looked as if it was embedded in the floor or under something, but it wasn't. It had been cut to pieces.

Andrew could also see that the tall man who had been leaning over David was now standing up in front of the girls trying to rip his shirt into strips. The material wouldn't give and Andrew could see the growing frustration on the man's face.

To brighten the mood Andrew spoke aloud: 'Look, Katie, things are getting better already. How often do you get a strapping man like that to rip his shirt off for you, hey Katie?'

The girls nodded but didn't say anything. They were growing weaker by the minute.

## St James's Park: Network Operations Centre control room

At St James's Park Andy Barr was pacing backwards and forwards in the Network Operations Centre control room barking questions at his staff. It had taken much longer than he would have liked to get a handle on what was happening on his network. Still, his team were doing their best, and he knew it; he just needed answers.

When Celia Harrison put in the first call from Aldgate station notifying Andy of a power failure and thick black smoke flooding the platforms, Andy had one problem. In the ensuing ten minutes dozens of calls from dozens of stations came in reporting similar power failures and smoke, turning what had been a problem for Andy into a crisis for the network. Trying to find out what had happened was like looking for a sheep in a snowstorm.

Andy's problem was that he was receiving calls from stations reporting power failures in the stations and on the tracks in clusters of stations at both ends of the Circle Line and in the middle of the Piccadilly Line. But because power is supplied locally, the power also went down in those stations, trains and underground lines that had not been bombed, but were in the same area as those that had.

As far as the Network Operations Centre control room was concerned, Andy and his team had two essential tasks: first and most important he had to find out where every train was so that he could move them into a station where passengers could be evacuated. Second, he had to work out where the emergency services needed to be sent. Unfortunately, one of the essential tools that would have helped solve the first problem had gone down at the very beginning.

Tracker Net, the electronic eye of the London Underground, was in the process of being installed on all underground lines but had not yet been set up on the Piccadilly Line. The Circle Line's Tracker Net system, however, had been completed. Despite the way Tracker Net can effectively show the control centre the position of any train at a glance, it has one fatal flaw: it relies on the same low-voltage power supply that supplies London Underground's signalling system.

When the bombs were detonated the explosions were powerful enough to destroy not only the trains, but also the cables and tracks running electricity throughout the system, thus blinding the electronic eye. Each line control room which had come to rely on the system now had no choice but to refer to their handwritten logs to tell them which trains had stopped at stations and which were trapped in tunnels.

Tracking down every train was slow. There were more than five hundred in service at the time and at least 200,000 passengers travelling on the network. Line controllers had to talk to drivers via radio, get their train numbers and locations and then cross them off the list in the log books one by one. To find the trains without working radios line controllers had to call each station and ask for the train numbers of the tubes at their platforms. Where trains were missing, staff had to be sent into the tunnels with torches to find them. Some trains would spend over two hours in a tunnel before they were found.

Working out where the trains were and ensuring passengers could be evacuated was Andy Barr's chief concern, but he also needed to know where to send the emergency services. Although the general public and station staff themselves had been putting in 999 calls from the outset, Andy needed to establish his own picture of where help was going and why. In emergency situations like these he was gold control, the primary contact for the emergency services.

Celia Harrison's initial calls from Aldgate to Andy and his team were early and clear. Within three minutes of the bomb injured passengers were already walking out of the tunnels, through thick clouds of smoke, looking for help. Whether it was a bomb or a power surge didn't matter to Andy. It was clear that there was enough smoke to summon both fire and ambulance crews to the stations on both sides of the trapped train and thus the response to Aldgate was both decisive and swift.

The first reports from Edgware Road, however, were, while still relatively early, much less clear. At 8.59, nine minutes after the explosion, a call came into Andy's team at St James's Park claiming that a tube leaving Edgware Road station had hit a tunnel wall and that there was a passenger under the train. The London Ambulance Service was contacted and appraised of the situation.

The truth was, of course, that the train had not left the tracks or hit a wall: it had been bombed and there was not one person under the train but several, who had been blown out of the carriage. Some of them had been killed instantly; others were fighting for their lives both on the tracks and inside the carriage.

The first ambulance reached Edgware Road at 9.12. Two minutes later medical crews placed a call saying that there had been an explosion resulting in up to 1,000 casualties.

The wide tunnels and close proximity of the explosion to the station allowed for as swift an assessment as that made at Aldgate. The paramedics on the scene might not have understood the reality of the situation in the bombed carriage but they knew it was serious.

The Piccadilly Line train that had been bombed between Russell Square and King's Cross, however, was a different prospect altogether. The tunnels the Piccadilly Line uses are not like the sub-surface tunnels used by Circle Line trains. The tunnels between Russell Square and King's Cross are round, and barely wide enough to fit the smaller, more tubular trains that run on the line. Most of the way through the Piccadilly Line there are only inches between the train and the tunnel wall, leaving no room for people to jump out of windows or doors and walk alongside the tracks, as they had done at Aldgate and Edgware Road.

To compound this sense of imprisonment, each of the Piccadilly Line train's six carriages was loaded to absolute capacity. No one could move. It felt as if there wasn't enough air to breathe and people quickly became upset and panicky. The train was also more isolated than those on the Circle Line because of its greater depth under ground. The tunnel between King's Cross and Russell Square is seventy feet below street level compared to barely fifteen on the Circle Line. The distance from the front of the train to Russell Square was almost 500 metres, with King's Cross station being 250 metres from the last carriage at the rear.

The train could not be seen from the platform and so its isolation made it difficult for London Underground staff in the stations and control centre to work out exactly what had happened. Smoke didn't flood the platforms as it had done at Aldgate either. The tight, enclosed nature of the tube slowed considerably the escape of smoke down the tunnel. What smoke that did slowly drift alongside the train had a long way to go before it reached a platform and so, at first, no one on the surface or in the Picadilly Line stations underground had any idea of the severity of the situation.

The man frantically trying to work out exactly what was happening between King's Cross and Russell Square was Gary Fitzgerald, back in the Piccadilly Line control room at Earl's Court. He was desperate for any information he might relay to Andy at the Network Operations Centre. He knew better than anyone just how crowded his trains were. After earlier calling Andy's team to tell them he had seen smoke and someone running down the eastbound Piccadilly Line track at King's Cross, he had been promised the emergency services. Help was on the way but still Gary wasn't satisfied: there was too much he didn't know about what was happening to his train. He needed answers. He needed someone to go into the tunnel and look for himself.

King's Cross is the busiest tube interchange in London. During the morning peak on any weekday, between 7.45 and 8.45 a.m. nearly 25,000 passengers will enter the station to board one of the six tube lines that meet in the tunnels beneath the street. Managing the flow of human traffic on the escalators, platforms and staircases is akin to herding sheep. That morning Simon Cook was the shepherd.

Simon was one of King's Cross's duty station managers. He had joined the London Underground's graduate trainee scheme after three years as an officer in the Royal Navy and at twenty-six was already considered to be one of the bright young men on the London Underground. At 8.50 he was standing above ground, where the up escalators of the Piccadilly and Victoria meet, when the power in part of the station suddenly failed. Five of King's Cross's nine escalators and the Piccadilly Line immediately ground to a halt. Simon knew the station would have to be closed. It wouldn't be safe to keep it open with so many passengers and no escalators to shift them around.

Within a couple of minutes of the power failure two of London Underground's customer service agents approached Simon and told him they smelled smoke on the eastbound Piccadilly Line platform. He decided to investigate and pushed his way past the flow of people now walking up the escalators, down to the platform below. Once there he did see smoke but not enough worry him. Assuming that it was nothing more than newspapers or rubbish that had got caught up in the tracks and was burning, he made his way back up the escalators to begin evacuating the station.

Back upstairs, he entered the station control room and started making calls. There were lots of people to contact: Gary Fitzgerald's team in the line control offices at Earl's Court; Network Rail, which operated the overground trains coming into the terminal at street level; the stations on either side of King's Cross on each of the six underground lines that ran through the station. All of them needed to be informed of the evacuation.

When he had finished making calls and delegating the rest to staff in the control room, Simon returned to the area at the top of the Victoria and Piccadilly Line escalators. It was now just after 9.00 a.m. The flow of people was now down to a trickle. Everything seemed normal and he was now slightly less concerned about the earlier power failure. Until, that is, he saw two passengers coming up from the Piccadilly Line covered in black soot.

They were clearly shaken.

Something was seriously wrong.

He decided to take a second look at where that smoke was coming from.

Pushing his way down the escalator again Simon reached the eastbound platform, now deserted but for two British Transport Police officers who were looking into the eastbound tunnel. Thick clouds of smoke were now pouring out and the three men agreed that this was no burning newspaper. There was a fire in the tunnel. There had to be.

Using his radio Simon called up to the control room with a message for someone to contact the London Fire Brigade. He didn't wait for a response. He told the officers he was going into the tunnel to investigate. He knew that sending someone down there – or going himself – was the only way to find out what was going on. The policemen tried to stop him but argument was futile: Simon was determined and jumped on to the tracks and marched into the darkness and smoke waving his small Maglite torch.

About thirty metres along the tracks Simon met two passengers walking towards him.

'How do we get out of here?' they asked him.

'Carry on past me and you will be right at the platform,' he said.

Simon continued walking another 300 metres or so into the eastbound Piccadilly Line tunnel, expecting to come across the stricken train, but instead, he was stopped cold by something else. It was to his left. It was the opening to another tunnel that linked his with the westbound Piccadilly Line tunnel running parallel. The opening was pouring with smoke.

Simon couldn't see what was on the other side of the crossover tunnel. There was too much smoke but he knew that the train he was looking for was at the other end. It had to be.

As he stood there it all started to make sense. Because

Piccadilly Line trains fit so snugly into the tunnels, with only inches on either side of the train, the smoke from the westbound tunnel was not able to waft down towards the westbound platform. The only escape route the smoke had was through the crossover, which led into the eastbound tunnel and platform. That was why Gary Fitzgerald, back in the line control office at Earl's Court, was so curious as to why a train on the westbound track was causing smoke to flood the eastbound platform.

Simon turned left into the smoke and walked forward through the crossover tunnel towards the parallel track. His eyes slowly adjusted to the darkness and before long he could make out the side of a tube train. It must have come to a stop across the opening to the crossover.

It was clear that someone had broken one of the side windows to the carriage and people were jumping out onto the tracks below and walking up the crossover towards him. It was the only way out. The train fit too tightly into the tunnel to walk alongside it to either end. Once out of the window the only way from there was through the crossover and back the way Simon had come.

He quickly worked out he was in a blind alley. The only way to the front of the train was by forcing the doors to the side of the carriage and then climbing into the train and walking through the cars, one by one, to the front to find the driver.

With the help of eight or nine of the trapped passengers Simon managed to prise open one of the pairs of sliding doors. They shouldn't have opened like that but they did. Once the doors were open, people started jumping down on to the tracks. Two male passengers who were among the first out of the carriage stayed with Simon as he helped people safely negotiate the four-foot drop to the tunnel floor.

'Walk through this tunnel, turn right and keep going,' he told them. 'The traction current is off and there will be London Underground staff at the station ready to help you.'

When the carriage was nearly empty Simon climbed in the side of the train and moved from the third carriage through the interconnecting doors into the second. When he reached the front end, he could see a teenage girl trying to climb through the tiny window in the upper half of the interconnecting doors between the first and second carriages. He helped her through and then tried to push the doors open. They would not budge. They were twisted and jammed.

Simon kicked them as hard as he could until they gave in.

When the doors opened about twenty people flooded forward, pushing him aside in their haste to get out of the carriage. Some were covered in blood and black soot and all were clearly panicking. Beyond them, in the first carriage of the train, there was almost no light. Everything was black. Looking past the escaping crowd Simon could see flashes of what they were leaving behind.

When passengers stopped coming through the door Simon walked into the rear of the bombed carriage and with his small torch panned around the car. It was completely destroyed. Two metres into the carriage the ceiling had collapsed inwards and hung in twisted sheets of metal right up to the front of the carriage. All of the windows were broken and the car itself looked as though it had been blown in half in the middle.

A French girl was crying. She couldn't have been more than sixteen. She was sitting on one of the benches along the right-hand side of the carriage. Her foot was badly injured and she couldn't stand. Simon could see she was terrified and he could hear it in her voice as well. She just kept repeating words to herself over and over in broken English as she rocked back and forth in her seat.

'When doctors come? When doctors come? When doctors come?'

The floor was thick with bodies. Some were still alive but most, it seemed, were not. Simon could hear moans, cries for help, but where to start? On the floor in front of him was a man with a badly injured knee. He took off his jacket and wrapped it around the wound, applying pressure.

'I am a duty manager from King's Cross,' Simon said. 'I just want to let you know that the police are aware and help is coming.'

That was Simon's hope anyway. The two British Transport Police officers on the platform should by now have been alerted to the need for the emergency services by the people Simon had already helped off the train. The blood-soaked faces of the passengers who had nearly trampled him when he had kicked open the doors to the bombed carriage would surely convey the message more graphically than words.

Simon toyed with the idea of leaving the train and going back up into the station to make sure Gary Fitzgerald in the line control room knew the extent of what was going on. Simon's naval training had taught him that the first person on the scene of an incident like this should go and get help, but he stayed where he was; he couldn't leave those frightened people alone in the dark.

Back at Earl's Court, Gary Fitzgerald was growing ever more anxious. He had reports from both King's Cross and Russell Square that station staff had gone into the tunnels from both stations to investigate the cause of the smoke and to find the driver of the train stuck in the dark, but twenty minutes had now passed and there was still no word from under ground.

On the CCTV monitor Gary could see more passengers arriving on the eastbound Piccadilly Line platform at King's Cross. He could see the smoke thickening. He could see police and station staff pulling passengers off the tracks. But he couldn't see what he most wanted to see: the train. It was hidden in the darkness of the tunnel. The passengers he was so proud to ship to work every morning were trapped underground like miners after a pitfall, and all Gary could do was wait.

## Aldgate: 8.50 a.m.

When Shehzad Tanweer's bomb blew up just short of Aldgate all the lighting in the second and third carriages was destroyed, leaving the most seriously injured in almost total darkness. The neighbouring track was empty. The only light came from the dirty and dim emergency tunnel lights high up on the walls.

The bulbs were weak and the plastic covers protecting them were caked in grime, years of tunnel dust kicked up by passing trains. They didn't afford enough light to see by at first. The smoke was too thick. Fortunately Benjamin Cotton had a torch. He was sitting at the front end of the second carriage fiddling with his BlackBerry when the bomb went off. Had he been at the other end of the carriage he might have been killed.

His first thought was that the battery in his BlackBerry had exploded, causing all the lights in the carriage to short circuit.

'I've made all these people late for work,' he thought. 'It is my fault. The other passengers will be furious.'

He looked at his BlackBerry again. The screen was still lit. It hadn't exploded. Something else had. People all around him were screaming.

He was blind to everything around him. That is when he remembered his bicycle headlamp. It was in his pannier, between his feet, on the carriage floor. He had ridden his bike to Princes Risborough station in Buckinghamshire that morning where he caught the train to Liverpool Street.

He reached into his bag and felt for the light. When he turned it on the cries around him seemed to stop. He couldn't believe how dark it was. He didn't think anyone at work would believe it either so he took a photograph with the camera on his BlackBerry. All that came out was one of the yellow vertical bars passengers hang on to when they're standing: it looked like the kind of photograph a deep-sea diver would take inside a shipwreck.

'What is happening? What is going on?' a man standing next to Benjamin asked. 'I'm blind. I can't see.'

'Well, then, this is one of those rare situations where I am not much better off than you,' Benjamin said in his cultivated voice, taking the man by the hand and guiding him to a seat. 'We've been in some sort of crash and all the lighting has gone. Stay here for a moment. I will come back for you.'

'I'm a doctor,' said a thin woman in her late forties, sitting close by.

'It sounds like they need help down there,' Benjamin said to the doctor, swinging his torch towards the rear of the train. 'What do you think?'

Silhouettes could be seen near to where the bomb had exploded. The doctor and Benjamin strained to see along the length of the torch's beam. To get a better look they would have to walk back into the carriage. When they reached the middle of the car Benjamin could see a woman lying on her back on a row of seats to his left. It looked as if she'd been thrown backwards by the blast, her head smashing through the glass partition behind her, before landing on the seats. She wasn't moving.

The doctor rushed over and dropped to her knees. The woman looked as if she was alive but only just. She had a serious injury to her neck. The doctor was trying to assess her but there was no response.

'Is she going to be okay?' Benjamin asked.

'No, she is not,' answered the doctor. 'We need to get her out of here.'

The ambulance crews were not going to make it on time. Despite Aldgate being the first incident reported to emergency services that morning an ambulance would not arrive at the entrance to Aldgate station until twenty-four minutes after the explosion. The paramedics would not get into the tunnels for a further twenty-five minutes or so after that. The young woman had no chance.

Benjamin bowed his head when he heard the doctor's words. He wanted to do something useful so he looked around to see if anyone else needed help. He could see four people sitting in a row of seats opposite the fatally injured woman. They were frozen. Their eyes were open but they were not moving or saying anything. Benjamin stared at them for a moment, wondering what to do.

'It is better to leave them,' he thought. 'I might make things worse if I go over there.'

As Benjamin was backing away a man came and stood close to him, next to the injured woman and the doctor trying to treat her.

Melvin Finn boarded the train at the previous stop and stood leaning his left side against the glass partition. It was the same one that had been shattered by the head of the woman now lying on the seats in front of him. She must have slammed into his left side, sending him crashing to the floor; at least, that was the most plausible explanation Melvin could come up with.

Whatever had hit him sent him crashing to the floor. Lying

there in the dark as the initial fireball from the explosion had washed over him and screams filled his head, he desperately sought an answer to what was going on.

'What the fuck was that?' he asked himself, still on the floor, confused.

'Have I just had a brain haemorrhage?

'Is this what a brain haemorrhage is like?

'Am I alive or dead?

'I must be alive, if I am asking myself this question, I must be alive.

'Get up. You have to get up.'

Melvin opened his eyes and stood up. He could see his clothes were ripped and torn. He was wearing his best shirt and suit that morning because he was on his way to a job interview near Victoria station. He had lived in Germany for ten years and was only now returning home to settle down with his Turkish wife and their five-year-old twins. Melvin's family was in Turkey on holiday; they had no idea where he was. They felt so very far away.

'Will I ever see them again?' he wondered.

He looked around and realised that he was standing in the middle of a doorway. The carriage was starting to come back into focus now. People were pushing past him to jump out on to the tracks. He looked down and could see a woman badly hurt lying on the seats in front of him. He backed into the aisle between two rows of seats and, without noticing, found himself beside Benjamin.

One moment Melvin had been standing in a train running through the answers he had prepared for his interview, the next he was standing in the middle of a train carriage, in the dark, choking on smoke and dust and watching a stranger die.

Melvin didn't think 'Bomb', he didn't even think 'Crash',

all he could do was wonder where he was, why his ears were ringing, what had happened and what was wrong with the woman lying across the seats in front of him. He didn't need to be a doctor to tell that she was in a very bad way.

Another woman – she looked slightly older than the injured one – was kneeling down next to her holding her head. She was a doctor. She was repeating something over and over again. Melvin could see them both but he couldn't pick out what was being said, his eardrums were damaged. He thought she might have been saying: 'Lady, lady, lady', or even 'Baby, baby, baby', he didn't know. He stooped over them to listen more closely.

The doctor turned around just as Melvin leaned in. She looked straight at him, indicating that she wanted to try and move the woman to a position that would better support her head. Melvin couldn't hear what the doctor was saying but understood her gestures and so stepped towards her. He put his hands under the injured woman's back and neck while the doctor supported her head.

They both tried to lift at the same time. The woman was heavy. Melvin couldn't lift her. His strength was all but gone and he wondered why: 'I'm a fit guy. Why can't I lift this woman? Shouldn't I be able to lift her? Maybe if I shake her she will come round and be able to help me.'

Melvin tried to push the woman's body with his left hand and a piercing pain shot through his arm. He lifted his hand and saw that it was covered in blood. The fingers didn't seem to be responding to what his brain was telling them.

'Why haven't I noticed that before now?' he thought.

When the bomb went off flying debris had slashed the tendons in his left hand to ribbons. All he saw was his mangled flesh and it worried him. He was left-handed. He worked with computers. He needed both his hands to be able to work, to support his family. 'What am I going to do?' he thought.

Standing back and looking to his left he could see that the doors of the train had been blown off and people from the carriage were queueing to get off. Two other passengers were helping them down, one of them the posh-sounding man named Benjamin he had bumped into earlier. He desperately wanted to join them, to get out of there, but he needed to be prompted to leave the injured woman.

Benjamin Cotton and another man were lowering passengers out of the carriage doors and on to the tracks. A gentleman in his fifties was sitting on one of the seats near the doorway. He looked a bit dazed. Benjamin was trying to wave him over to the doors to help him out of the carriage, but he seemed unaware of what was going on around him. He couldn't hear Benjamin calling. After a moment or two he saw the pair waving, got up and walked over.

His name was Terry Hiscock.

Terry was in fact almost sixty. Despite his age he was reasonably fit. When he got to the two younger men in the open doorway he stood there for a second to think before letting them lower him on to the tracks. He had his briefcase in his hand. He didn't feel right about taking it with him so he set it down on a seat and stepped towards the door before pausing to reconsider. He realised that if he was going to find his way home that night he might need his wallet. He opened the case, took it out, closed the case and left it on the seat. Then he allowed himself to be lowered on to the tracks.

Terry stood outside the carriage for a moment and helped Benjamin lower the two or three remaining passengers who could walk to the tracks. Everyone outside the train was moving towards Aldgate. Terry stood still. He was not ready to leave.

Melvin could see the exodus from where he was standing next to the doctor and the injured woman. He wanted to help the doctor but he was in a great deal of pain himself. His hand was bleeding badly. He couldn't hear anything unless the speaker yelled directly at him and his whole left side was aching. He looked towards the rear of the carriage and could see there were others worse off than him. They were still in the dark. He didn't want to go to them. He was afraid of what he might see.

Melvin turned his head back to the open door and saw his briefcase on the floor of the carriage. 'That's lucky,' he thought, picking it up with his good hand. At that moment Melvin, Terry and Benjamin could see three men in London Underground uniforms running along the side of the train from the direction of Aldgate. Steve Eldridge and two other drivers were following a passenger who had asked them for help a moment before. They were coming to offer that help.

Melvin felt an incredible sense of relief when he saw the London Underground workers' high visibility vests glimmer in the darkness. The men somehow emanated authority and calm. Benjamin simply thought how brave they were to be running into a tunnel, and a situation, that was so horrible. To those men and women trying to flee the horror that consumed the London Underground that day, those drivers were heroes.

'Everyone who is able to walk should leave now,' one of the drivers shouted up into the second carriage.

That was all Melvin needed to hear. He was desperate to get out. He hugged his briefcase to his chest and stepped towards the open door. There was no way he was leaving his case behind. It contained the notes he needed for his job interview and he was determined to keep them close. Somewhere in the back of his mind was the glimmer of hope that he could still make his meeting at Victoria.

Melvin stood on the edge of the doorway, waved away help from Benjamin and jumped down to the track, landing on both feet, with his briefcase. Terry was standing on the tracks. He saw a man jump down, clutching his briefcase to his chest as a child might a teddy. 'Maybe I should have brought my own case,' Terry mused.

Melvin left Terry on the tracks and lumbered through the tunnel and up the platform. Staff directed him out of the station exit where he turned left and sat down next to Emma Brown on the pavement. He could see she had a serious stomach injury. A member of the fire brigade was treating her.

The same fireman turned to Melvin and asked him if he was all right. Melvin nodded, despite the searing pain in his hand. He didn't feel he could complain. The young woman next to him was badly hurt. The girl across the seats in the carriage had surely died. There were so many worse off than Melvin, so he kept quiet as he bled.

Back in the second carriage Benjamin helped a blind man down into the tunnel and then jumped out after him. There was no way he could let the man stumble around on his own, but he wanted to stay with the doctor to see if he could be of any use to the dying girl. He crouched down next to the doctor and asked what was happening. The doctor shook her head. The poor woman was close to death.

'Here, you take my torch,' Benjamin said, not knowing what else to say. 'I am going to try and get this blind man out of here and fetch some help for you.'

Then, taking the blind man's arm, Benjamin walked him down the tunnel towards the lights.

Suddenly everyone had disappeared. Steve Eldridge had gone to the driver's cab to fetch a ladder so that he could help the people trapped in the third carriage. The other two drivers had walked down the tunnel to the rear of the train. They were intending to evacuate people in the four carriages behind the bombed car by the back doors. All of the less seriously injured passengers from the first and second carriages were already moving towards Aldgate.

There was only one man left alongside the train: Terry.

He wanted to leave too, to get away into the lights with the others, but instead he stood where he was, considering what to do next. Then he heard a voice, faint at first, but loud enough for him to pick up despite the damage to his ear. It was coming from inside the rear of the bombed carriage. It was a woman's voice. She was in pain: 'I'm losing blood. Help me. I'm losing blood.'

Terry walked back along the train to the last door of the second carriage. Inside he could see a crater in the floor, twisted bits of metal everywhere. If he was going to help the woman who was calling out he would need to climb up into the carriage again. The thought made him shiver.

He stood at the open door. He needed to prepare himself: 'Right, now you have to climb up there,' he told himself. 'You don't know what you are going to see when you get inside. Take a deep breath. Be prepared.'

He climbed into the carriage and stood up. Across from him in the last two seats of the train he could see a man in his thirties dressed in a suit and white shirt. He was sitting in a seat, perfectly still, as if frozen. Terry was about to step over to him when he heard the voice again, calling out from his left, in the two seats opposite the man in the white shirt.

'I'm losing blood, help me, pull me up,' it said.

Terry was amazed at how calm and composed the woman sounded. He moved over to her. She was sitting sideways in the last seat in the carriage facing the rear of the train. Her back was pressed up against the left side of the man in the second to last seat next to her who was sitting upright in the chair.

'I'm stuck. I can't move. I need to get upright,' she said.

'What's your name?' Terry asked.

'Martine.'

Terry looked her over. Martine's left side was pressed up against the back of her seat. Both of her legs were up and resting in the destroyed window frame in the rear bulkhead of the carriage. Her right leg was in horrible shape. It looked as if the explosion had blown most of the flesh off the bones. What remained was burned. Her left leg had either been blown off or was caught up in debris; whatever had happened, Terry couldn't see it.

He moved closer to Martine and tried to move her into a more upright position. He didn't have any idea where he was going to put her even if he succeeded. There was so much wreckage everywhere. No place was safe. When he tried to lift her he couldn't. Martine was like a dead weight. She wasn't going to move. Not by Terry's hand anyway.

He stood back to have a look at both Martine and the man next to her. Terry was in no condition to help either of them. The damage to his hearing was giving him vertigo and his head was spinning. He turned from Martine and took in the man next to her. He looked about fifty, was sharply dressed in jacket and tie and was broad-shouldered. Terry leaned over him and tried to loosen the man's tie but the knot had melted into a solid lump.

The man had flown in from Liverpool to London City Airport that morning for a conference. He was a naval air traffic controller. He got into London before the Docklands Light Railway started running and so took a bus to Liverpool Street to catch the tube around to Westminster for his meeting. It was a journey he made only three or four times a year.

His broad shoulders and thick build were the result of years of playing rugby and, latterly, coaching his kids. He was strong and fit and usually stood on the tube but when he got into the carriage and saw the vacant seat next to a young woman with long brown curly hair he decided to take it.

He put his small rucksack on the floor between his legs and leaned back in his seat to get comfortable. When the train left Liverpool Street a number of people were standing at the doors next to him, ready to alight at the next station. Somewhere among them was Tanweer, and somewhere in that crowd of standing passengers was where he let off his bomb.

The man was thrown further back in his seat and knocked unconscious for several minutes. The first person to come across him and the woman with the long curly brown hair named Martine sitting to his left was a man called Terry, who had tried to loosen his tie.

'Can you try and help me move my leg?' the man asked Terry in a weak but calm voice. 'I think it's trapped.'

Terry looked down the man's body and could see that his right leg appeared to be trapped under a small sheet of metal poking out of the floor. Terry took hold of the his leg and tried to move it. It was stuck against his shin.

'I think there is somebody down there,' the man said. 'Mind where you walk.'

Terry looked down and could see a hole in the carriage floor next to the man's trapped shin. Through the hole the tracks below were visible and on the tracks was a human hand. It was moving. Whoever it belonged to was alive. Terry stared at the hand for a moment, fascinated by its slow movements. After what seemed like an age he refocused. He didn't think there was much he could do for the owner of the hand so he turned back to the man with the trapped leg.

Terry moved some debris to one side and tried again to lift the injured man's right leg. This time it came free. For a second Terry was relieved that he had managed to help. Then he took a closer look at the leg. Its foot was missing. He had expected to see a black shoe on the foot, the same as on the other one. But where the man's trouser leg ended there was only empty space.

Terry and the injured man leaned over the leg at the same time for a closer look, their faces inches apart. 'My foot's gone,' the man said calmly. 'Oh my God, my foot's gone.' Terry tried to say something reassuring but the man just leaned back in his seat repeating, 'My foot's gone', over and over again.

Terry peered through the hole in the floor to see if he could locate the foot but all he could see was that same hand on the tracks. Swinging around to try to hide his disappointment from the man, Terry realised there was nothing he could do for him; he couldn't lift Martine; he couldn't find the other man's foot. What could he do?

Terry suddenly felt very ill. The horror was too much. He started to feel faint. He needed to get some air. He turned back to the door through which he had climbed and could see a young man sitting on the floor in the entrance. He was black from head to toe. He was staring at his hands. Terry had to leave.

'I'm not feeling well,' he thought. 'I'm not coping with this.'

Terry leaned over the young man and told him not to

worry, that help was on its way, but the young man couldn't stop staring at his hands. Terry moved over to the door and climbed out of the carriage on to the tracks. He thought he was going to pass out so he lay down on the gravel until everything stopped spinning.

He needed to leave that horrible place, so after a minute or so he stood up and started walking towards the lights at Aldgate station.

He felt terribly alone in the tunnel. Looking into the first carriage of the train as he passed he could see that it was empty. As he got closer to the station he saw several London Underground workers hovering near the end of the platforms. One shouted over to him.

As he stepped up on to the platform all he could think of were the people he was leaving behind. Those terribly injured passengers in the second carriage. The others in the carriage behind and everyone else still trapped in the darkness between Liverpool Street and Aldgate.

## Edgware Road: front of the bombed carriage, thirty minutes after the explosion

Despite the obvious signs that we were in the middle of a terrorist attack, the thought never occurred to me. I saw only the wounded, and those who, like me, were trying to help them survive until the emergency services arrived. It was as if I was looking through a telescope, afflicted by tunnel vision, able to see only within the circumference of the lens, oblivious in my narrow range of vision to the wider events framing this horror.

I – we – expected the paramedics to be there already. We had been below ground in the dark now for twenty minutes. If this had been a road accident we would already be on our way to hospital. But this wasn't an accident. No roads led to us; there was nowhere to pull up and park an ambulance.

I could only reassure David and the girls from Tennessee so many times that they would be rescued. I was afraid they would soon stop believing me. I was afraid they would die with my empty promises ringing in their ears.

It was frustrating not only for us below the surface but also for those sent to rescue us. The first ambulances despatched to the scene were mistakenly sent to Praed Street, several blocks away from Edgware Road station. They wouldn't get to the scene until 9.12 a.m., more than twenty minutes after Khan detonated his bomb.

When the flurry of calls went in to the emergency

services asking for help it was not at first clear where it was needed. Initially it wasn't obvious there was a bomb: staff at the station thought the train had hit the tunnel wall or that someone – Danny Biddle – had fallen under a train.

When the call went in for help it sounded somewhat routine. Someone throws themselves under a train on the London Underground almost every week of the year. There are incidences of smoke in stations and on platforms several times a day. The only way the emergency services could assess the kind of incident they were summoned to attend was to go to the scene and call in the necessary assistance. The only problem was that, at first anyway, they didn't even know where they were going.

When the train leaving Edgware for Paddington was bombed it came to a stop at the Praed Street junction. To the staff at London Underground that location is subterranean – in that it only exists underground. Halfway down the tunnel between Edgware and Paddington the track sends the Hammersmith and City Line outside in one direction and the District and Circle Lines underground in another, to Paddington.

When the ambulance services received news of an incident at the Praed Street junction near Edgware Road station ambulances were sent to the road above the bombing. But when crews arrived there was nothing for them to do. All the action was going on 4.5 metres below ground. This meant that our desperately needed medical attention was delayed while the ambulances turned round, drove to Edgware Road, assessed the situation and called for more help. All of this would take time. There wasn't any time to spare. People were dying.

The first to react were London Underground staff at Edgware Road station, and there were plenty of them around at the time. Edgware Road houses the management offices for a group of stations used by the Hammersmith and City as well as the Circle Line. Many of the drivers for trains, such as Ray Whitehurst, on both lines begin and end their shifts at Edgware Road.

At the time of the explosion most of the drivers in the station were in the canteen, while others were scattered in the dozen or so offices around the station. When the building shook with the explosion caused by the suicide bomb, staff from everywhere rushed down onto the platforms and into the tunnels to help get people off the trains. This was their territory and they knew what to do.

The tunnels are wide at Edgware Road, just as they are at Aldgate. Both of the trains that had been bombed at these two locations were also visible from the station platforms. It was therefore easy to tell where the problem lay. Even if the idea of a bomb had yet to register, staff were sure something serious was happening only a short distance away from their stations. As a result, calls were quickly put in to the emergency services.

Each of the trains stuck in the tunnel at Edgware Road contained close to a thousand people, and so, as London Underground staff helped the passengers off the trains and ushered them towards the platforms at the station, the exit started to jam with human traffic.

When the ambulances arrived at Edgware Road they were confronted with a mass exodus from the station, some of whom were the walking wounded from the bombed carriage, others from the one in front. They were bruised and bloody, and needed attention but the flood of injured people distracted ambulance staff from getting to the heart of the disaster.

From where I was standing in the middle of the second

carriage I could see that so many of us were in desperate need of medical attention.

There was David Gardner, a South African Shakespeare enthusiast, whose leg injury might prove fatal at any moment. There were the two American girls, Katie and Emily Benton, whose bare, exposed feet had been torn apart by the bomb. There was Danny Biddle, alone on the tunnel floor, both legs gone, one just below the hip and the other at the knee. There was Tim Coulson alongside the carriage trying to help a blonde woman named Alison who had somehow survived being blown out of the carriage.

These were just the most seriously injured people on my side of the carriage.

Straining to make out the front of the carriage, on the other side of the crater in the floor left by the bomb, all I could distinguish were shadows moving in the dark. It was too poorly lit to tell how many people were there, how badly hurt they were or if there was anybody besides Steve Huckelsby, a senior official in the Methodist Church, helping them. I would just have to hope they were all right.

Steve had come through the window with the rest of us and pushed forward in the carriage looking for someone he could help. When he reached the crater in the floor of the carriage, where Tim had watched a man die moments before, Steve stood up and saw a woman crouching on the other side of the hole. She was asking for help, for someone to tell her what to do.

The woman's name was Elizabeth Owen and she had been in the carriage when the bomb went off. In the moments after the blast she made her way to another, younger woman named Laura Webb who was lying on her back on the carriage floor. When Elizabeth got to Laura she was still breathing. When Laura's chest stopped moving Elizabeth called out for help and Steve swung across the crater using the overhead handles.

There were only four seats left in the front end of the carriage. Two pairs. Each facing the other. Each seat occupied. On the right were two builders from Manchester. On the left a middle-aged woman and a young blond-haired man called Kevin. All four were injured and needed help. The builders had lost most of their hearing when their eardrums folded in the initial shock wave. The woman sitting opposite them was in worse shape. She had lost her hearing as well but one lung had also collapsed. Next to her the young blond man's right leg had been cut to pieces by flying debris and was pouring blood on to the floor.

But when Steve reached them his first priority was the woman lying flat on her back who had stopped breathing. The rest would have to wait their turn.

In between the four people seated at the front of the second carriage was a body, that of a man who had died. Elizabeth Owen sat nearby watching, trying to rest up from her own injuries as the man she called over for help tried to save Laura Webb. She had moved aside when Steve arrived. As Steve tried to revive Laura using basic first aid two more passengers came through the connecting doors from the first carriage to see if they could help.

Of the new arrivals, one was a middle-aged man from South Africa, the other a young, attractive brunette, dressed like so many on her way to the office that morning. She stepped into the carriage and tied her scarf around the young man's leg to stop the bleeding. A moment or so later the driver of the train appeared and told the walking wounded to leave via the front of the train. The message did not register with Steve; he wasn't going anywhere. Neither was the young man with the badly damaged leg nor the woman

145

sitting next to him with the collapsed lung. They didn't classify as walking wounded.

The attractive brunette and the middle-aged South African could walk and so they left by the front of the train with the two builders from Manchester. They followed the driver on to the tracks and started down the tunnel wall towards Edgware Road, passing Steve in the second carriage as they did so. Only when Steve had finished trying to revive the woman on the floor did he realise that the others had left. He was on his own.

It was up to him now.

He had to do something for the young man with the badly damaged leg. He had to watch over the woman with the collapsed lung. He had to look after the woman sitting on the floor in the corner of the carriage who had called him over in the first place.

He had to do what he could to save them, because he was the only one on his side of the crater left who could.

Kathy Lazenbatt left her house in Hemel Hempstead that morning shortly after seven o'clock. She was a librarian at the Royal Asiatic Society and was heading in half an hour early to help prepare her office for a move to another building. It meant she could dress casually that day.

When her train pulled into Euston she walked around the corner to Euston Square to catch the Circle Line to Paddington. When she reached the platform the train was just pulling in. Usually Kathy boarded further back but she was in no mood to make a mad dash to another carriage and so just stepped straight on to the train where it stopped, at the front of the second carriage.

Once through the doors she turned left. The two seats at the front of the carriage were free. The seat right at the front was a little wider than the others and she made for it straight-away. It gave her somewhere to put her bag. Across from her she noticed two sturdy men in blue shell suits. They were speaking in northern accents. They were builders from Manchester.

Someone had left a copy of the *Metro* on the window ledge behind her. It was well-thumbed. She picked it up and began to read. When the train got to Edgware Road it stopped for longer than usual. Kathy remembered the delay because the natural light in the station made it easier to read the dog-eared newspaper.

A young man in his early twenties with blond hair got on before the train left Edgware Road and took the seat to her right. A number of other people came in as well and stood near her; she could see them through the corner of her right eye. She was glad to have a seat because she was tired. Kathy paid little attention to the young man and the people standing around her as the train eventually pulled away from the plat-form and into the black tunnel where the bomb would explode.

The explosion began with a metallic crash, like steel colliding with steel. It rang in Kathy's ears.

'The train has crashed,' she thought, looking up to the two builders opposite. The looks on their faces showed they were as surprised as she was. 'What going on?' she wondered, looking past the men.

In the window behind the builders' seats Kathy could see a strange reflection growing larger in the glass. A white flash of light wrapped in red flares twirled in the window like streaks of colour in a spinning marble. The flash was mush-rooming into a giant white blaze of light before her eyes. Everything slowed down and Kathy watched the reflection, unable to turn away, until it shattered the frame of the window and filled the carriage with blinding light and heat. Kathy could feel herself being engulfed in a roar of wind and fire for what felt like several minutes. She closed her eyes.

'This is it. I am going to die. Just let it be quick.'

Kathy tried to breathe but when she opened her mouth fire rushed down her throat burning her insides. Everything was so loud. She couldn't think. She couldn't call out. She was aware only of the orange glow of the fireball even through closed eyes and felt herself being lifted out of her seat, not knowing if she would come down. Then, just as Kathy was expecting the worst, the firestorm subsided and she was back in her seat in the corner of the carriage, in the darkness.

Kathy opened her eyes. She tried to move but it felt as if she'd been nailed down. In front of her shadow puppets seemed to be dancing in the dark, behind the men from Manchester. Confused as to what she was seeing, she stared harder at the movements until the light from another train started to break through the smoke. The puppets were people. They were moving around on the other train. It was parked next to them in the tunnel: 'How can that be?' she thought.

'Can anybody help? She's not breathing,' a female voice came from the floor near Kathy's feet. 'She's stopped breathing. I don't know what to do.'

Kathy looked down in front of her and saw Laura Webb for the first time. She was flat on her back, only partly clothed, the rest having been blown away by the blast. Laura lay quite still. A woman was kneeling down beside her, trying to help her, trying to revive her. Her name was Elizabeth Owen. She was the one talking, the one asking for help, for someone to tell her what to do.

Elizabeth Owen boarded the Circle Line at Baker Street at the same time as David Gardner. They stepped into the second carriage of Ray Whitehurst's train only one door apart. Elizabeth was engrossed in the *Financial Times* and didn't notice David with his script. She didn't notice anyone else on the platform either. Why would she?

When the bomb exploded Elizabeth was sitting in the same row of seats as Khan. He was three places to her right. The two people sitting between them, and the two or three standing up nearest to her, took the force of the blast. All she could feel was the whoosh of air from her right and her head being buffeted as things fell from the ceiling.

When the wind stopped she was still sitting in her seat but the people seated next to her and those standing nearby had disappeared. She looked at her hands and saw that they were shaking. It felt as if an electric current was running through her blood.

'I've got through the first bit of this,' she thought, 'but I don't see how I can survive the electric shock. I am going to die. I am going to die for sure.' Elizabeth remembered from her schooldays that if she was being electrocuted she should break contact with the ground. 'Maybe I can save myself.'

She jumped up and the shaking stopped.

Then Elizabeth's right leg buckled and she crashed to the floor on her knees and hands. Pain shot through her leg. Her right ankle had been torn to shreds. It was a mess of flesh and blood. She could not possibly walk. She scanned the floor of the carriage for a place to rest and saw a woman lying flat on her back a few feet to her right. Her clothes had been partly blown away by the blast. The woman was Laura Webb and she wasn't moving.

Laura's feet were little more than shoulder-width apart. Her arms were down by her side and slightly out from her hips, as if she was making snow angels. Elizabeth shuffled along the floor towards her for a closer look. When she got to Laura's side Elizabeth could see she was still alive. There was blood in each nostril and as Elizabeth put her fingers to Laura's nose she could feel her shallow breathing.

'What is your name?' she asked.

No response.

'Are you on your way to work?'

Still nothing.

Elizabeth tried to rouse Laura by putting her hands on her arm and patting her several times but to no avail. Laura wasn't moving. Elizabeth could see that the blood at Laura's nose was no longer moving as she breathed. She touched her nose once more and her fears were confirmed: the flow of air had stopped.

'Can anybody help? She's not breathing,' Elizabeth said. 'She's stopped breathing. What do I do?'

A South African named Chris Stones was standing behind Elizabeth watching from inside the connecting doors to the first carriage. When he heard Elizabeth call out for help, Chris added his own voice to her plea. From the other side of the crater in the floor of the carriage a man named Steve Huckelsby heard the cries and, like a monkey, swung across the hole in the floor holding on to what remained of the overhead handles passengers use to steady themselves.

When he reached Elizabeth, she shuffled back into an open space where the first set of doors had once been and found a place to rest. She could see Steve kneeling down next to Laura, checking her over. She looked past Steve and Laura into the fully lit train on the parallel track. Its doors had lined up almost perfectly with the doors of her own carriage when both trains came to a stop. The only difference was that the doors on Elizabeth's carriage had been blown off on both sides.

On the other train Elizabeth could see two young girls calling out to Steve through a crack in the doors on their carriage. They were giving him instructions. They were motioning with their hands, trying to tell him to straddle Laura and give her chest compressions in the hope that he could somehow restart her heart, save her life.

There Elizabeth sat, trying to catch her breath, trying not to feel the pain in her ankle as she watched Steve try again and again to revive Laura with CPR and mouth-to-mouth. It went on for what seemed like ages, the girls in the other train giving him instructions all the while.

Then Steve stopped and moved away.

The girls on the other train began to cry.

Laura had died.

As Steve tried to pump life back into Laura, eyes watched him from all around the carriage. I saw him from the other side of the crater, as did Jason Rennie. It was obvious to both of us that Steve's attempt, noble though it was, could only end in failure. Laura died when air stopped moving past Elizabeth Owen's fingers. Near Steve, Elizabeth watched from where she was sitting on the floor, as did Kathy from her extra-wide corner seat where she struggled to breathe the smoky air with only one working lung.

Standing in the connecting doors to the first carriage, Chris Stones looked on as well. Chris, like David and Jason, was South African. He was in his late forties, slightly below average height, bald and well built if perhaps a little heavy for his frame. As he watched, an attractive twenty-five-year-old woman named Susanna Pell, who was standing behind Chris in the first carriage, pushed her way past him to see what was attracting everyone's attention. When she saw Steve straddling Laura she froze.

Susanna was on her way to work that morning. Her long dark hair was tied back and she was wearing a black skirt suit that hid her slim figure. She was not in the carriage in which the bomb went off but she was injured none the less.

The blast was close enough to the front of the second carriage to blow out the windows into the first. Susanna was sitting in the last seat of the first carriage. When the bomb blew up her face was showered with glass and debris. Her head was resting against the window as it blew. She was knocked unconscious.

Susanna wasn't sure how long she was out. It couldn't have been more than a few minutes. When she came round she could see almost nothing. The carriage was dark and so she stood up to try and find out what had happened to her. As she stumbled in the dark, Chris Stones saw her pass in front of him and handed her a paper towel from his briefcase so that she could clean the blood off the side of her face.

'It's nothing serious,' Chris said to Susanna as she wiped her face. 'It was just bits of glass. You are going to be okay.'

Susanna looked at the blood on the towel. For the first time she realised she'd been injured. 'What happened to me, to this carriage?' she wondered.

For a moment the two of them stood near the back of the first carriage, examining each other for injuries. They could hear passengers in their carriage banging on the windows behind the driver's cab at the front of the train. When the banging stopped Susanna and Chris considered going up to investigate. They could hear the train's driver, Ray Whitehurst, talking to the passengers. Perhaps he could tell them what was going on.

Then they heard the screams.

They were coming from the carriage behind, and they were shrill with fear. Susanna was the first to move towards the screaming. Chris followed her. The connecting doors into the carriage behind had been badly damaged by the bomb. Susanna stepped aside. Chris grabbed the doors and forced them open before stepping into the bombed carriage. Susanna took a moment to sit in an empty seat before going through herself.

Susanna could hear a woman, and then Chris, calling for help. From what they were saying it sounded like someone injured had stopped breathing. When Susanna pushed past Chris and stepped into the second carriage she was shocked by what she saw, and for a moment couldn't move. Although the windows and lights in her carriage had been blown out it still looked like a train carriage. The second car, however, was like some Renaissance painting of Hell, every face tortured and hidden in half-light.

At first Susanna's eyes were drawn to Laura Webb's still and half-naked body lying on the carriage floor. Her skin was pale but there was something beautiful and peaceful about her. Susanna's eyes lingered as Steve straddled her and began a series of chest compressions. At her feet, just inside the carriage, Susanna could see the body of a man on the floor. He was missing his left leg from the knee down. He wasn't bleeding. He looked as if he were dead. Susanna turned to look at the four people sitting in the seats on either side of her. All of them needed help.

On her left she saw the two men in blue shellsuits from Manchester. Despite looking disorientated, they appeared to be relatively unscathed compared at least to Laura and the man missing a leg on the floor by her feet. In the two seats to Susanna's right she could see a young man with blond hair calling for help in a low, pained voice: 'My leg. Someone help me. I have a hole in my leg.'

Susanna had never taken a first aid course but both her

parents were doctors and she had managed to pick up a few things at the dinner table over the years. She trained her eyes on the blond man's leg but it was too dark to see exactly what was wrong. She leaned in closer. Despite the poor lighting she thought she could see bone sticking out of the man's shin, a hole in his flesh. She wanted to do something to stop the bleeding.

'Your leg is broken and bleeding,' she told the blond man. 'We need to elevate it, to get it up high. Do you understand?'

Susanna took off her scarf and stepped closer to the injured man. As she leaned over him she saw the woman sitting next to him: Kathy. Susanna had not noticed her before because Kathy was so still, so quiet. Susanna only saw Kathy's face briefly and that one glance convinced her she was dead. But Kathy was very much alive; she was just too weak to show it.

Kathy could see what was going on around her. She knew there was a young blond man next to her and that he was in agony. Although her eardrums had been crushed by the wind and fire that had threatened to engulf her not ten minutes before, she could hear the dull echo of his voice repeating over and over:

'There's a hole in my leg.

'There's a hole in my leg.'

A few minutes later Kathy saw a young girl with dark hair named Susanna come in from the first carriage. Susanna didn't say anything to Kathy; she didn't stop to see if she was okay either but just grabbed the blond man's leg and put it up on to Kathy's lap in an attempt to elevate the wound and stop the flow of blood. Susanna was doing her best to think clearly despite having been knocked unconscious herself only minutes before. She didn't intend to ignore Kathy and her collapsed lung; she was just doing the best she could.

When the blond man's leg was placed on Kathy's lap she could see that his injury was serious. His trousers had been blown to shreds, exposing a shin bone with a gaping hole in the front of it. Kathy could see thick beads of blood running down his calf and dripping on to her lap. She wanted to help but when she tried to move she felt like passing out, and so stopped. She didn't have enough oxygen for movement. All she could do was watch Susanna remove her scarf and tie it around the blond man's thigh.

'You have a cut on your head,' Susanna told him. 'You are going to be okay. People are coming to help. People are coming, you will be fine, fine.' Susanna didn't know if anyone was on their way but she wanted to find some way to make the young man feel better, to calm him down.

Just then the driver, Ray Whitehurst, poked his head into the second carriage. He had finished evacuating everyone in the first carriage through the front of the train, sending twenty or so passengers back towards Edgware Road between the bombed carriage and the tunnel wall.

'You can get out through the front of the train,' Ray told Chris Stones and Susanna. 'This way, come on, everybody is leaving now.'

Susanna grabbed one of the two Manchester builders by the hand and pulled him to his feet, helping him to walk into the first carriage. Chris grabbed the other man and helped him in the same way. Together the four of them walked to the front of the first carriage with Ray and left the train via a tiny wooden ladder that Ray had set up for them at the front of his cab. They were the last to leave the first carriage.

Ray followed them down the ladder and joined the rear of the queue of passengers trying to make their way along the tunnel wall towards the beckoning lights of the Edgware Road platforms. There wasn't much space between the carriages and the tunnel wall, perhaps no more than a metre; negotiating the debris from the train was a real challenge for them in their disorientated state, especially for the boys from Manchester who were battling dizziness brought on by their shattered eardrums.

All of them had to keep their eyes on the ground to avoid falling over.

They had reached the second carriage when the queue stopped moving. Something further up the tunnel was blocking the way. They would have to wait. Susanna's feet were hurting. She was wearing black open-toed heels and she needed to sit down. As she did so she made the mistake of looking under the train.

There, lying on the ground, she saw a man, or what was left of one. His entire body was missing from the waist down. It was a ghastly sight. It made her feel dizzy and weak. She tried to stand up to get away from the body, but when she did her head started to spin.

'Why isn't this queue moving?' she thought.

When Susanna and Chris followed the driver out with the two builders from Manchester, Steve Huckelsby left Laura Webb's side and moved over to a young man with blond hair who was resting his foot on the lap of the woman seated next to him. Steve was the only uninjured person left to care for the wounded on his side of the crater in the floor.

He could see the man's leg had been badly mashed by the explosion and would need treatment soon if it was to be saved. Most of the ankle had been crushed and there was a hole in the man's shin the size of a tennis ball. The scarf that Susanna had tied around his upper thigh had not stopped the bleeding but Steve felt it was doing some good and was glad it was there.

'My name is Steve. What's your name?' he asked.

'Kevin,' came the reply.

'Where do you work?' Steve probed further, trying to distract his patient from the wound in his leg.

'I am bleeding, aren't I?' Kevin replied, ignoring Steve's question. 'I can feel it trickling down my leg.'

'You are doing okay, you are going to be fine,' Steve replied.

Steve felt as if his mind was being torn in two. Outwardly he was trying to be the voice of calm, to put Kevin at ease, but inside he was terrified that Kevin would bleed until he passed out and died. It took all Steve's willpower to keep him from succumbing to the fear running through him. He had to stay lucid for Kevin. If not Steve, then who?

The side doors to the carriage next to Kevin's seat were open. The mechanism keeping it closed must have been destroyed during the blast, that or they had been blown off; either way they were gone. Steve could see people moving along the tunnel wall towards Edgware Road, Susanna and the builders among them. After a few moments a middle-aged man wearing a bright yellow London Underground coat appeared. Steve turned to him.

'We need medical attention here and we need it fast,' he said.

'Yes, I know,' the London Underground man said. 'We have been on to line control about what has happened. There was an incident at Aldgate as well.'

'Do they realise the severity of the incident here?' Steve continued.

'Yes, they do. They are doing everything they can,' the man in the yellow coat replied. 'In the meantime, do you need some water?'

'Yes,' Steve said. 'Water would be useful.'

The man in the yellow coat said he would be right back and disappeared into the tunnel.

When Ray had seen that all the passengers from the first carriage were out of his train he followed them down along the tunnel wall to make sure they were able to escape. As he passed the first carriage he came alongside the bombed car and stopped for a moment to survey the damage.

The screams he had heard in the aftershock of the blast had ceased. Most of the walking wounded were making their way down the tunnel wall towards Edgware Road. Ray became aware that something was blocking their way but it was too dark to see exactly what. As he waited for the line to start moving again, Ray looked around him. There were at least two bodies under the train; one had been torn in half. Inside the train Ray saw a number of passengers helping the injured, some of whom were clearly dying. There was almost no talking, and no sound from the engines either; it was silent in a way that a tube tunnel never is. The scene made Ray feel humble. Despite the horror of the situation, people who could have evacuated the scene had chosen to stay behind and help their companions. The atmosphere was calm. It was humanity at its best. London was working.

Standing on tiptoes to try and see why the queue had stopped moving, Ray suddenly saw a figure in a bright yellow London Underground coat pushing his way against the stream of people squeezing down the tunnel between the train and the wall. It was another driver. Ray recognised him. His name was Dave.

'My God,' Dave said, a look of shock on his face. 'You are going to need some help here. Have you called this in yet?'

'Yes, I used the signal phone but they don't seem to believe me. They are convinced it is a power surge,' Ray said. 'Come with me, will you, and tell them yourself.'

When they got to the signal phone Ray picked it up and hit the call button. It was 9.12 a.m., twenty-two minutes since the bomb had gone off. A voice answered. It was the signalman, Trevor Rodgers, the duty manager Ray had spoken to when he'd used the signal phone to call the incident in, who was by then in the tunnel helping with the rescue effort.

'Hello, Ray, is that you?' the signalman asked.

'Yes, it is. Look, this is definitely a bomb. Do you understand?' Ray said, describing once again the carnage that he and Dave had witnessed first hand.

'Are you sure, Ray?' the signalman asked. 'I have been on to line control and they are telling me that it's most likely a power surge.'

'Ray, give me the phone. Let me talk to him,' Dave said.

Taking the receiver, Dave told the signalman exactly what Ray had said down the same phone not fifteen minutes earlier. He told him about the debris in the ceiling, the blown doors, the blast injuries. There could be no doubt about what had happened. When he had finished, Dave put the phone back in the box.

'He is going to pass on the message,' he told Ray.

'I guess all we can do is go back and see if we can help,' Ray replied.

The two drivers then walked back towards the train. When they reached the driver's cab Dave told Ray he was going to walk back along the tunnel wall to see if he could help anyone from the bombed carriage.

'You do that, Dave,' Ray said. 'I am going to head back into the carriage from here and see if anyone needs help.'

When Dave got to the first set of doors of the bombed carriage he could see Steve Huckelsby inside treating a young man with blond hair. When Steve caught sight of Dave's high-visibility coat, he turned to him and said:

'We need medical attention here and we need it fast.'

When Dave left to get help, Steve turned back to Kevin and his injured leg. It was still bleeding and, although he'd only ever done a day's first-aid course, through work, Steve knew that he had to do something to elevate Kevin's leg if he was to stop him bleeding to death.

There wasn't much room at that end of the carriage in which to move. At Kevin's feet lay the body of a young man; Laura Webb's body was taking up most of the available floor space and everywhere else was littered with debris or other injured people. The only option was to try and move Kevin into the first carriage.

'We are going to have to move you into the space between the two carriages,' Steve told Kevin. 'There will be room for you to lie down there.'

Kevin nodded but didn't say anything. Steve leaned in and pressed his side up against Kevin's chest, taking one of Kevin's arms and wrapping it around his shoulder.

'I am going to try to swing your legs into the doorway. Help me if you can,' Steve said.

As he lifted him, Steve expected Kevin to cry out in pain but he didn't say a word. Kevin just got on with trying to move and together, showing remarkable stoicism, they managed to get him to his feet. Hopping gently, Steve supported Kevin until he was standing on his good leg in the passage between the first and second carriages.

'Well done,' Steve said. 'Now let me just lower you down here.'

Once on the floor Kevin was blocking the passage between the two carriages. The lower part of his body was in the first carriage with only his chest and head still in the second. Steve crawled over Kevin and into the first carriage to examine his leg wound. He could see that he was still bleeding and Steve worried about his right ankle.

Steve didn't feel as if he was in control any more. He was moving on automatic pilot, on hope, his mind numbed by what he had seen. He knew there was not much he could do for Kevin's leg – he didn't have the skills, the equipment – and so he sat facing Kevin and propped the wounded leg up on his lap in the hope that the elevation would slow the flow of blood.

'I have pain in my chest,' Kevin said.

'Can you breathe?' Steve asked.

'Yes, but it's painful,' Kevin replied.

'If you can breathe, and you can talk, there is nothing to worry about. You are going to be fine.'

Steve hoped what he was saying was true. The wound to Kevin's ankle was clearly serious. It didn't look as if it could get much worse. Steve could do little more now but prop up Kevin's leg and wait for the emergency services to arrive.

What followed next was a sustained period of assessment, a pause for respite, where the injured had been identified and those who could help them now offered comfort and quiet assurance, a shoulder to lean on, a hand to hold while they waited. There were no more windows to break, no more heroics.

'Stay awake,' Steve said. 'I will take care of you. I am watching.'

As he sat there Steve realised there was no one left in the

front of the bombed carriage to look after the two women he had left behind: Kathy, with the collapsed lung, and Elizabeth with a similar, although less serious, leg injury, were on their own.

'Are you okay in there?' Steve called through the connecting doors. 'Are you all right?'

There was no answer, only darkness.

## Earl's Court line control room: 9.30 a.m.

It was approaching half past nine and Gary Fitzgerald still had no information from the staff at King's Cross and Russell Square stations about what was happening to his trapped train.

By this time word had reached him in the Piccadilly Line control room that there had been explosions on trains just short of Aldgate and Edgware Road stations. At first the blasts were not thought to have been caused by bombs, but were rather a consequence of a massive power surge from one of the Circle Line's power generating stations. Still, bomb or no, the situation was serious and, with smoke flooding out of the Piccadilly Line tunnel, Gary was worried the same might be happening to him.

At 9.10 a.m. the City of London Police had decided that the incident at Aldgate should be declared a major incident. At Edgware Road the situation was less clear and it would take the police until 9.32 to give it the same priority. The train trapped between King's Cross and Russell Square, however, would have to wait until 9.38 for the true gravity of the situation to be recognised, a full forty-eight minutes after the bomb had exploded. Until then the people trapped down there were on their own in the dark.

Delaying the diagnosis was a lack of information. Gary could only stand at the back of the Earl's Court control room and wait for one of the staff who had run into the tunnel on the Piccadilly Line to call him with a first-hand report. Until then everything was speculation. While he waited he busied himself with the job at hand. An Amber Alert had been issued by Andy Barr and his team at St James's Park at 9.15. It meant that all trains had to be brought into the stations and passengers evacuated. Gary's team had a number of trains stuck in tunnels and they were working to get them into available platforms while they waited for word.

It was deeply frustrating. Radios and mobiles did not work in the tunnels and the radio system the drivers used to communicate with their line controllers was patchy at best. The only other way a driver could talk to line control was to stop his train and clip his tunnel telephone on to the copper wires that ran along the tunnel wall. It would discharge traction current along the track, yes; but it would at least work. The tunnel telephone's great flaw, however, was that it assumed conditions were normal. A bomb on a train, such as those on 7 July, was something extraordinary. The explosions tore the cables running along the tunnel wall to pieces, putting them out of operation. What the drivers needed in such a situation was a wireless radio system that worked underground. They didn't have it. They should have had it, but they didn't.

After the official inquiry into the 1987 King's Cross fire the lack of communication between the underground tunnels and the surface was identified as a major hindrance in the effort to save lives. As that fire raged not only could staff not communicate with colleagues on the surface but the emergency services sent underground to quell the flames had no way of communicating either. Since the King's Cross inquiry's findings, successive governments have failed to invest the necessary money or effort to install a radio system that would allow proper, reliable communication between the tunnels and the surface. Eighteen years of complacency leading up to the London bombings meant that on 7 July London Underground staff in the control rooms, and at street level, had to wait for runners from the tunnel to spread the call for help.

Until that news came Gary was stuck in a prison with walls that flashed, beeped and hummed useless information about the Piccadilly Line. That little round room above the entrance to Earl's Court station was packed with technology telling him which signals were showing what colour along his line. The CCTV screens were giving him images of passengers being pulled up from the tracks on to the platforms at King's Cross. But Gary had no answers to the most vital questions. All he did know was that the situation was serious, that there were passengers trapped who needed help, but he could do nothing to help them until he knew the reality of their situation. For that he would have to wait.

The phone rang.

It was David Boyce, a young station supervisor from Russell Square. He was talking fast and breathing heavily.

'Look, there's been an explosion on the train,' David said.

Gary pressed the receiver into his ear and listened as the worst possible news was relayed to him. The incident had begun with someone operating a tunnel telephone, or so Gary had thought. In reality, that telephone had never been used. There had been a bomb on the first carriage of the Piccadilly Line train that had left King's Cross on its way to Russell Square.

Gary listened as David Boyce told him how he had run into the tunnel when people, blackened and covered in blood, had started appearing at the Russell Square platform having walked half a kilometre through the tunnel to get there. He told him how he had made it into the bombed carriage and seen people with limbs missing, dead passengers, people who were dying. He told Gary that it could only be a bomb.

When Gary put the phone down his head was spinning. Ever since the King's Cross fire had claimed thirty-one lives Gary had lived with the fear that the same tragic loss of life would occur when he was at the helm. Those fears were now reality and he began his well-rehearsed personal monologue. He told himself to accept what he was being told, that if he could do that he could respond to the crisis instead of becoming part of it.

Picking up the phone he put in another call to the Network Operations Centre. When the duty manager picked up at the other end Gary started talking:

'We've had an explosion on one of our trains as well,' he said. 'The train was reached by staff deep in a closed section of tunnel. Our information from staff at the scene is telling us that our situation here is at least as bad or worse than the reports we have been getting from Aldgate and Edgware Road.'

There was silence at the other end of the line. It was now 9.30. Gary could almost hear the news sinking in down the telephone. Until that point it might have been logical to assume that a power surge on the Circle Line had affected two trains on that line: but on the Piccadilly, too? That was too much of a coincidence. This was an attack. Gary felt it. The voice at the other end of the phone felt it. It was happening. The nightmare was upon them.

After explaining in detail everything David Boyce had told him, Gary put the phone down and told the dozen or so staff in the Earl's Court control room what they were dealing with.

The Piccadilly Line control room is a place where trains are managed, where decisions are taken about which signals should be changed or ignored, which trains should be rerouted or delayed. It is a place where the line as a whole is managed and where trains are little more than a flashing light on a console. Once the news of the explosion had been passed on to the Network Operations Centre all Gary could do was trust in his staff on the ground to manage the incident. He could only watch, and wait; his job was to manage the line from a distance and he had to maintain that distance in his control room.

The frustration of being trapped in the control room when he wanted to be at the scene was overwhelming. Gary knew how tightly packed those tube carriages were. He knew people had already been down there for forty minutes, in the dark, pressed up against each another, breathing in smoke. He knew the cramped conditions would be unbearable and he wished he could lend a hand. But the only people who could help now were the staff at King's Cross and Russell Square. It was up to them, and the staff who had run into the tunnel to help the trapped and wounded, to try and make a difference.

Natalie Whitney had been walking along the tracks in the dark for what seemed like a very long time. It was hard to gauge distance in the dim light of the Piccadilly Line tunnel. Everything looked the same. The walls, the tracks, even the feeble tunnel emergency lighting spaced evenly along the ceiling, were all part of a repeat pattern, giving no clues as to distance.

Natalie had been sitting two seats behind the driver's cabin in the first carriage of the train when everything went dark. The light disappeared into a loud, yet dull, thudding sound that boomed right through the carriage. The train came to a sudden stop and she was thrown against the person sitting next to her, where, for a brief moment, along with everyone else, she sat in the darkness.

Without being able to see anything, she tried to work out what had happened. Then she smelt something: burning plastic. She thought that wires must be on fire but she didn't know where. She was a lawyer, not an engineer. The smell was soon replaced by a metallic taste in her mouth. She licked her lips. She wasn't to know it until much later but the taste of iron was actually that of blood from the people around her.

The quiet after the thud seemed to Natalie to last for only a few seconds before a middle-aged man in a business suit standing over her started to yell. He set off everyone else in the carriage and before long dozens of the other people around her were beginning to panic as well.

'I can't breathe. I can't breathe,' the man shouted. 'Someone break a window.'

Natalie was struggling to breathe as well. She leaned back in her seat to see if she could push open the window but it wasn't there. Her hand went right through the frame and only stopped when it hit the tunnel wall inches away from the side of the train.

'There's no window,' she thought. 'There is no air in here and there is no window. How are we going to breathe?'

Natalie struggled to draw enough breath to satisfy her need for oxygen, but no matter how hard she inhaled she always seemed to come up short. Her heart was beginning to race. Her breathing quickened.

The moaning and screaming around her was getting louder. People were terrified, panicked. She suddenly realised that because they had come to a halt another train might hit them from behind. She reached for the bar next to her to pull herself back upright in her seat but it was no longer fixed to the floor and came away in her hand. A woman opposite was screaming, shrieking something about her leg. The businessman standing up was yelling for the driver again and again, and, through it all, someone else could be heard trying to get everyone to calm down.

It was chaos in the dark.

Natalie wondered how this had all changed so quickly.

Just a few minutes earlier she had boarded the train at King's Cross. The platform was packed and she'd had to wait for two trains to clear the crowds before she made it into pole position on the platform. She passed the time chatting to a young blonde woman standing next to her, on her way to a job interview. Everything had been so normal.

When the train pulled up the doors to the first carriage opened directly in front of Natalie. She stepped in just as someone was vacating a seat two spaces back from the driver's cab on the left hand side of the train. The blonde woman remarked how lucky Natalie was to get a seat in such a packed train. Natalie had settled down for the ride to Leicester Square where she would change for the Northern Line to Charing Cross.

Apart from the unusually cramped conditions that day everything had been normal, safe, predictable. Her train from Wellingborough that morning was late but that wasn't unusual either. She was on her way to what was promising to be a very average day at work. She'd even chatted to someone on the platform. But now she was trapped in a dark carriage, screaming, choking on smoke, with the taste of someone else's blood on her lips. The world she knew had gone.

Then came a voice.

It was the driver of the train. It sounded as if he was

speaking through the door to his cab. 'Everyone stay calm,' he said. 'Everything is going to be all right. I am trying to contact line control. Just stay calm.'

'What happened, what happened?' people sitting and standing around Natalie began to shout.

'It was an electrical problem,' the driver replied. 'Stay calm.'

Natalie sat quietly and listened to what was being said. When the driver mentioned an electrical fault she could hear the self-doubt in his voice. It did not reassure her.

A short time later the driver opened his door into the carriage and told the passengers that he could not raise line control. It wasn't the news they wanted to hear. They threatened to force their way off the train. Once again the driver told them to stay calm and to wait, that he was going to open the emergency door to the front of the train and lower a ladder down for them.

As the driver spoke Natalie strained to make out his face but it was too dark. All she could see was the outline of his body and the emergency tunnel lighting behind, silhouetting him. Leaving the door to his cab open, the driver disappeared to prepare the exit. A few minutes later Natalie found herself in a queue of eight or nine people on their way out of the front of the train.

'Okay, you can start walking down now,' the driver said. 'The tracks may be live so be careful. You are going to walk straight ahead to Russell Square station.'

King's Cross station was much closer, about 300 metres away, compared to the half-kilometre from where she was to Russell Square. The train was so tight in the tunnel, however, that there was no room to walk alongside the train back to King's Cross. The only way out was forward, through the front.

As she waited to go Natalie turned to look at the carriage she was about to leave. Thick smoke obscured her view. Through the murk she could see that the carriage had imploded. Twisted metal sheeting hung down at unnatural angles. Bars and handrails lay intwined like discarded straws on a bar floor. At her feet, and strewn across the seats, was a tangled mass of people. It was too dark to separate out individual suffering from mass death. Everything, steel and flesh, had become one entangled horror.

Natalie turned away. She could bear the scene and the accompanying smell no longer, but as she climbed down the ladder the cries from the carriage followed her into the tunnel. 'My leg, my leg, I've lost my leg,' one voice shrieked. It was much easier not to see the horror than it was not to hear it.

She followed the people in front of her for what seemed like forever. Natalie was unsteady on her feet, stumbling several times. The distance was far and she was neither very fit nor blessed with the natural balance needed to negotiate the tracks in her office shoes. She needed to rest every now and then. Every time she stopped a fellow passenger would halt to offer encouragement. It kept her going, knowing that people around her cared. Eventually the lights of Russell Square could be seen glowing ahead of her.

Leading the queue was a London Underground driver who had been riding shotgun in the driver's cab on his way to work. When the driver of the train stayed behind to look after the injured his colleague stayed with the walking wounded to make sure they got to Russell Square safely.

From Natalie's place in the line she could see the second driver reach the platform first. He started talking to a couple of London Underground staff who, on seeing the state of the people emerging from the darkness, jumped on to the tracks and raced down the tunnel past Natalie towards the bombed train.

One of the two members of staff was David Boyce, a young station supervisor from Russell Square. He and a colleague sped past the injured into the dark. Their intention was to find out what was happening so that Gary Fitzgerald in the Piccadilly Line control room at Earl's Court could call up the emergency services that were now swarming around Aldgate and Edgware Road stations.

Once inside the front of the bombed carriage David Boyce and another duty station manager named Gary Stevens waved their torches around in the dark to survey the scene. From the rear of the carriage, on the other side of the crater caused by the bomb, Simon Cook, the duty station manager from King's Cross, shouted at them. London Underground staff were now inside both ends of the carriage. But they couldn't reach each other.

Simon had only been in the bombed carriage for a few minutes before he saw the lights of two torches dancing around in the front of the carriage. He was kneeling, having just tied his jacket around a male passenger's knee, in an attempt to stop it bleeding. When he saw the lights he stood up, intending to walk towards his fellow staffers to discuss what to do next.

When Simon tried to do so, however, it quickly became obvious that the carriage was impassable, so tightly had it been packed with passengers when the bomb went off. Now they covered every inch of the floor. With his tiny light it was too difficult to tell who was alive and who was dead and with every step he made moans of pain rose from the floor.

Even without people littering the carriage floor it would not have been safe for Simon to negotiate the carriage anyway. The bomb had destroyed most of the floor, practically cutting the carriage in two. The ceiling had collapsed inwards to such a degree that only at the ends of the car was it possible to stand without running the risk of cutting one's head open on the dangling sheets of metal. The explosion had all but destroyed the entire carriage.

The bomb that was used was a five-kilo charge of organic peroxide, the type of material that could be purchased easily on the internet. Its strength lay in its efficiency. Once detonated, in this case with a small electric charge generated by a normal nine-volt battery, the entire five kilos of peroxide exploded and burned instantly, creating a massive fireball and consuming every gram of explosive material packed into the device. When investigators later scoured the carriages looking for residue they found none. This told them it had to be peroxide. It is the only kind of explosive that burns completely once detonated.

The power of the bomb relative to its size was considerable. If the same bomb were to be detonated in the middle of the pitch at Wembley Stadium, for example, it would have enough force to knock back someone standing behind the cheapest seats high up in the stadium's perimeter. By detonating these devices underground in a confined space the suicide bombers ensured maximum destruction. In the two Circle Line trains at Aldgate and Edgware Road the blast had more room to dissipate. Both trains were in double-track tunnels which allowed the explosion to travel through the windows and doors and out into the wide subways. On the Piccadilly Line train the tunnel was so tight the force of the blast had nowhere to go but back ·into the carriage, destroying not only the roof of the first carriage, but also making it impossible to walk from one side of the car to the other in the aftermath.

Faced with the state of the carriage, Simon knew he would have to content himself with treating the people at his end of the car as he waited for the emergency services to arrive.

To the casual observer he must have seemed calm, ordered even, in his actions but Simon was slowly being overcome by the sheer destruction all around him. He could feel his hands shaking. They would not stay still. Yet he pressed on, remaining in the carriage to lend a hand.

'When doctors come? When doctors come?'

It was the teenaged French girl again. She was being comforted by a woman who also seemed to speak French. Simon could see she was still terribly distraught and desperate for someone to take her out of there. He tried to tell her help was coming soon but it didn't seem to register.

'When doctors come?' she said again.

Lying on the carriage floor, Paul Mitchell could hear the French girl's repeated cries for a doctor in her broken English. Paul propped his head up to look across the carriage and saw that she was being embraced by a woman in her early thirties seated next to her. It made him feel better to know that someone was trying to help her. Paul would have liked to have been that person himself but he couldn't move. Quite apart from being tangled in a mess of debris and people on the floor his left calf was missing. Standing wasn't an option.

The bomb had exploded near the middle of the carriage and Paul had been standing five or six people away from the bomber, Jermaine Lindsay, fighting for space with the person next to him at the time. The rucksack containing the bomb had been placed on the floor of the carriage and when it went off those closest to the blast took the full force of the explosion. The first to die protected to an extent those next in the line of fire, but because the space was less densely packed below waist level the explosion ripped along the floor of the carriage taking with it the legs of several passengers. Paul was, to a degree, fortunate in where he had chosen to stand that day; he still had his left leg, but he was losing blood and couldn't move from the spot in which he had come to rest on the carriage floor.

Paul was twenty-seven. Normally he was out of bed by 7.30 every morning but on 7 July he slept in, for no particular reason, until just after eight. He lived in Islington and that morning, as every morning, was on his way to work at Piccadilly Circus where he was an administrator for a technology company. Knowing he was not going to make it into work for his usual nine o'clock start, he dressed quickly in black trousers and a blue shirt before rushing out of the door to Old Street tube station where he took the Northern Line to King's Cross to change for the Piccadilly Line, his usual route to the office.

When he got to the Piccadilly Line platform Paul was surprised at how packed it was. He had never seen it that busy before: people were standing six deep. He stood at the same spot he did every day knowing that it would line up perfectly with the exit at Piccadilly Circus where he got off. When the first train arrived, however, it emptied enough people to allow just about all those on the platform to get on. Paul pushed his way on to the front carriage and stood there, the last one in, just inside the doors, when he had a change of heart.

Although he only had a few stops to travel and was already late he decided the carriage was too crowded and that the doors would not close if he stayed on. So, with seconds to spare, he hopped off and waited for the next train.

When it pulled up he pushed his way into the carriage

and turned to the right where he found a spot to stand in the rear third of the car. It was so tightly packed that he couldn't stand with his feet together so he put his right foot in front of his left and held on to the handrail above him as people continued to push their way in behind him. Looking out of one of the windows he could see the platform filling up again as the train doors closed.

To Paul's right, a few feet closer to the bomber, two young men were talking and laughing. The one right next to Paul kept bumping into him, knocking him off balance. Paul was in a bad mood that morning; he didn't like being late, and their banter was getting on his nerves. As the train pulled away and into the darkness of the tunnel Paul sighed and shook his head. This journey was going to be a real pain.

Seconds later, an intense white light burst over Paul's right shoulder and he instinctively closed his eyes as tightly as he could. The flash was followed by a loud popping that made him think of champagne. And then, as quick as that, Paul was on the floor. It was so fast. It seemed as if there was no time in between the burst of light and his back hitting the ground.

Paul kept his eyes squeezed shut as a powerful gust of wind swirled around him. It was so strong that it felt as if the carriage had disappeared and he was somehow out in the open, being ravaged by wind and fire, somewhere else – anywhere but in a tube carriage. He felt butterflies in his stomach, almost as if he was falling through air, and the shock of the sensation prompted him to yell at the top of his lungs.

'Oh my God,' he cried. 'Oh my God. We're going to die.'

He could not think. His life did not flash before him. Paul succumbed entirely to the force of the explosion, was bound up in the moment, felt every possible sensation afflicting him. The whooshing sound lasted for several seconds. From his position on the floor he could feel intense heat surging over the left side of his body.

'Oh my God,' he cried again. 'I'm on fire. I'm on fire.'

Paul felt as though his mind and his body were falling to pieces. He thought the fire swirling through the carriage would tear his body apart, burn him into nothingness. He tried hitting his head with his right hand in an attempt to stop the heat from searing into his skull. As he did so he felt something slip from his hand and fall on to the floor. 'What was that, what just fell?' he wondered.

But before he could give it any further thought, the wind stopped, the fire died away, everything went quiet and from behind his still closed eyelids he could see that all the light in the carriage was gone. He opened his eyes to find he was in almost total darkness. There appeared to be some dim light coming from the tunnel. Opposite him, on the seats, he could recognise the outlines of his fellow passengers.

He began checking over his body. His head felt fine, as did his torso. Relieved, he moved his hands down his left leg and that relief soon disappeared. Touching his left calf Paul thought, 'That doesn't feel right.' When his hand went up to the knuckles in a hole in his calf, he knew he was in trouble.

Pulling himself upright, Paul could see that most of his calf was missing, gone; it had been blown away to the bone.

'Oh my God,' he cried for a third time. 'My leg. Something has happened to my leg.'

'Its okay, calm down, you are going to be okay,' a female voice assured him.

'Who is that?' Paul replied.

'My name is Julie,' the voice said, leaning forward from the other side of the carriage so that Paul could see the shadowy features of a young woman. 'People know that this has happened. They know we are down here. Don't you worry; everything is going to be okay.'

The woman seemed to have a northern accent. Paul was from the north as well and her familiar tone was a comfort when no face was visible in the darkness.

Julie looked at Paul's leg and within seconds went into action. With a scrap of cloth she tied a tourniquet around Paul's thigh and then removed a sanitary towel from her bag. Putting it across the open wound on Paul's left calf, she took another piece of cloth and wrapped it around his lower leg to keep the towel in place.

As Julie worked on him Paul looked around the carriage from his position on the floor. To his left he could feel that he was leaning up against someone who was in an almost identical position. Opposite he could see people on seats. They could have been asleep or dead: in the poor light it was difficult to tell. Further to his left he could see a man lying face down on the floor. He was certainly dead. His skin looked cold and scaly. It was a terrifying sight and it wasn't long before Paul started to panic again.

He thought first of those who loved him. 'My wife, my wife,' he thought. 'She doesn't have a clue I'm here. She has no idea where I am.'

As he thought of his wife, Paul squirmed about on the floor of the carriage, trying to shake off the worry consuming him. As he moved, he banged into a man lying on the floor to his left. Every time he did so the man moaned. Paul stopped for a second and looked at him. It was one of the two men who had been talking loudly and bumping into him as the train left King's Cross not ten minutes before.

'What's your name?' Paul asked.

The man answered him and then fell silent. His feeble

voice told Paul that, no matter how bad he was feeling, the man beside him was much worse off. It was humbling.

'Come on,' Paul said. 'You're going to be okay.'

When Paul's leg had been bandaged Julie let him rest it on her knees so as to keep it elevated. Paul settled into the most comfortable position he could and started making small talk with Julie and the other people sitting close by. Every now and then the man lying next to him moaned horribly, as if he were dying. It upset Paul; he continued to talk to those around him until there was nothing left to say.

Lying on the floor in the dark in the midst of so much human suffering, Paul needed something to distract him. That something was Monty Python and he started humming quietly to himself 'Always Look on the Bright Side of Life', as he did so imagining the swinging feet of Eric Idle dancing in the darkness above him. Paul thought he was going to die there in the dark and he wanted to hear the sound of a happy song before he went.

More than twenty minutes had now passed and Paul was beginning to drift off, his mind full of music and memories, when he heard a commotion at the rear of the carriage to his right. At first it was a bang and then the movement of people as they poured out of the first carriage into the second. 'Someone must be coming,' Paul thought. 'Who?'

When almost everyone who could walk had left, a young man stepped into the carriage carrying a tiny torch. It was Simon Cook.

'I am a duty manager from King's Cross,' Simon said. 'I just want to let you know that the police are aware of what has happened and help is on the way.'

Paul put his head back against the base of the seats. Until Simon's appearance he had been prepared for death, had accepted its inevitability, had mouthed that little ditty as if it was the last song he would ever sing. But now help was at hand. Someone was coming. Someone knew he was there.

'See, Paul,' Julie said. 'They're coming. They're on their way.'

Simon didn't try to speak to Paul. He was distracted by a man at his feet with an injured knee. Without a first aid kit to hand all Simon could do was tie his jacket around the wound and apply pressure. There on the floor he sat with his hand on a stranger's knee for a while when the size of the rescue effort doubled.

A police officer appeared from the second carriage, a large torch in his hand. As soon as he entered he swept the flashlight around, painting the darkness bright with the faces of the terrified and the dead. Passengers, unmoving, were in piles.

The torchlight was unsettling. People screamed, hysterical until the torch was switched off. Simon stood up to talk to the policeman and together they tried to work out what was needed – stretchers, ambulance crews, the London Fire Brigade. That done, the policeman turned and headed back to King's Cross where he could radio for help.

Several more minutes passed before another member of staff from King's Cross entered the carriage with a station issue first aid kid. It was tiny, the sort you kept under a desk in the control room to treat paper cuts and blisters. It contained plasters and butterfly stitches, stuff that was utterly useless in the present situation. Simon looked at the kit and laughed. It was ridiculous. His colleague turned and went back to King's Cross to try and find something more practical.

At about 9.45 two firemen and two paramedics came in through the interconnecting doors from the second carriage.

They fanned out to start assessing people. Simon stood back to watch them get to work as more police and paramedics started to enter the rear of the carriage.

At first the rescue workers seemed unable to decide where to start. Lack of communication with the surface meant that they had no idea what to expect when they entered the first carriage. Faced with the terrifying reality of the situation, they were dumbfounded. Sensing the confusion, a newly arrived air ambulance doctor assumed authority and began to assign levels of priority to the wounded. With someone in control, the emergency services fell into line, their training taking over.

Simon continued to hold back but soon found himself moving dead passengers into the second carriage to give the medics more room to help the living. He lifted several bodies into the second carriage with the help of a fireman as the paramedics brought stretchers into the bombed carriage.

When a few bodies had been cleared Simon walked back into the bombed carriage where, on the floor in front of him, he saw a bare foot. It wasn't attached to a leg. It wasn't near a body. It was small. Perhaps it had belonged to a child or a small woman. Simon didn't know. He didn't want to know. He had seen enough.

From the moment that Simon Cook had come into the carriage to the moment the emergency services had started to tend the wounded Paul Mitchell had been lying on the floor listening to the man next to him. As the minutes passed, he could hear him drifting away, complaining of being tired. Then he suddenly went silent.

At that point emergency service members entered the carriage and started to work on the injured. With so little space in which to move, a policeman asked if anyone who could walk should do so and leave. A man deeper in the carriage was the first to move. He did so in such a hurry that as he stepped over Paul he kicked him in the head.

'Well, that's brilliant isn't it,' Paul yelled after him. 'Thank you very much.'

Julie, the woman who had bandaged Paul's leg with a sanitary towel, was the next to go.

'What is your name?' she asked him for the first time.

'Paul Mitchell,' he replied.

'What, like the hairdresser?' she wanted to know.

'I wish I had his money,' Paul said.

'Right,' Julie said laughing lightly. 'I'll keep my eye out for you.'

And then she was gone. Suddenly Paul felt alone. At that moment a policeman came over to him and told him they were going to get him out. 'Could you hold my hand?' Paul said. 'Please?'

The officer took Paul's hand and held it tightly until two paramedics appeared with a stretcher. Paul tried to roll to his right but found that he was wedged between some of the bodies on the floor. Putting both hands down to help himself he noticed how strange and soft the floor seemed. Feeling something in his hand, he picked it up. It was a chunk of human flesh the size of a cigarette packet. It might have been his; it might have been anybody's. When he tossed it back on to the floor, discarding it like a stone from a shoe, it seemed, in the full, horrible reality of the situation, a perfectly normal thing to do.

Once he was on the stretcher Paul was moved back into the second carriage where Simon Cook was busy laying out the bodies of the dead. All the way to King's Cross Paul could think about nothing else other than what was wrong with him. In panic he patted down his body but he seemed to be in one piece. Then he noticed that something was wrong. The ring finger on his left hand. It was bare. The penny dropped. That something he'd earlier felt slipping from his hand must have been his wedding ring.

Resting his head back on the stretcher and sighing deeply, Paul wondered how he was going to explain this to his wife. 'She is going to kill me,' he thought. 'Only married seven months and I've lost it already.'

## Edgware Road: about thirty minutes after the explosion

Those who had rushed into the bombed carriage at Edgware Road to help the injured had administered all the first aid they were capable of. They were now spent. Having bandaged wounds, applied tourniquets and made the victims as comfortable as possible, there was little more they could do other than talk to them, keep them awake, away from death.

David Gardner was telling Jason Rennie about the adaptation of *Julius Caesar* he was directing and starring in. Jason promised to come and see him play Brutus when they got out of there.

Andrew Ferguson was talking to two girls from Tennessee about their taste in music and why they didn't like country and western, about the West End musical they had seen the night before, and about home.

Steve Huckelsby was talking to the wounded at the front of the second carriage, what they did for a living and how he had friends who did the same thing.

Conversation was sporadic, superficial, but it served its purpose: it distracted the injured, helped them to focus on staying awake and not giving in.

We had been underground for half an hour and not a single policeman, fireman or paramedic had made it to where they were most needed. In the first few minutes after the bomb exploded people had died. We had watched them die. There was no way they could have been saved even if ambulance crews had been on the train when the bomb went off. Now those who had tried to help were afraid that people injured in the initial blast would die waiting for proper medical attention.

Although we couldn't see it from inside the bombed carriage, help was on the way. Passengers were now flooding out of the carriages and into the tunnel from both of the stricken trains, clearing the way for emergency crews to push through to our assistance. It would take time to clear the carriages and, until all the passengers were out, it would be like trying to swim upstream to get to us.

Drivers who had been waiting to book on for shifts or who were having their breakfast breaks in the station canteen were quick to react when they heard the explosion in the tunnel. Like the staff at Aldgate they didn't wait for orders. They didn't stop to consider the dangers. It didn't occur to most of them that this had been a terror attack and that there might be other devices waiting to be exploded or chemicals in the air. They just raced along the tracks to the stranded passengers and started preparing them for an emergency detrainment. They acted instinctively.

The first of the two tube trains at Edgware Road to get help was Ray Whitehurst's. It had been leaving Edgware Road when it was bombed and the last of its six carriages was only 100 metres from the platform. The other train, the one on the parallel track, was heading into Edgware. It was another few carriage lengths deeper in the tunnel and, because of the bend in the tracks, it was slightly obscured by Ray's train.

When Edgware Road's duty manager, Trevor Rodgers, had finished speaking to Ray from the telephone in the signal cabin in the minutes after the bomb, he walked out of the booth and down on to the tracks to help the other drivers lead people out of the tunnel to safety. The smoke that had flooded the platforms after the bomb went off was thinning rapidly and Trevor could see where he was needed.

Because the bombed train was closer to the platform there were already at least half a dozen drivers and staff swarming around its rear doors. They were helping people out of the last carriage, down a set of wooden steps and on to the tracks. Staff scattered along the tunnel from the train to the platform were then marshalling people across the complex set of points that helped direct trains in and out of Edgware Road's four platforms.

Trevor walked past them and pushed towards the front of the train that Tim, Steve, Ben and I had been travelling in when the bomb went off. When he got there two other drivers had already secured the train and were starting to help the first few people down the steps and into the tunnel. The train's windscreen had been smashed by flying debris that now littered the tracks.

Trevor moved to the side of the ladder and stood a couple of metres in front of the space between the two stranded trains. He watched people climb slowly and cautiously down the steep, short wooden ladder leading out of the driver's cab. There were more than a thousand passengers on the train. It was going to take time to get them all off like this.

As he waited Trevor peered between the two trains and into the tunnel. In the distance, where the bombed carriage was, he could see debris scattered all over the tracks, sheets of metal, bits of the seating, pieces of clothing. And no more than a couple of metres from his feet, he could see the body of what he thought was a female passenger on the tracks.

His eyes were drawn to her pale, exposed legs.

When Trevor was a twenty-year-old trainee tube driver a woman had thrown herself in front of his train. Attempted suicide. She was only eighteen. Trevor didn't have to look at the body but he feared that what he didn't see his imagination might fill in. So he had left his cab to look at the poor girl.

It was a sight that would never leave him, something he could never un-see. Over the years Trevor had witnessed many more scenes like his first one. Each time it was as horrible as the last and he didn't want any of the passengers now leaving the train to have the same experience.

Now, Trevor looked around for something he could use to cover the body and found a blue tarpaulin. He placed it over the body and stood in front of it, blocking it from curious eyes, and instructed the passengers coming down the ladder to walk towards Edgware Road, hoping to direct their attention to the exit and away from what was under the blue tarp behind him.

After a little more than twenty minutes Trevor walked over to the rear of the bombed train parked next to the one he was helping to clear. Passengers were still clambering down the steps of the last carriage when he got there. Two other drivers followed Trevor as he stepped through the flow of people and into the rear of the bombed train. Once inside he was determined to make his way towards the bombed carriage he'd seen earlier while standing between the trains in the tunnel.

When Trevor reached the carriage behind the bomb it was empty. He looked out of the windows to his left and saw a queue of people wedged in between the train and the tunnel wall. They were trying to get to Edgware Road station but something was blocking their way. Trevor and one of the other two drivers flipped up the seats in the third carriage and disabled the air pressure system that fed the locks on the sliding doors.

The three drivers then opened the doors into the tunnel and beckoned people into the carriage.

Back in the bombed carriage two trainee nurses arrived to help the wounded. They were on their way home from work at a nearby hospital. They had been on my train, the one that had not been bombed, the one still burning with fluorescent lights on the neighbouring track, but as the news filtered through the carriages of the seriously wounded people in need of help, the two nurses pushed their way forward.

Ben Thwaites helped them through the window from his side as he had done for Tim, Steve and me not half an hour before. Andrew Ferguson worked with Ben to get the nurses through the window.

'Who needs help?' one of them asked. She spoke with an Ulster accent.

'Over here,' I said. 'We have a serious leg injury.'

One of them came over to where Jason Rennie and I were crouching on the floor, stroking David Gardner's head. I indicated his leg and she went down for a closer look.

'Are you a doctor?' she asked Jason.

'No,' he replied. 'I am a first aider. I tied a tourniquet around his thigh. I had a look for other injuries but there was nothing as serious as his leg.'

'Do you have a light?' she asked.

'I have this,' I said, holding up my mobile phone. 'We could use the light from the screen.'

'Here, take mine, too,' Jason added.

I took Jason's phone and with my own tried to throw some light on David Gardner's leg. The nurse tried to do the same with her own phone but it was still too dark to

make any kind of diagnosis. All we could see was the tourniquet. The rest was in shadow.

'I am not going to touch this,' she said, standing up. 'I
think it is better to leave it as it is. It looks like a good job.
Is there anybody else who needs help?'

'I haven't been towards the front of the carriage,' I said.
'If you are going to go through, let me lower you on to the
tracks. You can make your way more safely from there.
Trying to climb across that hole in the floor doesn't look
easy.'

'Okay,' she said.

I took both her hands and helped her slip down to the
gravel surface of the tunnel floor. I thought the other nurse
would follow her but she had disappeared into the darkness
of the carriage and I couldn't tell where she'd gone. When
I turned around Jason was on the floor next to David again,
checking his wounds over and talking to him, trying to keep
him awake. It was a task that became increasingly difficult
as David continued to lose blood.

Standing there, shirtless, covered in soot, I was filled with
a very strange yet somehow inappropriate sense of relief.
That morning I had tried to persuade Donna, my wife, to
take the Circle Line with me to Farringdon but she had
decided not to. Had she been here she would have been
scared, stressed: it might have affected her pregnancy. It
might even have brought on her labour.

I thought for a moment how fortunate this all was. If there
had to be a train crash on the very day my wife was making
one of her last tube journeys into work before leaving to
have our child, at least I knew she was safe, because, well,
she wasn't here. I was at the epicentre of the train crash and
that meant she wasn't, that I knew. In the confusion of the
moment it was the only thing I did know for sure.

It was hard to know anything else. I was scared to the point of delusion. My mind was behaving in a way typical of psychological stress patterns. My creative and logical brain had shut down and I was relying on memory, instinct, to survive. I might not have been able to make a decision about what to do with a pair of cufflinks, or work out how to rip a shirt, but I could remember that Donna was safe, and so was our baby. I needed something certain in the world to hang on to. The wellbeing of Donna and our unborn child was my hook.

It was holding me together.

'Bastards, those fucking bastards,' I heard someone shout.

I turned around.

It was the Irish nurse, the one I helped out of the train. She had climbed back into the carriage and was shouting and crying.

'They killed us.'

'Who? Who did what?' I asked, confused by what she was saying. 'This was a train crash,' I said. 'You can't blame anyone for this.'

She lifted her chin and shot me a look drenched in exasperation. Her eyes said everything: how could this tall shirtless man with the Canadian accent standing before her be so stupid?

'This wasn't a train crash, this was a bomb. Look at what they did,' she said pointing to the two lumps of meat hanging out of the carriage that had once been someone's legs.

'That is what they did, that's what bombs do,' she added, walking past me towards the rear of the carriage.

When she left my eyes trained on what was left of the body hanging out of the carriage door. I had looked at those legs many times in the half-hour I had been in the carriage but never for longer than a second. It had not occurred to me that all this horror and death could have been caused by a bomb. I had assumed the sound of metal on metal as the trains passed in the tunnel could only have been a crash. It was logical. It fitted. Train crashes happen all the time. Bombs? Well, bombs explode in war zones, in Iraq, in Afghanistan, not in London. Not near me.

I turned away from the legs hanging out of the train and tilted my head towards the ceiling of the carriage. I could see a huge hole directly above the crater in the floor. They matched perfectly, as if someone had blasted a hole through the carriage with a cannon. They were the only two such holes in the carriage. I was right in the middle of what had happened. I looked to my right, past the end of the carriage and into the first car where I could see the lights from the neighbouring train illuminating a carriage that, although dark, seemed almost undamaged.

To my left, through the connecting doors into the third carriage, the scene was made even clearer. The lights there were still on. It was almost empty of passengers. There was no damage at all. We were in the only affected carriage on the train, not in the front or in the rear, those that one would have expected to have been destroyed in a crash.

This had to be a bomb.

For the first time I had turned off my tunnel vision. I stopped looking at the wounded, the dead and could see the situation for what it was – a terrorist attack. I knew that now. Someone had either planted a bomb, as they had in Madrid in March 2004, or detonated it themselves, and for all I knew those legs falling out of the open doors of the carriage might be all that was left of the suicide bomber.

A surge of nausea slammed into my gut.

'Fuck,' I thought. 'If this is al-Qaeda, if this is like Madrid or the 9/11 attacks or the African embassy explosions then there has to be other bombs. There always are other bombs. Coordination is the key to inflicting terror with these guys. It's what al-Qaeda do. They might have bombed Donna's train as well. She might already be dead. These attacks are never a one-off. I have to get the fuck out of here.'

Standing there, faced with the naked truth, I wished that the Irish nurse had kept quiet. Now what would I do? If Donna was still below ground there was be no way I could get to her. I had been here for over half an hour and we had yet to see even one member of the emergency services. If the emergency services couldn't make it from the platform to this carriage in the thirty minutes since the bomb had gone off, how on earth could I get to Donna?

What should I do?

Should I leave now and find Donna?

No. I would never find her in the chaos.

I could try.

I could leave now.

I could run and run and run, but that would mean leaving David in Jason's hands and Jason was losing blood as well. What if his condition deteriorated and he could no longer help himself, let alone David?

What about everyone else here?

I couldn't leave them simply to tear around the city in a panic looking for Donna. Everyone in London would be trying to find their loved ones. It was probably mayhem out there. I had to stay. I had to stay calm. David needed me. The girls from Tennessee needed me. I could do something here. I could help. I could make them feel that they were not alone, if nothing more. I had to stay until help arrived.

Where was that help?

After I caught my breath I walked over towards the carriage doors facing the tunnel wall and leaned out to try and see Edgware Road station. I saw the light shining on the platforms a few hundred metres up the tracks. Along the tunnel wall I could detect people trying to make their way towards the light. They had come from the first bombed carriage. They were stuck. Not one of them was moving. There must be debris in the way, something stopping them. But what?

More than two dozen passengers had ground to a halt, one behind the other, between the train and the tunnel wall. Most of them had been ushered out of the first carriage by the driver, Ray Whitehurst; others had jumped out of the open doors of the bombed carriage in an effort to escape the mayhem. All were desperate to reach the sunlight ahead of them.

The first few people in the queue stumbling down the line towards Edgware Road made reasonable progress, but they stopped when they came across Danny Biddle lying on the ground in front of them. By now two people were helping Danny: a passenger from the front carriage, who'd appeared on the scene quite quickly after hearing Danny's screams, and a driver from Edgware Road who was among the first to run into the darkness to help the stranded passengers.

In desperation the people at the head of the queue started stepping over Danny's broken body to get out. The third or fourth to do so was Jacqui Putnam, the middle-aged blonde woman who would have boarded the bombed carriage at King's Cross that morning had it not been for the peculiar behaviour of an autistic young man. Jacqui knew it was wrong to push her way past Danny but she was panicking.

'You can't come out this way,' said the tube driver kneeling down to help treat Danny.

'Please don't make us go back there,' Jacqui answered back, her eyes pleading, her hands shaking. 'Please.'

Like everyone else in the queue Jacqui had shuffled past the bombed carriage to get to where she now was and the thought of passing it again, of seeing the bodies, the blood and the mutilation, was more than she could bear. She looked down at Danny: he was more flesh and bone than man. She had to get out of there. Edgware Road was only a few yards away. So, against her better nature, she stepped over Danny and stumbled on down the tunnel.

After a dozen or more people had forced their way past Danny, the other man who had arrived to help him stood up from his kneeling position on the tracks and ordered everyone to stop. They couldn't go on climbing over Danny; he was getting stepped on. They would either have to wait for him to be moved or turn around and go back the way they had come. But no one turned. They just stopped, backed up like traffic, and waited for someone to tell them what to do next.

Five or six places back in the queue was thirty-one-year-old John Nabdoo, a website developer who, like Danny, had been on his way to Wembley that morning. He had been in the front carriage of the train when the bomb blew apart the one behind his and now he wondered why he was being asked to stop. He thought he had almost made it home, away from the carnage of the bomb.

The explosion was the loudest noise John had ever heard, eclipsing even the sound of the Clapham rail crash in 1988. As a schoolboy, John had been walking on a path beside the tracks with his friends when, just a few feet away, two trains collided and a third crashed into the wreckage, killing thirty-five people on the other side of a chain-link fence. John had witnessed the crash, had seen the horrible injuries, the injured

194

and the dead until a paramedic on the scene had pushed him away, kindly, through an opening in the fence.

When the bomb blew up between Edgware Road and Paddington John didn't think 'Bomb' or 'Crash'. The lights had gone out instantly in his carriage and so he immediately assumed there had been some kind of electrical explosion.

In the first few minutes after the bomb he heard cries coming from the second carriage. He thought about going back there to help. He had taken a first aid course through work – he might be of some use – but he didn't go. The carriage was then filling with smoke and he decided the scene was not safe; it was the first lesson of first aid: don't endanger yourself. He stayed where he was and waited for the driver to tell them when to exit via the front of the train.

Once on the tracks John followed the people in front of him towards Edgware Road, stepping over debris and steadying himself with his hands on the dirty bricks and wires of the tunnel wall. As he passed the rear of the bombed carriage he saw a blonde Australian woman in fishnet tights lying on the gravel. Her name was Alison and she was screaming something about her leg. Next to her was Tim Coulson. He was supporting her back, telling her that he was going to stay with her until he was told otherwise.

John looked down at Tim and Alison and thought they were a couple; they had to be. They seemed too intimate to be strangers. John had no idea that Tim had jumped through a broken window from the train on the opposite track to get where he was, that he had held a dying man in his arms, said a prayer for him and then moved on to help someone else, that he hardly knew Alison at all.

John wanted to stop and help. He thought that perhaps he could make a splint for Alison's leg but, looking around, he couldn't see anything to make a splint with. Tim was helping Alison – John could see that – and so he decided to press on, to get out, to look after himself. As John passed Alison he looked away. He was riddled with guilt for not stopping, terrified, and ashamed of himself for leaving the wounded woman behind. He couldn't look her in the eye as he passed.

His legs weakened as he walked and he felt as if he was going to fall with every step. After another dozen or so strides forward he found himself at the rear of the third carriage where the queue came to a stop. John stood there for a few minutes, wondering why they were not moving, when a man inside the carriage started banging on one of the sliding doors.

The man wanted John to help him try and prise apart the doors so that he could get out. John stepped forward and the two men tried to open the doors, but to no avail. Just then, out of the corner of his eye, John saw a figure in a fluorescent jacket pushing his way towards him along the tunnel wall from Edgware Road. When the figure was only a few feet away John could see he was a London Underground driver.

'Don't bother with the doors,' the driver told John without stopping. 'They won't open like that.'

John joined the queue again and the line started to move. Just ahead of him several passengers seemed to be climbing over something as they moved towards Edgware Road. A few steps on and the queue stopped again. John had reached Danny Biddle. There were a few people in front of him, but, standing to one side, he could see there was a man lying on the tracks and two others kneeling down next to him. One of the men looked like a London Underground employee; the other, John thought, must be a passenger.

It was dark but John could see that the man on the tracks

had lost his left leg. There was no stump; it was virtually gone from the hip down. Danny's right leg was at least partly there. It looked as if the two men were trying to find enough of Danny's left leg to tie off and prevent further bleeding. It made John feel better to see them work. Someone was helping, taking charge, administering first aid.

John stood there with the two dozen other people for ten to fifteen minutes, waiting for paramedics to come and stretcher Danny out, but no one showed up. All John could do was wait. Rumours began to filter down the queue. Someone mentioned Madrid and the commuter trains that had been bombed by terrorists, how many people had died and how this was probably the same thing. Someone else was repeating the name al-Qaeda over and over again. John could see what was happening to Danny, what had happened to the people in the second carriage he had walked past, and the horror of the scenes started to crush what was left of his capacity for rational thought.

He could almost touch the light in front of him. Edgware Road was just there. Light was his salvation. If he could only walk into the sunlight he would be okay, he could get away from the horror. It was torture to be so frightened, to see the light but to be unable to get to it. The only other way out was back into the darkness and around the other side of the train and he couldn't do that. He couldn't walk back into the dark, past the second carriage. Not again.

John was afraid. The smell of burning steel and oxidised blood hung in the air. He had smelled this stench before. He had been this afraid before. It had been a long time ago – 1988. When he was a child, on his way to Emanuel School in Clapham, south London. John was walking beside a chain-link fence that separated him from the railway line. There was a loud bang, the loudest his young ears had ever heard.

Now, nearly twenty years on, John once again found himself on a railway track witnessing another tragedy. Standing in that tunnel, underground, watching a similar horror unfold was too much. This time there was no hole in the fence through which he could escape. Smelling the same repulsive smells, feeling the same uncontrollable fear, was oppressive. All he could think about was getting out of there, out to the light ahead of him.

Unable to go forward, unable to muster the strength or the will to turn around and go back, John faced the wall of the tunnel and started to claw at the bricks with his finger tips. His breathing raced, matching his pounding heart. Sweat ran from his scalp and down his face as he clawed at the wall. There was no logic now, only panic and memories of that day on the tracks in Clapham, when he was just a boy.

After a minute or so his fingers started to bleed. The pain from his hands sobered him up. John looked at his hands, then at the man on the floor of the tunnel who was fighting for his life. John had not gone into the second carriage when he heard the screams for help; he had stepped over the blonde Australian woman on the tunnel floor as he tried to get out, but that was as far as it would go. He couldn't run forever. It was time for him to do something, anything, to help.

'Does anybody have any scissors?' one of the men helping Danny shouted down the line.

'I have a penknife,' someone behind John said.

'Here, I'll take it,' John said, grabbing the knife and taking it to where Danny lay on the tunnel floor.

'Is there anything I can do to help?' John asked, handing over the penknife.

As John moved closer he could see just how badly Danny had been injured; he looked barely human. His head seemed unusually swollen. It was sliced apart from one side of his forehead to the other, one of his eyes didn't seem to be there and he lay in shadow, giving the impression that whatever lay in darkness, whatever John couldn't see, was much worse.

The only thing remotely human about Danny was his voice. It sounded normal, almost calm.

John could hear Danny talking to the man hovering above what was left of his legs. Danny was explaining that he was a football fan, that Arsenal was his club. The man kneeling over him didn't like football; he preferred rugby. They promised to take each other to their preferred sports if they ever got out of there. John could detect an accent in the first-aider's voice. Where was he from? Australia? New Zealand? John couldn't tell.

In fact, the accent was South African. The man helping Danny was Adrian, a professional bodyguard. He had been one of the first people into the tunnel when Ray had opened the doors to the first carriage. He'd hit the gravelled surface of the tracks just as Danny was coming to terms with the horror of his situation. Adrian heard screams of terror down the tunnel and quickly set out to find where they had come from.

Like Jason Rennie in the second carriage, Adrian was also ex-army, except that he had seen action, in Kosovo. Adrian had heard screams like Danny's before; he knew the cries of broken and desperate men confronted by their own mortality. Adrian ran down the tunnel in between the two trains until he was level with Danny. Crouching down on his knees he looked under the train to where Danny was lying.

'My name is Adrian. What do I call you?' he said, clambering across the tracks.

'Danny, my name is Danny,' came the reply.

'Stay calm, Danny, I am on my way. Stay calm,' Adrian said.

Wriggling out from under the carriage Adrian stood up and looked at Danny before bending over and lifting away the door that was pinning him to the ground. Tossing it aside he knelt down and looked over the man whose life he was going to try and save.

'I am ex-military,' Adrian said. 'I have been in this situation before. I have never lost anyone yet and I do not intend to start now.'

From the determination in his voice Danny knew that the man who had come to his aid had seen injuries like these before. He knew he was now in the hands of someone who could help, but not for a second did Danny believe he would survive. He fully expected to die in that dark and lonely place. His only sense of relief at Adrian's arrival was that he no longer had to die alone.

Before Danny could speak again a London Underground driver named Lee Hunt appeared up the tracks from Edgware Road carrying a torch. He shone the beam into Danny's face.

'Please don't shine that light into my eyes,' Danny said, unaware that he now only had one eye.

Adrian told the London Underground driver to take off his high-visibility vest and give it to him. He applied it immediately to the stump of Danny's left leg. There wasn't much there but Adrian was determined to tie it off. Even with a proper first aid kit it would have been difficult, with nothing but a plastic vest it was near impossible.

Danny lay still as Adrian worked on him. He could not feel any pain. He didn't think about his body. He thought about the life he was minutes from losing. He thought about his fiancée. He thought about the wedding day they had been planning together. He thought of the things he would never do, of holding his child in his arms for the first time. He thought about how much he had been looking forward to his life and how none of that was going to happen now.

Danny was certain he was going to die in that tunnel. He looked at Adrian and Lee, shadows fidgeting in the darkness around him, and he thought that these two men, two strangers, were the last people he would ever see. It broke his heart. He was going to die in the dark, with no one who loved him by his side, with no one who knew him even aware of what was happening.

The thought terrified him.

'I don't want to die. I don't want to die,' he thought. 'I am twenty-six. I don't want to die this way. Not like this. I have a lot of things left to do. Not like this, please.'

With the panic came guilt. He was going to leave his fiancée behind, alone without him. For the rest of her life she would have to live with the thought that he had died in the dark, afraid, staring up at the dirty ceiling of some filthy tunnel with no one to tell him they loved him.

He had to pass on a message to her.

Lifting his head Danny caught Adrian's attention and told him his fiancée's name.

'You have got to find her, do you hear me?' Danny said. 'You have to find her and tell her I am sorry.'

'It won't come to that,' Adrian replied. 'I am going to get you out of here.'

There was something in Adrian's voice: confidence. It was genuine, too. Danny began to think, for the first time since he'd hit the ground, that he might not die there in the tunnel after all. He still thought death was inevitable, that there was no way he could survive his injuries, but he hoped he would be strong enough to make it into the sunlight above ground before he breathed his last.

If only he could have one more look at the blue sky.

If only he could feel the sun on his face once more before he died.

If only.

Adrian took what seemed like ages to stabilise Danny's left leg before turning his attention to his right. Locating the end of the stump was tricky. Danny's trousers had been destroyed and were caught up in the wound. Needing something to cut away the material, Adrian stood up and asked if anyone in the queue now gathering behind Danny had a pair of scissors.

Seconds later John Nabdoo stepped forward and handed over a penknife he had collected from someone further down the line. When he'd done so he stayed close to watch Adrian and Lee work to try and save a man who looked as if he had no right to be alive.

It had now been over half an hour since the bomb had exploded and there was still no movement in the queue. John looked up into the carriage and could see that people inside the train were moving towards the rear of the train. It was progress at least. As they left he could see several London Underground workers moving back through the train towards the bombed carriage.

A few minutes later news began to filter down the queue that the best way out was to turn back, walk along the train and then climb through the carriage doors which had been opened behind them. People started to leave. Among them were Susanna Pell, Chris Stones and the two builders from Manchester. John and another man, who was tall and wearing a suit, stayed behind with Danny to help. Before long everyone but the four people helping Danny had gone.

The first call to the Network Operations Centre claimed

that the train Ray was driving had hit the tunnel wall and that there was a person on the tracks. When the paramedics arrived at Edgware Road most of them stopped to treat the walking wounded but one of them ran into the tunnel looking for the man he had heard about on the radio.

Almost forty-five minutes had passed before Danny caught sight of a paramedic's reflective bag bouncing down the tunnel. The man carrying it was called Graeme Baker; he also had a stretcher with him. Immediately, Graeme joined Adrian and Lee as they worked to stabilise Danny sufficiently to get him to hospital.

John stood back, waiting to be told what do to, as he watched Adrian, Lee and the paramedic try to scoop Danny up. The stretcher came in two long pieces that had to be slid under the patient and clicked into place. The poor lighting and uneven ground made it difficult to secure and they had several goes before they got it right.

Danny could hear the voices above him discussing how they were going to put the stretcher under him but the voices came and went as he faded in and out of consciousnes. Their every movement caused Danny to wince in agony.

John could hear Danny's groans as they shifted him about the tunnel floor, but they sounded like no other that John had heard that day. There was a strength, a determination, in Danny's voice. He was terribly injured but he was still trying to suck up the pain and get himself on that stretcher. He was utterly determined to make it into the sunlight before he died.

John drew strength from Danny's desire to live.

Then, to John's relief, he heard the parts of the stretcher clicking into place. They were going to get out of there. Graeme told John to take his first aid bag; then, Adrian, Lee, Graeme and the man in the suit picked up Danny's stretcher and walked down the side of the train as John followed behind with Graeme's bag.

The ground was uneven and strewn with bits of metal and loose stone, and great care had to be taken not to drop the patient. At one point they encountered a signal light blocking the way and Danny's stretcher had to be lifted to chest height to clear it.

John thought the men in front of him were bound to drop the stretcher. Danny was just as convinced. He had somehow survived being blown out of a carriage and into a tunnel with such force that the loose change and the keys in his left trouser pocket were now embedded in his right leg. He had had the strength to scream for help and to remain conscious while he was being cared for; surely he wasn't going to die now as a result of falling from a stretcher?

Danny could feel himself wobble but then just as quickly he was steady again. They had made it over the signal and past the end of the train to the point where the tunnel opened up wide enough to allow them to walk with relative ease. When they reached the platform John dropped the paramedic's bag on to the ground, leaving it with an ambulance attendant on the platform who was waiting for permission to go into the tunnel. Someone handed John a cup of water and he knocked it back as he watched Danny being taken up the stairs towards the station exit.

As he passed under the blue awning covering the entrance to Edgware Road Danny felt himself being carried into the light. Relief. He was outside. He didn't have to die breathing that horrible rusty air that tasted of human blood. The sun was on his face again.

Danny began to relax, his determination to get out of the tunnel now realised. When the ambulance pulled into casualty at St Mary's Hospital, Paddington, it hit the kerb and jolted Danny on his stretcher. Graeme swore at the driver from the back of the ambulance.

The doors were opened and Danny was carried into Accident and Emergency. A doctor ran over and looked at his latest patient. Even with only one eye, Danny registered the shock on the doctor's face before he turned away for more help. Within seconds he was surrounded by doctors and nurses, a babble of voices calling out instructions.

Then he passed out.

## Aldgate Station: 9.10 a.m., twenty minutes after the explosion

About twenty minutes after suicide bombers tore apart three underground trains across the city of London the entrance to Aldgate station was swollen with the walking wounded and uninjured passengers who had fled the stricken train trapped between Liverpool Street and Aldgate.

The first to emerge were those from the front carriage. The driver let them out through his cab and directed them on to the tracks shortly after his train came to a stop. Following those from the first carriage were the walking wounded from the second, those who had jumped clear of the train when the doors were blown off by the explosion. The seriously injured still trapped in the wrecked carriage – those unable to move – were still waiting for help, as were the four carriages full of people trapped behind them.

Despite the fact that the Aldgate bombing was the first incident reported to the emergency services that morning, it still took ambulance crews until just after nine o'clock to reach the gates of Aldgate station, where everyone was being taken to or directed. Some ambulances had made it to Liverpool Street at 9.03 but they were in the wrong place and had to be redirected.

The British Transport Police, who have an office at Aldgate, were the first to arrive on the concourse, a few minutes after the blast. They quickly cordoned off the station to prevent more people from entering. Next were the London Fire Brigade at nine sharp. The first firemen fanned out quickly to treat the wounded who were being lined up along one wall of the station entrance and on the pavement outside.

By the time Emma Brown made it into the sunlight, less than ten minutes after the blast, still clutching her stomach, which was bleeding quite badly, she only had to wait a few minutes before a fireman was looking her over, offering her treatment. People were still showing up at the station expecting to get on a train, only to be told by police that Aldgate was now closed. When Melvin Finn emerged from the tunnel a few minutes later, clasping his briefcase to his chest with his wounded hand, Emma was being treated on the pavement.

Melvin sat down next to Emma and couldn't help but stare at her stomach wounds. When a fireman asked Melvin if he needed help he declined. He was wrong to do so. The tendons in his hand were severely damaged – he would later require two operations and five days in hospital – but complaining about his hand while Emma's stomach was in such a state seemed petty to a man of Melvin's character, so he kept quiet.

Aldgate's station manager Celia Harrison was running between the phone in her office and the bridge overlooking the platforms, relaying messages from the London Underground staff who were directing the walking wounded from the mouth of the tunnel to the sunlight above. When everyone from the first two carriages of the train who could walk had made it past her, an eerie silence filled the station. Smoke continued to waft out of the tunnel but no one else appeared. She wondered why not. There were hundreds more down there.

Celia started to get messages from the staff she had sent into the tunnel. They were requesting paramedics, ambulance crew, firemen, anyone who could help the dying in the second carriage, all of whom were now completely on their own in the dark. She rushed over to a police officer standing in the station entrance.

'Can you get some paramedics on to the tracks?' she pleaded. 'There are people dying down there.'

Deep in the tunnel, with the stranded passengers, there were only the three tube drivers. There were no paramedics, firemen, police or teams of London Underground staff. Aldgate wasn't like Edgware Road. There was no station canteen, no despatch office, no drivers congregating to book on and off from their shifts who could run into the tunnel to help. At Aldgate there were only a handful of staff and they were doing their best.

Two of the three drivers who went into the tunnel had gone to the rear of the train in an attempt to open the doors and evacuate the hundreds of people stuck in the four carriages behind the one that had been bombed. Next to the bombed second carriage Steve Eldridge had given up trying to get people out of the third via a broken window. The stepladder he had retrieved from the driver's cab was too short for the job. He decided to stay near the second carriage and direct people towards the station as they filed down the tunnel.

A few feet away and up from Steve, inside the front of the third carriage, there were at least a dozen people with injuries that needed attention. They had been waiting there for over twenty minutes, expecting some kind of help, but none was forthcoming. Their situation was becoming desperate. Most of the injuries in the third carriage were cuts and bruises, but one at least was far more serious.

The bomb had been very close to them, just on the other side of the interconnecting doors. The shattered glass blew into their carriage with such force that people twenty feet away had pieces embedded in their skin. The worst injury, though, belonged to Ross Mallinson, a middle-aged Tasmanian with curly salt-and-pepper hair.

When the train came to a sudden stop he was thrown sideways with a force that sent the right side of his head crashing through the glass partition to his right. The impact fractured his skull. For the moment Ross was coherent enough to understand what he was being told but if he didn't get to hospital he would die. His life was in the hands of his fellow passengers.

Among the crowd stood a middle-aged, handsome man wearing a well-tailored blue shirt. Seeing the situation deteriorate for those around him he walked back towards the connecting doors into the fourth carriage. Stepping through he told the people sitting there he was going to get help for the injured in his carriage. When he reached the end of the fourth carriage he stepped through the doors into the fifth and introduced himself as Nigel.

'There are some very badly injured people back here. Does anybody know first aid?' Nigel asked loudly. 'Can anybody help?'

Standing just inside the fifth carriage was an off-duty policewoman named Lizzie Kenworthy. She was a schools' officer. That morning she was on her way to Westminster for a conference about safety in education at the Department for Education and Skills. She was dressed in casual business clothes. Her long blonde hair hung loosely down her back.

When the bomb went off she had tried to stay still and remain calm. Like almost everyone in the last three carriages of the train she was so far from the explosion that the idea of people bleeding to death only a few carriages up had not entered her mind. Now, with the arrival of the man in the blue shirt, all that had changed.

'I am a police officer,' she said flashing her warrant card. 'I'll go.'

Standing a few feet away was a young woman named Laura Morris. She was travelling with her mother, Katie. Laura had graduated from college three days earlier and was on her way into her mother's office at Tower Hill where she had landed a summer job.

When Laura saw the blonde off-duty policewoman follow the blue shirted man back into the fourth carriage to help the injured she wanted to go with them. Laura had spent a season as a ski instructor in Canada. As a result she knew basic first aid and wanted to help if she could. Her mother held her back.

'Mum, I'm trained. I have to go,' she said.

Laura could have gone. She knew that – she was old enough to decide for herself – but when she saw the look of fright on her mother's face she agreed to stay put.

Ian Webb had spent the last twenty minutes crouched on the carriage floor in his uncomfortable new shoes. He was trying to claw his way back from a claustrophobic fit brought on by his combined fear of underground trains, smoke and fire. Some of the people standing above him, most of them injured, were moving about, talking, kicking the broken glass that was covering the floor at the front of the third carriage. Others were in the same state of paralysed fear as Ian, unable to move.

The smoke that had initially flooded into the carriage had been thinning since the explosion and Ian was beginning to realise that he need no longer fear being burned to death. Something in him was beginning to lift. Raising his head from his knees he looked around. Outside the carriage, on the tracks, he could hear voices so he stood up to look out of the window and see whose they were.

A London Underground tube driver was standing on the tracks just outside the bombed carriage. He was directing people around the debris that Ian could now see was covering the empty track alongside his train. The driver was telling one of the passengers not to worry about the electric current: it had been shut off. The passenger clearly didn't believe him. To prove his point the driver did a little dance on one of the rails and the worried commuter smiled as she continued on towards Aldgate station. Ian laughed at the driver's jig.

Word soon spread that people were leaving via the rear of the train and someone near Ian could be heard addressing the walking wounded, telling them to start moving back. Unhurt passengers in the carriage moved to the sides to let those worse off than them pass through. Ian followed the wounded from the back of the queue.

When the dozen or so who had been injured reached the rear of their carriage a woman with long blonde hair in a black trouser suit, waving a police badge, pushed past them on her way towards the bombed part of the train.

Ian kept walking.

Once inside the fourth carriage he decided to rest and so sat down on one of the seats. Although he had some cuts and bruises and was covered in the blood of his fellow passengers, he didn't feel he was injured enough to warrant being one of the first to leave the train. Now that he was away from the damage in the third carriage, and the smoke had almost gone, he was regaining his composure.

As the wounded walked through the fourth carriage on their way to the back of the train the rest of the passengers in the carriage moved to the sides and stood up on the seats to let them pass. For the people in the fourth carriage this was their first sight of blood that day. Despite their uneasiness, and a universal desire to escape, there was no pushing and shoving. No one needed to be asked to move out of the way. Some offered words of encouragement.

'Not much further now.'

'Keep going, you are almost there.'

'You are doing really well, just a little longer now.'

If the bombers had hoped that fear would turn into mass panic, they were to be disappointed. The quiet words of comfort and support offered to the injured as they passed showed that kindness, virtue and courage would, that day in London, triumph over cruelty.

When the wounded got to the back there were two drivers and a couple of passengers waiting on the tracks to help people through an unused driver's cab at the rear of the train and on to the tunnel floor. Once on the tracks everyone was directed to turn left and walk back along the length of the train towards Aldgate station, the lights of which could be faintly seen in the distance.

Most of the wounded could walk unaided but Ross Mallinson, whose skull had been fractured when it slammed into a glass partition, had to be helped by two of his fellow passengers. Had it not been for the assistance he received, Ross's doctor would later tell him, he would not have made it out of that tunnel alive. His injury was life-threatening and Ross would undergo urgent brain surgery before the evening was out.

Following the wounded were the rest of the passengers from the four carriages behind the bomb. It took about half an hour to get them all out of the rear of the train. Progress was slow. Many of the women were wearing high heels which made it difficult for them to climb down the ladder at the rear and side doors of the unused driver's cab, let alone walk along the gravel surface of the tunnel floor.

Some of the passengers insisted on taking their bags with them. Others, some pregnant, some elderly, slowed general progress. Nonetheless everyone waited patiently for their turn to leave; no one pushed or shoved. In the middle of the pack was Ian Webb in his uncomfortable shoes, and right in front of him Laura Morris and her mother, Katie. Like the rest of the passengers now escaping the train, both of them thought the worst was over; but before they would feel the sunshine on their faces, there would be one more horror for them to endure.

To get to Aldgate all the passengers would have to walk past the terrifying scene of the bombed carriage further up the tracks.

Lizzie Kenworthy followed the man in the blue shirt through the fourth carriage and into the third. She knew instantly that something serious was wrong. The wounded from the front of the third carriage had started to move towards the rear of the train. They were covered in blood and looked shocked, terrified.

Looking at them as she made her way past, Lizzic thought: 'If there are people walking around with injuries as these passengers are, there must be more back there too badly hurt to walk. They might even be dying.'

'Can I help anyone?' Lizzie called out to the bloodied faces limping towards her. 'Does anyone need help?'

They just looked at Lizzie as they passed, most of them in a daze. The man in the blue shirt – Nigel – stayed with the walking wounded as Lizzie pressed forward alone into the front of the third carriage. When she reached the twisted connecting doors between the third and second carriages she could see that all the windows had been blown out. Blood spattered the inside of the carriage and the floor was covered in an inch of shattered glass.

'Don't go in there,' one of the few remaining people at that end of the carriage, an uninjured man standing among the twisted debris, told her. 'Just don't go in there.'

'I have to,' Lizzie replied. 'I'm a police officer. I need to know what is happening.'

Lizzie could hear yelling from somewhere in the darkness in front of her but she couldn't tell where it was coming from. She would have to get closer. Moving right, she squeezed past the sheets of twisted metal until she was inside the bombed carriage.

Just inside it, on the corrugated rubber floor, was a woman. She was pinned to the ground. One of the interconnecting doors looked as if it had been blown off and landed on her arm. The woman couldn't move. Lizzie looked down at her and considered lifting the door to free the woman but then she stopped. Perhaps the woman's artery had been severed. The door might have taken her arm off but it might also be the only thing stopping the woman from bleeding to death.

To Lizzie's right she could see that there were two very seriously injured people in the last two seats of the carriage. The first to catch her eye was the air traffic controller from Liverpool. He was sitting quietly and apparently normally in the second seat, looking across to the tunnel wall in front of him. Twisted sideways and doubled over in the neighbouring seat, so that her back was leaning into the man's left-hand side, was a petite woman with long curly hair named Martine.

Martine's right leg was stretched out and resting up in the window frame that faced into the carriage behind. Her leg was still in one piece, her shoe still on her foot, but almost all the skin and muscle had been blown away with Martine's trousers, exposing the bones of her leg from the thigh to the ankle. It was impossible to see her left leg. Either it had been lost in the explosion or was trapped under debris at the back of the seats.

Looking at Martine, Lizzie thought, for the first time, that this had been no accident. A crash would have compressed the train, thrown it, and everyone in it, around; here, though, everything had been blown out, blasted, charred by fire. This had been some kind of explosion: the engine might have exploded; or it might have been a bomb. She wasn't sure, but it didn't really matter. She had first aid to administer.

Lizzie's police training started to kick in. Her instinct was to put an exclusion zone around the carriage and then leave the area to report on what she had discovered. This was a crime scene now. Her training had taught her that she should not stay where she was lest she disturb vital evidence. But just as quickly she realised she couldn't leave. There was no way to report what she had found; she was alone with people who needed help. She had to stay calm and go through the ABCs of first aid: Airway, Breathing, Circulation.

There was no one else.

Just then someone, a young man with dark hair, casually dressed, stuck his head through the window from the third carriage. 'Can I do anything to help?' he asked.

'Can I trust you?' Lizzie asked.

'Yes you can,' the young man replied.

'Okay, then. Go up the carriage and get me some ties or scarves. Whatever I can use for first aid. I need shirts, too, anything I can make bandages with.'

The young man turned and ran back into the train and Lizzie removed her own jacket. She turned back to Martine and wrapped the jacket around her right leg, tying it as tight as she could. The fire that had followed the explosion seemed to have cauterised the wounds on Martine's leg. They didn't appear to be bleeding, but it was dark and Lizzie wanted to be sure.

'I've lost my leg, haven't I?' Martine said.

'Yes you have, but you are going to be okay,' Lizzie replied, squeezing Martine's hand tightly. 'I am going to look after you.'

Just then the young man returned with a few T-shirts and other articles of clothing. He handed them to Lizzie through the window from the third carriage. She thanked him. Martine was bent forward, making it almost impossible for Lizzie to see the extent of her stomach wounds in the darkened carriage.

'Here, let me put this in your belly to stop the bleeding,' Lizzie said, pressing an item of clothing into Martine's stomach. As Lizzie pushed it into her abdomen Martine gritted her teeth but didn't cry out showing great strength in adversity. Lizzie could tell that, despite her appalling injuries, the young woman was strong and utterly determined to survive.

Lizzie turned to the man sitting next to her, the air traffic controller, to see if he was still alive. He had been calm and silent the whole time. Lizzie introduced herself and the man told her his name. She knew from her first aid training that she had to remember it. The use of a person's first name can be the most comforting thing in the world.

In order to remember Martine's name, Lizzie thought of the tennis star Martina Navratilova. The air traffic controller's name would be easier. It was the same as that of the son of a close friend of the family. She repeated both names over and over again to herself. Crouching down on the balls of her feet, Lizzie took Martine's hand in her left and the man's in her right.

She had done all the first aid she could. Now she had to comfort them, to keep them awake, alive, until help arrived.

Behind her Lizzie could still hear the woman she had seen lying on the carriage floor when she'd first entered the carriage. To her left was a young man. Most of his clothes had been blown off and he was slumped on the carriage floor looking at his hands. Lizzie thought about going over to try and help him but she didn't want to leave Martine and the man, both of whom seemed to have benefited from her presence, so she stayed where she was.

Looking outside the carriage, Lizzie could see that people were now starting to move past it on their way to Aldgate. 'They must have got out through the rear of the train,' she thought. It was too dark to see their faces as they passed in the tunnel but she wondered if the injured people she had seen walking past her when she first reached the third carriage were among those now escaping.

She hoped so.

Outside the bombed carriage tube driver Steve Eldridge stood a few feet in front of a pile of bodies that had been blown out of the second carriage. He faced the rear of the train, his back to the scene of mayhem. He didn't want to look at the dead again and he didn't want any of the passengers, those being evacuated out of the rear of the train, who were now walking towards him, to witness the horror either.

The image of the dead, strewn about the track, the wreckage, and the man's body on the edge of the pile wearing nothing but a pair of underpants, one sock and one shoe, was not something anyone needed to see. It was horrifying. The man's flesh was so charred, and the sight of his skin and the gaping wound on his face where his left eye had once been would certainly traumatise anyone who saw it.

Steve knew that the best way to prevent people from seeing the full horror of the carnage as they passed was to distract them.

'Keep looking straight ahead. Follow the lights towards Aldgate station,' Steve said. 'Keep looking at the lights. Watch your feet; there is debris all over the tracks.'

It was dark, the ground was covered in pieces of twisted metal and train parts. Walking was a challenge. They needed the light to see, so following Steve's instructions made sense. At least half the people lumbering down the tunnel towards him never turned their heads.

The four carriages behind the one that had been bombed were carrying between seventy and one hundred people each. People were still moving towards him in what seemed to be an orderly fashion and Steve hoped to keep distracting them until the last had passed. There was still no sign of the emergency services; more than half an hour had now passed since the bomb exploded.

When about half the remaining passengers in the last four carriages had passed Steve on their way to Aldgate, he turned slightly, picking up the glow of Aldgate in his left eye and the passengers walking towards him in his right.

'Keep looking at the lights,' he repeated. 'Keep looking at the lights.'

Everything was starting to settle into a pattern. But then Steve saw something out of the corner of his eye that disrupted that pattern. At first it was no more than a large shadow. It blocked out the light over Steve's left shoulder and moved past him. He turned around for a better look and what he saw almost knocked him over.

It was the naked and burned man.

The one he'd seen lying on the edge of the pile of bodies.

The man whose skin had been impossibly charred; the man wearing one shoe, one sock, blackened underpants. He had been on the ground with the dead for over half an hour, showing no signs of life, and now he was standing up. Walking.

How could that be?

How could that *possibly* be?

Phil Duckworth was having a bit of a lazy morning. He was supposed to be up by 6.15 but his wife Heather had to kick him out of bed at 6.45. If she hadn't, he would have missed his train to work. Still, when Phil eventually left the comfort of the duvet, he was in no hurry to leave the house.

He put on his lucky white shirt and tie. He had worn that same shirt when he interviewed for the job he now had at an investment bank near Aldgate. Heather said goodbye through gritted teeth; she was annoyed with Phil for running late again. He disappeared down the road on his way to St Albans station to catch the Silverlink into Farringdon.

Phil reached Farringdon and switched to the Circle Line for Aldgate, as he did every day. When the train pulled up to the platform he stepped into the rear of the second carriage and stood within a metre of a suicide bomber carrying a bag of explosives. At Liverpool Street a young woman called Emma Brown, wearing combat trousers, with curly blonde hair, would step aboard and stand near Phil. They would both leave the train the same way.

Phil had his journey down to a tee. Every turn in the tracks was familiar. When the train left Liverpool Street, the station before Aldgate, he prepared to move towards the doors. He didn't need to look up from his book, *Angels & Demons*, to know his next move. The train always jiggled a bit when it went over a set of points a minute or so before pulling into the station.

That was his cue.

Instinctively Phil pushed past several people and made his way towards the doors, still reading his book. He had stepped away from the suicide bomber. There were now several passengers between him and the bomb. As he waited sparks were lighting up the tunnel where the wheels of the train connected with the points. Normally Phil wouldn't have noticed them. They flicker out as quick as they ignite, like flashbulbs in the dark.

This time, however, one of the sparks seemed to get brighter and brighter, until it consumed everything around him. The train disappeared, then the book he was reading; then his own body gave itself over to the light. All Phil had left was a great whiteness, a void. He could feel it all around him as if he were standing in the darkest of rooms, unable to see even his own hand in front of his face; except that now everything was as white as the electrical spark he had barely noticed moments before.

He was pure thought, he couldn't feel his body.

'What's wrong with me?' Phil thought. 'Why is everything so bright? Is something wrong inside my head, making me think that everything is gone? Where am I?'

There was no banging or smashing of metal to tell Phil what was happening to him. All he could hear was a deep ringing in his ears.

'Have I fallen out of the train? I must have,' he thought. 'How could I do that? I will have made all these people late for work. How stupid of me.'

Then everything went from white to black, and Phil was out.

Phil had been blown through the doors of the carriage and into the tunnel. The force of the blast was so strong that it tore the clothes from his body, leaving him in his underwear, wearing one shoe and a sock. As he flew through the air the fireball caused by the explosion burned his exposed skin almost completely black. Those passengers between Phil and the bomber had their clothes blown off as well, but they absorbed more of the explosion.

Phil landed on his back on the tracks on the edge of a pile of his fellow passengers. Unconscious and unable to move, he lay there for more than half an hour with Steve Eldridge, a tube driver, standing next to him for much of the time. No one walking past stopped to check on him. No one thought for a second that there might be a chance he had survived. He was left alone, all but naked, in the dark.

But then again, anyone who looked like that couldn't possibly have survived. Could they?

Apart from his blackened skin, Phil's left eye had been destroyed when a piece of the bomber's shin bone flew into the socket. His face was a bloody mess. The bomber's bone was still inside his skull. Remarkably, however, not a single bone was broken in Phil's body.

After lying naked for more than thirty minutes in the dark, a last burst of adrenaline surged through Phil and he could feel himself starting to wake up. Return to consciousness was slow and difficult. He lay there for a long time, trying to work out where he was, which way he was lying. Lethargy seemed to cover him like a blanket of stone. His chest felt tight and every breath needed a concerted effort.

He started to feel his body come back to him. He was on his back. He was sure of that now. His head was resting on one of the rails. His leg felt as if it were caught up in something. Turning to his right he could see a train still at the platform of Aldgate station, its dull red lights dancing in the darkness stretching out in front of him. Through the haze he could see the beams of torches swinging through the smoke. Behind them were the yellow high-visibility vests of London Underground staff.

People were coming. He wasn't alone.

Phil knew something awful had happened to him but he told himself not to worry about that now. He had to focus. He sat up and convinced himself that if he could do that he could also stand.

'I've got to get up. I have got to get to my feet and get home for Robert and Heather's sake.'

The thought of his young son and wife was all Phil had to spur him on and it was the driving force that kept him moving. Thinking of his family he rocked from side to side until he managed to roll up on to his feet using his hands to support him on the ground.

As he stood up he was overcome by a sudden awareness that everything was getting smaller, harder to see. He stumbled forward, past the left shoulder of a London Underground tube driver named Steve Eldridge, until he came to a rest against the tunnel wall. There he stood, his palms against the century-old brick, supporting himself as he tried to catch his breath.

Steve and another passenger walking by hurried after Phil as he staggered towards the tunnel wall. They told him to breathe, to look straight ahead at the wall; they told him over and over again. Steve didn't know what to do. The very idea that someone could have survived an ordeal such as Phil's seemed inconceivable. There was no time to think anyway, only to react to this dead man now walking away from him.

Laura Morris and her mother Katie were passing the bombed carriage when Phil stood up to move. They could hear Steve and the other passenger shouting at him, 'Look at the wall. Just look at the wall.'

Laura took one look at Phil, standing there in his under-wear, the band of elastic around his waist cutting into his burned skin, and she stepped forward to help. Her mother held her arm. This time Laura didn't argue. She just took Katie's hand and tried not to look at the man who surely would not survive his injuries. Laura couldn't leave her mother to walk out of the tunnel alone.

Ian Webb heard the shouting as well. His feet were still hurting him and he stopped for a second to look at this naked and blackened body trying to prop itself up against the tunnel wall. 'His chances of getting out of here are fifty/fifty at best,' Ian thought, turning to walk away. 'I hope he makes it.'

Phil could hear Steve and the other passenger shouting at him. His ears had been badly damaged by the blast and it was difficult to separate their words from the ringing in his head, but just the sound of their voices was reassuring. He was glad they were there.

Phil knew he couldn't stand against the wall for very long; he knew his strength would give out if he did not move and so he tried to walk. He wanted to go home. It was an optimistic attempt. Phil's leg buckled and he went crashing to the gravel. He didn't have the strength to support his body. That sudden burst of adrenaline was beginning to evaporate. It might not have given him the strength to walk but it had turned him from a mere body on the tracks, a blackened mess ignored by everyone, into a living individual who needed help. That, at least, might be enough to save his life.

Steve and the passenger tried to pick Phil up but he was a dead weight. Despite being only five foot nine, Phil weighed over 240 pounds. He wasn't going anywhere under his own steam and he was too heavy to be carried without a stretcher and more help, so Steve tried to make him as comfortable as possible on the tunnel floor, reassuring him that everything was going to be all right, that help was coming.

When Laura Morris and Ian Webb reached the platform at Aldgate about half a dozen firemen marched past them into the tunnel towards the bombed train carrying a ladder. It was now at least forty minutes since the bomb had gone off and these men were the first to arrive at the scene of the explosion.

When the London Fire Brigade got to the bombed carriage they ran straight over to the tunnel wall where Steve was comforting Phil. They quickly agreed that he needed to be taken out if there was any chance of saving him and so they put the ladder to use as a stretcher.

Two of the firemen then lifted Phil up and started to walk,

but he was too heavy for them; they lost their balance and all 17 stone of Phil went crashing to the tunnel floor. They hurried to help put Phil back on to the ladder and the six of them then carried him towards Aldgate, leaving Steve to continue directing people around the debris outside the second carriage.

Phil could hear the firemen talking to each other as he was carried down the tunnel. When they reached the station steps one of the firemen turned to a colleague and said: 'Why is it that I always get the bloody heavy ones?'

Phil smiled. He was alive.

He lay back and watched the overhead lights pass above him as he was taken out of the entrance to Aldgate station. Sunlight poured down on to his face and Phil could see the blue sky above as he was bumped into a waiting ambulance.

Information about the scene in the tunnel had now filtered through to the police and ambulance service at the station; within minutes they were heading down into the tunnel to the second carriage, where they were most urgently needed.

Lizzie Kenworthy was still crouching down on the balls of her feet in the second carriage. She had been holding hands with Martine and the air traffic controller next to her for close to twenty minutes. Her awkward position on the floor was cramping her legs and causing pain in an old back injury. She wanted to move but space was too tight; she would have to wait.

The man could hear Lizzie talking to him, attempting to keep him awake, but he tried not to speak more than he had to. His cheekbone had been broken from the corner of his eye to his jaw. He could feel the bone moving around inside his face every time he spoke so he kept his conversation to a minimum.

Behind Lizzie a woman had arrived from somewhere back

in the train and was now treating the woman on the floor whose arm had been pinned down by the interconnecting doors when they had been blown off. Lizzie did not turn around to look at the woman but could hear her talking to her patient, asking questions, doing what Lizzie was trying to do: keep her victim awake until help arrived.

Lizzie looked out of the carriage door and could see a London Underground driver standing on the tracks directing people.

'For Christ's sakes get me a first aid kit. Get a move on,' she yelled.

'They are on their way, help is coming,' the driver replied, seeing uniformed emergency services crew now running towards him from Aldgate.

'Well, tell them to get a bloody move on then,' Lizzie replied.

Less than a minute later a police officer in jeans and a T-shirt jumped up into the carriage.

'I am a police officer,' the man said. 'My name is Neal.'

'Good, so am I. My name is Lizzie,' she answered. 'This is Martine. She has a stomach injury and this man here has lost a leg.'

Neal went straight to the injured man and started looking him over.

'I am glad you are here,' Lizzie said, and she meant it. She had been there for something like half an hour. The polluted air was making it hard for her to breathe. Her awkward position on the carriage floor was causing her back and leg pain and she was covered in blood.

Neal gave Lizzie the chance to stand up while he assessed the two people she had been looking after. It was several more minutes before the fire brigade and a team of para-medics arrived. One of the firemen offered to help Lizzie out of the carriage but she wanted to walk out on her own and so turned around and marched through the back four carriages of the train, all now empty of passengers, before climbing out and on to the tracks.

A fireman walked with her down the tunnel. As she passed the carriage she could see now beyond doubt that this had been a bomb. She hoped that both the air traffic controller and Martine would live.

'They have to survive,' she thought. 'They have to live, they just have to.'

At about the same time police arriving on the scene started to fan out on the track and take control. An officer walked up to Steve Eldridge, the last London Underground worker still in the tunnel.

'Okay, you can leave now, out you go,' the police constable said.

'Hey, don't you talk to me like that,' Steve snapped, his anger fuelled by shock and distress. 'I have been down here all morning looking after these people. Who do you think you are?'

'I am sorry,' the officer replied. 'I didn't mean to sound rude. You have been doing a great job but it is time to go now. We've got it from here.'

Steve knew the policeman was right. Like Lizzie, who had tried to help the wounded in the second carriage, Steve had done all he could that day. The people who were still, even then, struggling to survive in the second carriage, and those who had died, were in the hands of the emergency services now. He and his fellow drivers had done more than could ever have been expected of them that day. While the three men were unable to do anything for those passengers who had died before and after they reached the scene of the explosion, the living, the survivors, would never forget their relief at the sight of those figures in distinctive London Underground uniforms hurrying to their aid. They knew then that they were not alone.

## Edgware Road: 9.20 a.m.

Nearly half an hour after Tim, Steve and I disappeared into the darkness of the bombed carriage, Ben's attention was drawn to two young women, both of whom had suddenly appeared from one of the forward carriages. They said they were trainee nurses and wanted to know if they could help. Ben told them where they were needed and, with the aid of Andrew Ferguson on the other side of the broken window, helped them across into the bombed carriage. When they were gone Ben wondered what to do next.

He knew our situation was growing more desperate and that we needed help. Deciding that the only thing to do was to get that help himself, he started pushing past the people in his carriage who were by this time queuing up to walk out of the front of the train. In so doing, he disrupted the relative calm and orderly behaviour of those queuing, but he knew he had to do something.

In a seat next to the broken window Rhian Jones had been sitting quietly, patiently waiting for someone to tell her how to get out of there. After her experience when leaning up against the window – seeing the blood-soaked man banging on it from the bombed carriage, watching his bloody hands try to claw their way across into her carriage; standing back while the window was smashed and people around her jumped through into the darkness – she didn't know what to do.

She looked across into the bombed carriage and contemplated going through herself but Ben had told her not to, that the people who had gone across could manage on their own. Of course, he had no real idea and nor could he justify what he was saying. He just saw how scared Rhian looked and decided she was better off staying in the light.

Rhian sat down and began to fidget. She expected the emergency services to arrive but after twenty minutes had passed and there was still no sign of rescue effort, she started to feel trapped. She tried to calm herself by talking to an elderly couple sitting next to her but she couldn't concentrate or sit still. She pulled out some of her work papers and tried to read them but it was no use. The thought that she might die there, that the trains might catch fire, ran wild in her mind.

Rhian's thoughts turned to her family. She yearned to see them one more time, to say goodbye, she was heart-broken at the thought of dying without ever seeing them again. She contemplated writing them a note to tell them that her last thoughts had been of them but realised if there was a fire it wouldn't survive the flames.

Then the idea of writing a text message struck her and she pulled out her phone. Perhaps it could survive a fire, she thought.

'Mum, Dad, Brother, Sister,' she wrote, in her native Welsh. 'I love you. Remember me. Thank you. Rhian xxx.'

Saving it in her drafts folder Rhian thought her sister would be the one to find it if anyone would. Leaving a text message for her family comforted Rhian and she sat back without moving until word started to filter through the carriage that people were getting out at the front of the train. When Ben stepped forward and pushed his way through the queue looking for help she followed close behind.

Ben got to the front of the train and walked down the

steep, short, narrow wooden ladder. He marched along the tracks and up to the platform where he saw several paramedics standing around, waiting for clearance to enter the tunnel.

'There are people with blast injuries back there,' Ben told them. 'There are four dead and four dying. There is also someone under the train.'

'Where are they?' one of the paramedics asked.

Ben told them exactly where and then moved up to the station exit. He could see that the ambulance crews on the platform were anxious; he could tell they wanted to go in to help the wounded but that they had yet to get permission. It frustrated Ben to see them waiting there, knowing that our situation was desperate, that we had now been waiting nearly forty minutes for help. How could they just stand there and wait?

Ben wanted to go back into the train himself but was ordered out of the station. When he reached the top of the stairs someone handed him a bottle of water, one of many donated by the Marks & Spencer next to the station entrance. He twisted open the cap and took a gulp as he walked out into the sunshine. The water was cold, refreshing; he hadn't realised until then just how dry his throat was.

Back in the second carriage Jason and I had moved into a collective state of panic.

We had both been watching over David Gardner for three quarters of an hour and with every passing minute he was getting worse. He had stopped talking about his play, he had stopped waving his hands around as he spoke, and he had gone a pale grey colour. Both Jason and I knew that if he didn't get out of there soon he was going to die in front of us.

'If I can find something we can use to carry him, will you help me get him out of here?' I asked Jason.

'Yes, but what? There is nothing here,' he replied.

'I know but let me have a look around,' I said.

I turned and walked up towards the rear of the carriage. Some of the seats had been blown apart and I was hoping that we could tear away one of the benches to use as a stretcher. I yanked at a few but nothing seemed to budge so I considered making one. Some of the metal rails from the carriage with which passengers had been supporting themselves before the blast were now lying on the carriage floor. 'Perhaps I can use them and some coats to rig something,' I thought.

I could see two of the rails wedged under the girls from Tennessee. When I tugged at one David let out a yelp of pain, as did the girls. It was evident that the injured and the debris among which they were lying were tangled up. Moving anything on the floor almost certainly meant hurting someone. There was no way that was going to work.

What I didn't know was that there was a stretcher only a few feet away. Every tube train on the Circle Line has six carriages, three of which contain a driver's cab – one at the front, one at the rear and one somewhere in the middle of the train. The rear of the bombed carriage at Edgware Road connected to a driver's cab in the front of the third carriage. In each driver's cab was a panel behind which tools were kept: ice scrapers, circuit breakers and a set of collapsible poles that could be extended and fitted with a canvas stretcher pad which is kept in another panel in the same cab. Of course, I didn't know that and neither did Jason. And Ben was equally unaware that had he looked further when he had tried to help us find tools to pry the sliding doors apart in the moments after the bomb exploded, he would have found the stretcher we needed.

'There is nothing here I can use,' I said, rubbing my head. 'We have to get him out of here.'

'I know,' Jason replied.

But what could we do? We couldn't carry him in our arms. In his condition David would be as heavy and as unmanageable as a bag of sand. There'd be a danger, too, of loosening the tourniquet, causing David to bleed to death. Jason was limping now, the injury in his leg getting worse; he wouldn't be much use carrying a heavy load. There was no one else to help us. We would have to wait until the paramedics arrived. That was the only answer.

Never before had I felt so frustrated, so torn between what action to take, so useless. I wanted to leave to find my wife; I wanted to stay to help David, I wanted to carry David to safety – but I couldn't do any of these things. I had made a decision to stay with the wounded until the paramedics arrived. I had to stick to that now. I had to stay, whatever happened.

David Gardner had been lying on the floor of the carriage for almost an hour. The lucidity he had shown in those early minutes, the strength he had used to help Jason tie a tourniquet around his own leg, the calm and almost logical way he spoke about his play and his interest in rugby, had left him. Everything was blurring: sound, light, dark, smell.

David was coming close to losing consciousness. At about forty-five minutes he was still able to respond when someone inadvertently stepped on his wounded leg, hidden as it was in the darkness, long enough to politely – always politely – ask that person to watch where they were standing. As he continued to lose blood, however, every minute, every second, became a life and death struggle against the overpowering urge to sleep.

Jason and I could only watch him drift slowly away in

front of us. With each passing moment my heartbeat charged with the terrifying anticipation of his death until it threatened to overrun me completely. It was such a strange experience, to feel this way about a man I had only just met.

I didn't know David Gardner. I didn't know his wife, Angela, or his son, Matthew. I had never met his brother in Australia. I knew almost nothing about David, but I felt an overpowering connection with him that manifested itself in a desperate hope that he would continue to live. The fear that this hope would be dashed had taken hold of me. I could think of nothing else except that David might die and that I would have to stand there and witness his death.

Despite having no shirt on, I felt hot and feverish. I started to sweat and to rub my palms together like a nervous gambler. I was desperate now, more than I ever thought possible. What made that feeling so much stranger was that I was not the only one experiencing it. Jason was in the same state of anxiety as me; we were like psychological twins.

What made it even odder was that I didn't know Jason either; nothing about his plans to become a father; his service in the South African army; his job as project manager; his penchant for playing video games on his mobile. Jason, like David, was a stranger to me. But with him I shared an emotional attachment to David that was, in those brief, intense moments, all-consuming.

How could it be that I cared this much about people I had only just met? An hour earlier I would have ignored them both, as they would have me. Had one of them stepped out of the London Underground and been run over by a bus, would I have cared? Would they have cared if the same had happened to me?

Of course, everything was different now. We had invested in one another. Jason had surely prolonged, if not saved,

David's life by tying off his leg. I had watched over David, promised him he would make it out of that tunnel alive. Help had to come soon or our efforts would be for nothing, and, like the man through the hole in the floor, or Laura Webb on the other side of the carriage, David would die in front of us, too.

Desperate for some indication of when that help would arrive, Jason looked out of the carriage towards the tunnel wall where he thought he he had seen someone in a brightly coloured coat pass. Stepping forward and leaning his head out of the doors to look alongside the train, he could see it was a fireman, racing up the side of the tunnel and back again just as quickly.

Less than a minute later paramedics started pouring into the carriage from all directions. I could see them coming up between the tunnel wall alongside the train and in from the third carriage behind. 'I could leave now,' I thought. 'I could go and find Donna.' I wanted to rush out of there but not until I had made sure someone was treating David.

'Over here,' I called. 'This guy needs to get out of here right now. He can't wait.'

One of the paramedics looked at me but I could see my words were not registering. He was trying to take in the horror in the middle of which we had been trapped for the last hour. I could see his frantic movements and those of his colleagues. My words were just bouncing off him. They were all completely overwhelmed by the scene before them. They were scared now, too.

One of the paramedics came over and pointed at Colin Morley, still lying face down opposite David on the carriage floor. Turning to Jason the paramedic asked: 'Is this guy okay?'

'No. I mean, I don't know,' Jason replied. 'I think he's dead.'

'Has anyone checked him?' the paramedic asked.

'I haven't,' Jason admitted.

As the words left Jason's lips the gravity of what he had just said sunk in. All of his army first aid training told him he should have gone straight to the quietest victim first but he had never even touched Colin. He'd gone directly to the man stuck in the hole in the floor who was crying out for help. When that man died Jason had moved over to David Gardner. He had never given Colin a glance, had assumed his silence was final, and the thought bothered him deeply.

The paramedic felt for a pulse in Colin's neck and then took a tag out of his pocket with the word DEAD on it and tried to attach it to Colin's ankle.

'Here, let me do that,' Jason said, taking the tag.

The paramedic turned and looked over David's leg. Jason and I leaned in. I was satisfied now. Someone was going to take care of David. I could leave. I looked around for a bag or something to put behind David's head. When I found one I knelt down next to David, took my folded jacket from behind his head and replaced it with a satchel I had found on one of the seats.

Slipping on the jacket, I grabbed my own bag and turned to Jason to say goodbye. I should have stayed with David until he had made it to hospital but the desire to see my wife, to find out if she – and the baby she was carrying – had survived, overpowered my sense of loyalty to David. The paramedics would have to care for him now.

'Look, I am going to take off now, mate,' I said to Jason, extending my hand.

'It's a shame about your shirt,' Jason said, shaking my hand.

'Not really,' I said. 'I never liked that shirt anyway.'

'Well, this was my favourite shirt,' he said, pointing to the collar still tied around his forehead.

We both laughed. I am not sure why. It wasn't a particularly funny thing to say but it was the first time in more than an hour that we had said anything to each other that was even remotely normal or light-hearted. It didn't involve a diagnosis or a fear of death; it was just a simple, stupid joke.

I turned to leave, stepping over Andrew Ferguson and the two American girls as I did so, and walked to the end of the carriage. Before I went through the interconnecting doors into the light I turned for one last look. I could see Jason leaning over Colin's lifeless body. He was attaching that tag to Colin's foot. The single word written there, printed in white on a black background, was so final. So unquestioning.

Walking into the third carriage I was struck by how normal it looked. Everything was perfectly undamaged, from the lights, to the rubberised floor, to the cheap polyester seat upholstery. All it took to get away from that horror was to step through a doorway. So simple, why hadn't I done that earlier? I could see that most of the passengers had left but in the next carriage back I stumbled across two guys in blue shell suits, and a young, attractive woman in a black skirt suit who appeared to be helping them.

The men were the two builders from Manchester who had been sitting at the front of the bombed carriage and the woman was Susanna Pell from the first one. They had been among the people waiting between the train and the tunnel wall for someone to move Danny Biddle. A London Underground worker had eventually opened the carriage doors from the inside and the three of them climbed up with all the others. Everyone else had by now left but the two builders were having trouble walking. Their eardrums had been crushed by the explosion, destroying their sense of balance, and they decided to stop inside the carriage and rest. I could see blood coming from the ears of one of the guys as I walked past.

When I got to the back of the train I stepped down the ladder and on to the tracks. Trevor Rodgers was standing on the tunnel floor. He looked at me in my shirtless state, probably wondering where it had gone. I must have looked odd wearing a suit without a shirt. I didn't notice Trevor staring at me as I passed. The two trainee nurses were next down the ladder and when they were safely on the tracks the three of us walked to the platform together.

The Irish nurse seemed composed but her companion, an American, was crying and shaking. She had been in New York when the Twin Towers came down and kept asking me over and over why someone would do such a thing. I had no answer. I just put my arm around her as we walked upstairs to the station exit and out into the sunshine.

The scene that met our eyes was manic. The whole road had been cordoned off. A sea of fire engines and ambulances filled my vision. A police officer came over and directed us into the Marks & Spencer next to the station which had been set up as a temporary gathering point for the walking wounded. But before the policeman would let me pass he wanted to know something.

'Was it a bomb? Do you think it was a bomb?' he asked, looking me straight in the eye.

'Definitely,' I said, finally sure of myself. 'Without question.'

Once inside Marks & Spencer I could see dozens of people lined up on either side of the entrance and grouped around the clothing racks. I walked over to the flower stall and buried my face deep into roses and lilies, taking one deep breath after another, desperate to erase the stench from underground.

Andrew Ferguson had barely moved since he'd arrived in the bombed carriage. He had stayed behind Katie, supporting her, his back towards Edgware Road, sitting on the floor for almost the entire time. When the paramedics came rushing into the carriage from behind him he took his mobile phone from his pocket and checked the time.

It was 9.50.

It had taken help an hour to arrive but at least it was finally there. Green-uniformed London Ambulance workers surged into the carriage. Andrew looked into their faces. They clearly had no idea what they would see when they got there. Utter disbelief registered on every face. Their usual daily routine was to answer calls about heart attacks, women in labour, minor car accidents or the odd broken bone in a school playground.

What they had come upon was something else altogether. It was like a war zone, complete with battlefield injuries.

There was little warning on the platforms and the station entrance of what lay in the tunnel between Edgware Road and Paddington. Above ground, ambulance crews were dealing with cuts, burns, broken bones and skin that had been sliced open. But underground, in the darkness, the paramedics were faced with pieces of people and bodies blown in two. Before they could even start to treat the wounded they had to separate the living from the dead. It was the worst of all possible calls for the emergency services to answer.

'We need neck collars, spine boards and IV bags,' one ambulance worker shouted. The call echoed down the tunnel where other paramedics were gathering to join the rescue.

It was obvious that there was a shortage of equipment. In the next few minutes calls for saline bags and other supplies could be heard all around the carriage so frequently that they became an almost reassuring background noise, reminding Andrew that help had now arrived.

Andrew stood up and surveyed the wounded and dead around him and the utter destruction of the carriage. Up to that point he had only thought of Katie and Emily. Those two girls from Tennessee were the only things that mattered. Now he could see not only the rest of the carriage but the frantic ambulance crews buzzing all around him, blood dripping off everything. The severity of the situation finally hit home. 'People have died here,' he thought. 'People have died all around me.'

A paramedic arrived at Katie's feet and handed Andrew one of the few saline bags available.

'What do I do with this?' he asked.

'Just hold it,' came the reply.

At first the ambulance crew thought Katie could stand and they tried to pull her to her feet. It was too dark to see the extent of her injuries. Her legs buckled and she seemed to pass out. A stretcher was brought over and Katie was strapped in as Andrew held the saline bag and watched. When Katie was stretchered out Andrew told the paramedics that the two girls were sisters and wanted to stay together. He repeated that they were not to be separated.

Andrew walked behind Katie as she was stretchered off the train and taken to the platform. As he passed through the empty, undamaged carriages behind the one that had been bombed, he was in a state of disbelief.

'What the hell happened back there?' he thought. 'What the hell?'

Once at the surface Katie was slotted into the first available ambulance and Andrew was directed across the street to the Hilton Metropolitan Hotel. Everybody was being moved there from Marks & Spencer because of a bomb scare. Someone had left a laptop bag unattended but it turned out to be nothing.

Once inside the hotel, Andrew pushed through the crowds and made his way to the bar on the far side of the lobby. He looked at his mobile again to see what time it was – 10.25 a.m. At the bar he ordered a drink and stood glued to *Sky News* on the plasma screens in the hotel foyer.

The image on all the television screens was of the outside of the hotel. Andrew turned around and through the windows could see the camera crews on the streets. The ticker at the bottom of the screen said there had been a series of explosions across London. It wasn't until then that Andrew had realised it was a terrorist attack.

Andrew turned to talk to the guy next to him at the bar. He needed someone to listen to his story. The man listening to Andrew was called Adrian, a South African. After Andrew had finished speaking, Adrian revealed that he had run into the tunnel to help a man named Danny Biddle who had been blown out of the train. He had lost both legs. When they finished, both men stood quietly next to each other and watched the plasma screens.

Tim Coulson was comforting Alison near the rear of the bombed carriage when the paramedics arrived. She was flat on her back on the floor but her legs were sticking out of the carriage doors where Tim stood tall to let her badly injured ankle rest on his shoulders. Despite Alison's occasional ear-crunching screams of pain, she afforded distraction for Tim. She was alive; she was seriously wounded, yes, but not so badly that she might have died in his arms, as the man in the floor had earlier.

Tim had moved Alison up from the tunnel floor to the edge of the carriage and made her comfortable some time ago. He had stayed with her, holding her hand, talking about her work and his, about her life and his, until he saw the light of torches flickering down the tunnel and from inside the train. Help had finally arrived. The beams came closer and behind one of the sweeping lights he could hear a female voice.

'Hi, my name is Lisa and I am a paramedic,' the voice said.

'Hello, Lisa, my name is Tim and this is Alison,' he replied.

Lisa stood there for a moment, looked around the carriage with her torch and then turned back to Tim, shaking. She had begun to cry.

'You've got a bag there,' Tim assured her. 'Put it down and let's see what's inside.'

Lisa knelt down, took a deep breath, collected herself, and opened the bag.

'Thank you,' she said.

Tim smiled.

Now composed, Lisa's training kicked in and she started to look Alison over. Grabbing a saline bag, she explained to Alison that she was going to give her some fluids to help stabilise her condition. She told Alison she would feel a stabbing pain in her arm.

'Don't worry,' Alison replied. 'It can't be any worse than the pain I feel in my leg right now.'

Lisa stabbed the needle into Alison's right arm and then gave her some gas and air to help relieve the pain in her leg and eye. A few minutes later another paramedic arrived with a stretcher and the three of them rolled Alison on to her side and clicked the stretcher into place underneath her. With Lisa at one end of the stretcher and another paramedic at the other, they picked Alison up and started walking back through the train carriages towards Edgware Road.

Tim stayed with them, Alison gripping his hand the whole way. In the last carriage of the now empty train some of the side doors had been opened by London Underground staff. Outside on the tracks was a track trolley that looked like something out of a Buster Keaton film. It was being used to move people on stretchers between the train and the platforms at Edgware Road.

Tim climbed aboard and a London Underground man pumped the handles to get the track trolley moving. When they reached the station Alison was hurried up the steps and into an ambulance. The paramedic who had helped to carry her turned to go back into the station and stretcher the next person out. Lisa however, jumped in the ambulance and sat next to Tim, who was still holding Alison's hand.

'This is Tim and this is Alison. He goes where ever she goes,' Lisa instructed the driver.

When they got to St Mary's, hospital staff had divided up the emergency room into major and minor injuries. Alison was rushed into major. The hospital was pulling doctors down from all the wards and the one seeing Alison identified himself as a consultant gynaecologist.

Tim stayed with Alison during the initial assessment of her eye injury and then as doctors began sewing up some of the gashes in her legs. They held hands the whole time. Tim was completely focused on Alison, on her wounds, on her treatment and on her wellbeing. Not for a moment did he think of himself, nor did anyone else, until Alison was taken away some time later for surgery.

When she left the room Tim was finally alone with his thoughts for the first time since he had said a prayer over the body of the man who had died in his arms. Alison, the focus of his attention since then, had gone. He no longer had the distraction of trying to help someone to free his mind from the horror he had witnessed a short time before.

A nurse saw him sitting on the edge of Alison's now empty bed and asked him if he wanted something to eat. 'Yes, a sandwich would be nice,' Tim replied, but before she could turn away to fetch it for Tim, he started to shake and to cry uncontrollably.

The nurse asking Tim if he was hungry was the first time anyone had taken an interest in him; the first time that anyone had asked how *he* was, how *he* was coping. Until that moment he hadn't thought about himself, but now that he had been asked if he was hungry, if he needed anything; now that he had taken the time to consider the prospect – the sense of shock and loss overwhelmed him.

The nurse put her arm around him and told him to let it all out. She told him not to worry, and he didn't; but he was never the same man again. That kind school teacher, father and husband who had answered a simple call for help, who had climbed into a bombed train, in the dark, had given the best part of himself to people he didn't even know.

If every action really does have an equal and opposite reaction then Tim's response that day was the counter to the cruelty of the suicide bombers. In the same way that those men with rucksacks selfishly took the lives of innocent people, Tim, like several others, selflessly gave of himself to save others.

\*

Ray Whitehurst had evacuated everyone from the first carriage through his driver's cab, just as the driver of the bombed train at Aldgate had done. Ray had made four separate trips to the signal phone along the tracks to call for help and to find out why it had yet to arrive. He had walked down both sides of the train to look for passengers who might have lost their way. And in so doing Ray covered more ground than anyone in the tunnel that day.

Ray became one of the few people to get an almost complete picture of the blast zone. The rest of us were trapped in our own little bubbles, aware only of the person we were treating, but Ray had seen bodies and parts of bodies on both sides of the train, under it, across the tracks, splashed against the tunnel walls from a distance and close up. It was more than anyone should have to see.

About an hour after the blast Ray found himself standing on the tracks in front of his train when something caught his eye. He looked to his left, towards the illuminated train on the next track, and saw three paramedics being rushed towards him by a duty station manager in a high-visibility London Underground vest. Ray walked towards the rear of the neighbouring train to wait for them to climb down.

As he stood there he could hear the radio in the unused driver's cab at the rear of the train crackling away. He couldn't make out what was being said but wondered if, unlike his radio, it could be used to call for help. When the paramedics hit the tunnel floor, Ray introduced himself and quickly went about telling them where the wounded were. He suggested that one of the paramedics walk between the train and the tunnel wall to look for wounded there and that the other two follow him into the first carriage, where Steve Huckelsby was looking after a man named Kevin with a tennis-ball-size hole in his leg, a woman with a collapsed lung named Kathy Lazenbatt and another woman with a crushed ankle called Elizabeth Owen.

Once inside the carriage Ray turned to the ambulance crew. 'You are about to see injuries you have never seen before and wouldn't have thought possible,' he warned them. 'You might want to take a moment to prepare yourselves.'

The medics, however, ignored Ray and advanced but they were prevented from stepping into the bombed carriage. Kevin was still lying on the floor in between the two carriages, blocking their way. Beyond him, one of the medics could see dead bodies and the accompanying horror of the second carriage. What he saw caused him to throw up. The other medic knelt down close to Steve Huckelsby, still hunched over his patient, trying to keep him awake.

'Do you need anything?' Ray asked.

'Tell them we need stretchers and saline,' one of the paramedics said.

'Right,' Ray replied.

Ray thought about the crackling radio in the rear driver's cab of the train next to his and reckoned that if he went over there to get the first stretcher he could try to radio through to tell someone the paramedics needed IV bags at the same time.

When Ray left his train another medic appeared and pushed Steve aside to have a better look at Kevin. Steve stepped over Kevin and back into the front end of the bombed carriage. The scene was now bustling with activity. Paramedics were swarming around the victims, on both sides of the crater in the floor, and Steve could see that several tags had already been attached to the dead victims on the floor.

One of those tags was attached to Laura Webb whose face

had been covered by someone's cardigan. Seeing her lying there, her face covered, with that tag hanging from her ankle, all seemed so impersonal to Steve; somehow improper. He had tried to save Laura earlier, and although he didn't know her, he felt a connection with her. A sense of loss was now confirmed by that tag.

Kathy was sitting across the two seats at the front left-hand side of the bombed carriage next to where Steve was looking down on Laura. She had stretched out when Steve took Kevin out of the seat next to her to move him into the doorway. Kathy's collapsed lung was making it increasingly difficult for her to suck in enough oxygen to stay awake so she had busied herself by trying to talk to Elizabeth Owen, who was sitting just below her on the carriage floor.

Steve stood across from them both, watching as a paramedic arrived and began to look them over. He was impressed by the paramedic's efficiency. The ambulance crews were working quickly, assessing who was dead and who needed help, before swiftly starting to treat the wounded. They might have taken an age to arrive but, once on the scene, they were in full swing.

'How are you feeling?' the paramedic asked Elizabeth.

'I think I have broken my leg,' she answered.

The paramedic looked over Elizabeth's leg by the light of his torch and then handed it to Steve. 'Hold this while I bandage her leg,' he said, reaching into his bag for something to wrap the ankle in.

Standing there Steve could see the paramedics treating Kevin. They had already put a drip into his arm and were working to stabilise his leg. Within minutes he was loaded on to a stretcher and taken out of the front of the train. 'Great,' Steve thought, 'he is in safe hands now.'

After the bandage had been secured to Elizabeth's leg she

was put in a splint and given a drip. She screamed in pain as the splint was fixed to her badly damaged ankle. Once stable, she was made to lie on her back on the carriage floor for a quarter of an hour before a fireman appeared in the tunnel outside the now open sliding doors to the carriage.

The fireman hopped up on to the train and Elizabeth was strapped into the stretcher and moved out of the doorway. She was carried past the wrecked carriage towards Edgware Road before being brought back into the train through the same set of open doors in one of the undamaged carriages that had been used by Susanna Pell and all of the other people who had earlier queued up behind Danny Biddle.

Steve walked behind Elizabeth's stretcher and, as she was carried through the undamaged carriages at the rear of the train, she was filled with relief, not because she was finally on her way out, but because, in those lit and undamaged carriages, she was looking at something normal again. For more than an hour she had been trapped in a place that was dark, twisted, burned and soaked in blood. That had finally come to an end.

Ray never made it to the radio in the unused driver's cab at the rear of the neighbouring train. Halfway there, two London Underground duty managers appeared from the Paddington station end of the tunnel and stopped him. They had been at the Hammersmith and City Line station of Royal Oak, one station beyond Paddington in the other direction, overseeing track maintenance, when the bombs went off.

A tube train had just left Royal Oak when they heard the bang. When it came to a halt only the last carriage was still at the platform at Paddington. The two managers walked down the tracks and helped the driver evacuate the passengers through the front five carriages, into the sixth, and then out on to the platform. When the passengers were clear, one of the managers, Alex King, called into the Circle and Hammersmith Line control centre at Baker Street.

The control centre told him that there had been some kind of power surge across the network and that the traction current was off between Paddington and Edgware Road. Beyond that, line control was still trying to piece together what was actually going on and so Alex told them he was going to walk the tracks towards Edgware Road and have a look for himself.

Leaving the other manager at Paddington, Alex disappeared into the tunnel and walked as far as the Praed Street junction where he could see that two trains had come to a halt, side by side, in the tunnel. The train lights were still on but he couldn't see any people. There was thick smoke and the smell of burning metal in the air. He tried to call in what he saw but, now that he was in the tunnel instead of in the open-air section of track between Royal Oak and Paddington, his radio could not get a signal.

Walking back to Paddington to find the other manager he had left behind, Alex raised line control again, this time telling them about the two trains and giving their location.

'I think there has been some kind of explosion,' Alex said over the radio. 'I have another duty manager with me. We are going to walk back and see what we can do.'

By the time Alex and his colleague were once again at a point in the tunnel where they could see the two stricken trains it had been over an hour since the bomb had gone off. As they approached the train they were confronted by a man in a suit carrying a briefcase. He was walking away from the trains towards Paddington: 'You don't want to go back there, mate,' the man said. 'It's worse down there.'

The two managers turned the passenger around and told

him to walk back towards Edgware Road with them. On the way they found several others wandering the track, including Ray Whitehurst, the driver of the bombed train, on his way to fetch a stretcher and to use the radio in the train next to his. For Alex this was all new. He had yet to see any of the carnage first-hand but Ray had seen just about all he could take.

Alex could see the strain on Ray's face as he told the two managers what had been happening for the last hour. Talking to Alex helped to put Ray at ease. Finally someone had arrived from management; responsibility was now being passed to them. He could breathe again. Alex told Ray that he should leave, that they would take charge now, but he argued with them, determined to stay with his train until everyone was out of the tunnel.

Rank eventually won the argument and Alex decided to go into the bombed carriage while the other duty manager took Ray by the arm up the ladder at the rear of the neighbouring train and walked him through all six carriages, along the tracks and into the staff canteen at Edgware Road where he could rest. Ray had done his duty and it had taken its toll.

Inside the second carriage most of the living had been evacuated. The only remaining injured person was Kathy Lazenbatt who was sitting quietly on the two seats at the front of the bombed carriage. Paramedics had put an IV into her arm and bandaged her leg, but she was sitting alone. All of the ambulances above ground had left to carry wounded to nearby hospitals and they didn't want to move Kathy until they could put her straight into the back of a vehicle.

And so began the wait.

Alex, two of his colleagues and another two paramedics stayed close to Kathy for a further hour and a half as they waited for an ambulance to return to take her to hospital. It was too dangerous to move her without an ambulance, but nevertheless her condition was deteriorating. To stay awake Kathy tried to follow their conversations but she could only understand the words when they were spoken loudly. Occasionally one of them would kneel down to talk to her and make sure she was still awake.

It would be three hours after the explosion before Kathy would finally get out of the tunnel and into an ambulance. She was the last person taken out alive. As she was carried out of the station she gave her husband's phone number to a member of London Underground staff and asked him to call and let him know she had survived.

When Kathy was loaded into the back of the ambulance the paramedic told the driver that she had been waiting too long. There was, he said, almost no chance that she was going to survive. Kathy had no way of knowing, in her weakened position, just how wrong that assessment was. She, like the city of London, would prove far more resilient than anyone could have hoped.

## St James's Park: 9.15 a.m.

That morning, Andy Barr took a conference call with security and operational staff working for, and with, London Underground. Conversation was brief.

No decision had yet been taken as to whether or not the chaos affecting the network that morning was the result of a terrorist attack. It was still believed the problem was caused by a series of power surges. The reality, from the perspective of London Underground, was that it didn't matter what the cause was. The concern was the same, regardless of whether the explosions were accidental or deliberate: the safety of the 200,000 people still travelling on the network.

When the call had come to an end, Andy left his office at the back of the Network Operations Centre and issued an Amber Alert to everyone working for the underground via the breakdown broadcast messaging system. He couldn't afford to wait any longer to find out what was going on. Everyone had to be evacuated from every train and from every station. The entire tube network was being shut down.

Making a decision like that is not easy. London is a congested city. On a normal weekday morning the streets are jammed with cars, buses and people. Stopping the tube was like trying to dam a fast-flowing river. There was going to be overflow. By 9.15 police had started closing down the streets around King's Cross, Aldgate and Edgware Road. This meant that traffic had to be rerouted around the stations and it wasn't long before the streets near the affected stations started to gridlock.

Andy's decision to add to that congestion by dumping 200,000 people on to the streets of London – and at the same time removing the most widely used piece of transport infrastructure in the city – meant that London's network of buses was going to have to work overtime. Andy's team put in a call to the London Bus Control Room. He needed to speak to Alan Dell, the network liaison manager and the man in charge of London's system of buses.

Alan Dell and his team had been keeping an eye on what was happening to the tube network all morning, so when he got the call from Andy saying that an Amber Alert had been issued he was not surprised. A ticket collector near Edgware Road station had called a few minutes after the bomb to tell Alan's team that there had been an explosion and that people were emerging from the station under a plume of smoke.

Alan called the Network Operations Centre and was told that it looked as though a train leaving Edgware Road had jumped the tracks and hit a tunnel wall. He sent out a message to drivers in the area of the station to accept tube tickets from passengers emerging from the station. Then he decided to have a look at what was going on for himself.

The London Bus Control Room has access to the network of CCTV cameras that cover the whole of London. Controllers working for London Buses use these cameras to keep an eye on traffic and reroute buses so as to keep people moving should there be an accident along a bus route. That morning, however, Alan Dell would use the camera to take a look at something else.

253

Training in on the Edgware Road station entrance Alan could see on his monitor that people coming out of the exit were not the usual crowd. He could see a cloud of smoke behind them. The passengers were dazed and stumbled across the street outside the station. Alan had taken part in Exercise Atlantic Blue in April 2005, a mock-terrorist attack designed to help prepare the emergency and transport services in London for just such a day as this. Seeing those people emerge from a smoke-filled tunnel made Alan think he might now be on the verge of applying all the training he had received during Atlantic Blue.

Over the course of the next hour the problem spread to Aldgate and then King's Cross. Alan's team had to reroute buses around the affected areas as the police started to close roads. To cope with the sudden surge of pedestrian traffic in the heart of London, Alan issued an order for blanket acceptance of tube tickets across all bus routes operating in the city's core.

One of the buses being rerouted was the Number 30. Driver George Psaradakis was told by Alan's team in the control room that he was not going to be able to proceed towards Hackney, as scheduled, because the Euston Road was being cordoned off. George was told to turn instead on to Upper Woburn Place, which leads into Tavistock Square.

Progress was slow for the Number 30. The roads were jammed with diverted traffic and the pavements were full of people who had either been evacuated from the tube or who were being turned away from the stations. Passengers asked George if they could get off his bus in the middle of traffic because he was moving so slowly; he let a few of them off.

George's bus quickly came to a stop in Tavistock Square, just outside the front doors of the British Medical Association. He was stuck behind a row of cars, buses and vans. There he waited for traffic to move while a male passenger named Hasib Mir Hussain, sitting at the back of the top deck with a rucksack at his feet, waited to join the three friends with whom he had travelled into London that morning.

Just before four o'clock on the morning of 7 July three British-born Asians in a rented blue Nissan Micra were heading down Hyde Park Road in Leeds on their way towards the M1. Shehzad Tanweer, a twenty-two-year-old from Beeston, had hired the car in his name and he was now on his way towards Luton railway station with two companions, both of whom were also from Beeston. They were Mohammad Sidique Khan, a thirty-year-old married father of one, and Hasib Mir Hussain, an eighteen-year-old who had one month earlier completed a course in advanced business studies.

Just under an hour later the trio pulled into Woodall Services on the M1 to buy petrol. Tanweer went in to pay. He was dressed like many twenty-two-year-olds: in tracksuit bottoms, a baseball cap and a white T-shirt. He picked up some snack food, paid for his fuel and complained about his change to the cashier. When he was satisfied he looked directly into the station's CCTV camera and left.

A few minutes later, at 5.07 a.m., Jermaine Lindsay, a nineteen-year-old Jamaican immigrant and a convert to Islam, arrived at Luton station car park in a red Fiat Brava. He had time to kill. His three accomplices, by then working their way down the M1 to meet him, were still ninety minutes away. While he waited Lindsay walked around the station, checked out the departures board and moved his car a few times.

At 6.49 a.m. the three men from Beeston reached the Luton station car park and pulled up next to Lindsay. They opened the boots of their respective cars and pulled out four similar sized rucksacks, each containing five kilos of organic peroxide explosive, and slung them over their shoulders. Leaving behind several smaller backpacks containing lesser bombs, and a 9mm handgun, the four young men walked into Luton station and through the ticket barriers.

They boarded a train for King's Cross where they were all seen hugging each other around 8.30, before splitting up and heading in different directions. Khan walked towards the westbound Circle Line platform for Edgware Road. He stepped aboard the second carriage, taking a seat just inside the second set of doors from the front. Tanweer went to the eastbound Circle Line towards Aldgate and stepped on at the rear of the second carriage. Lindsay headed towards the southbound Piccadilly line towards Russell Square. He was delayed getting on to the train at the platform because of the crowds which had built up because the service was delayed. When he eventually made it to the front of the platform, Lindsay stepped into the middle of the first carriage. Fully loaded, and ready to kill, all three young men sailed off into the darkness.

Hussain, the fourth bomber, seems to have been walking towards the Piccadilly Line's northbound platform. For some reason he never made it. At 8.55, five minutes after Khan, Tanweer and Lindsay had detonated their bombs on their respective trains, Hussain was seen walking out of King's Cross underground station and on to the Euston Road. For the next few minutes he tried, and failed, to call his three friends.

Behaving almost casually, Hussain walked back into the station, through Boots and into WH Smith on the station concourse. There he bought a 9-volt battery before dropping briefly into McDonald's on the Euston Road. He walked out ten minutes later and shortly afterwards stepped aboard the Number 30 bus bound for Hackney.

The bus's driver, George Psaradakis, didn't remember Hussain getting on but passengers did recall a man fitting his description fiddling with a rucksack on the lower deck. At some point Hussain decided to go up to the top deck where he took a seat, by himself, at the rear of the bus.

Back at the London Bus Control Centre, Alan Dell was frantic. Reports of suspect packages left on buses were coming in from one end of the city to the other. Almost every bus in the centre of London was on diversion. Things weren't getting better, only worse.

Then, at twelve minutes to ten, Alan's team got a call from a bus travelling through Tavistock Square in the opposite direction to the Number 30. Alan was ushered over to the phone. The driver said that across the square from where he was he had seen a bus blow up. Alan immediately tuned the large plasma screen at the front of the control room into a CCTV camera with a view of Tavistock Square. The image was grainy, and the angle was from a distance, but there was no mistaking what had just happened to one of Alan's buses.

Hussain had blown it up.

The control room staff sat gripped by the screen for several minutes until the British Transport Police, which has an office in the same building, turned off access to the CCTV cameras in Tavistock Square. They were afraid that television networks would tap into the system and broadcast the images. Their efforts were in vain. A few minutes later a news helicopter had moved into position over what was left of the bus and was broadcasting the images on a twenty-four-hour news channel which was by then filling the plasma screen in front of Alan and his team.

One of the great symbols of London, the red double decker bus, had been torn to shreds. The destruction underground which had been unfolding for the last hour had been brought into the light of day for all the world to see. Thoughts of power surges were a thing of the past. This was no electrical fault. London was under siege.

Soldiers in battle fall into what is sometimes called 'the zone'. It is a place where the capacity to make logical or creative decisions is diminished and the part of the brain that works on training or instinct takes over.

The logic is simple. The better a soldier is trained, the more experience they have of battle, the better they will be able to cope when the bullets start flying. It sounds simple because it is. This is why the special forces are so effective. They train longer and harder than ordinary troops or reserve units, so when they come under fire and the logical and creative is stripped down, they have a great deal of instinctual reserve to draw upon. Their 'zone' is big enough to carry them through the task.

The four men who blew themselves up in London on 7 July didn't have a great deal of training and, for obvious reasons, had no experience of carrying out a similar task. Mohammed Sidique Khan, Shehzad Tanweer and Hasib Hussain all visited Pakistan in the years and months leading up to the attacks and it is believed they received some training at the hands of Islamic militants while abroad. Just how much training is unknown but it was certainly brief and left the men with just enough skill to plan and execute the attack.

Members of the security services believe that had the bombers trained longer or to a higher standard, many more lives would have been lost. The most 'successful' of the four attacks, from the perspectives of the bombers, was the

Piccadilly Line where twenty-six lives were taken. The number of fatalities on that train could, in part, be put down to the congested nature of Piccadilly Line that morning. Germaine Lindsay only had to step aboard the first carriage of the tube train and the sheer number of people around him would guarantee a massive death toll. On each of the Circle Line trains however, the carriages were less congested and so, logically, the number of fatalities at Edgware Road, six, and Aldgate, seven, were far less by comparison.

But this is only part of the story. Reports from people who were on the trains, and off-the-record briefings from security officials, suggested that the bombers simply walked into the first carriage they saw, not thinking about where to stand to cause the most damage. The men, in their tiny 'zones', were not able to consider the fact that they could have caused more destruction by trying to find the most congested part of the most congested carriage. Had they been able to think creatively, or had they had more training, it is likely they would have found the thickest part of the densest crowd before unleashing their cruel betrayal upon their fellow citizens.

Nowhere was this lack of creativity and training more obvious than on the Number 30 bus that was destroyed outside the doors to the British Medical Association in Tavistock Square, only a few hundred metres from King's Cross Station.

When Hussain stepped aboard the bus, he moved to the rear and fiddled with his bag before moving to the top deck where he took a seat at the back of the bus, alone. The seats around him were empty, many had been vacated by passengers who got off the bus, frustrated with the dense traffic and slow progress along the roads. Had Hussain waited below, on the lower deck, where there were more people, or had he chosen to step aboard a busier bus in the first instance, he could have been more deadly. Despite his decisions that day, however, Hussain still managed to kill thirteen people, bringing the death toll of the bombings to fifty-two.

The Number 30 bus bombing was different from the other acts of barbarism that day because there was no mystery about what had happened. Thousands of people who had offices facing Tavistock Square just had to look out their windows and, with a glance, know what had happened. There were cars stuck in traffic on either side of the bus, and the pavements were jammed with pedestrians; everyone could see.

The bombing occurred at 9.47 a.m., almost an hour after the three simultaneous explosions underground, so the emergency services were in full crisis mode by the time the fourth bomb hit. The state of alert made it easier to get out the message that help was needed, despite the fact that there was by then a shortage of ambulances because of the growing demand for assistance at the other three locations.

If there was any fortune in the location of the bombings of the Number 30 bus it had to be in the fact that it was right outside the British Medical Association, which was full of doctors and other medically trained staff. Within minutes of the explosion a contingent of passers-by, employees from the surrounding buildings and doctors from the BMA had turned the inner courtyard of the BMA building into a battle-field-like medical unit and all those present were working hard to save the lives of people who had been injured. It would take until 11.31 a.m., almost two hours after the bus bombing, for enough ambulances to be available to take all of the most seriously wounded to hospital.

Those who had suffered only minor injuries, the walking wounded, in many cases just wandered off into the crowds.

Some, about 700, went to hospital to get checked out but most went home. It was not an easy task. There were no buses or tube trains and in the hours that followed people walked. Those who had driven into the city that morning offered to drive home strangers they had met on the street that day. Co-workers shared taxis or took trains to outlying towns where they were picked up by family or friends.

A number of workers for London Underground were put up in hotels overnight and the very next day were hard at work again to get the network up and running. Andy Barr and his team at London Underground were determined that they were going to run a limited service and that is exactly what they did. The passenger numbers were about half but the trains were running and London was, once again, soldiering on.

## Epilogue

When her husband left Edgware Road station on Circle Line train 216, Ros Morley was sitting in a café in Sudbury drinking a cup of coffee and reading the morning newspaper.

The art teacher and mother of three was early for her lithography course and so decided to kill time before it started that morning. When her course began at 9.20 a.m., the instructor led Ros and the other students through the lesson. Just before 11.00 he tuned the radio to Classic FM and let the music fill the room. Ros settled into her course work and forgot about the time.

It was not until 11.30 that the instructor came back into the room after collecting some supplies to tell everyone what had been happening in London. He explained that there had been several bombs on the tube and on a bus. Immediately Ros's heart sank. Her youngest son, Jake, took the London Underground to work every day.

Turning on her phone she tried to call Jake but got no answer. A text came through as she was leaving a message on Jake's voicemail. It was Oliver, another of her three sons who was at the time working in Liverpool. Oliver's message said he had received a call from Jake and that the two of them were okay, but, despite trying, they had had no contact with their dad.

Colin Morley spent most days working in Milton Keynes but the nature of consulting meant he often moved around.

The previous night Ros had called her husband from her B&B to talk before they went to bed. For some reason they did not discuss where Colin was going the next morning so Ros assumed it was to Milton Keynes. Since her sons could not raise him on the phone she started to worry.

She tried to call Colin as well but with no success. To settle her nerves she walked down the road and bought herself a salad roll which she didn't have the stomach to eat. Until she had word of what was happening she decided she would try to press on with her course, but, as time passed, and there was still no word from her husband, Ros could no longer concentrate on the course.

Shortly after 1.00 p.m. Ros got a call from her sister. She listened as she explained that her son, Ros's nephew, had narrowly missed a train at King's Cross, how he had stood on the platform as it sailed into the tunnel and how he'd jumped with shock when a loud boom came rocketing out of the darkness. It was a good news story for the family, but at the same time it was a misleading omen.

Ros told her sister she was glad her nephew was safe and rang off so as to keep the line open for news of Colin. Fifteen minutes passed and she could no longer stand the tension. She grabbed her bag and left the course. She told herself that Colin was probably just in a meeting with his phone turned off and she asked the instructor to keep her materials safe, saying that she would return the following day to finish her work.

Back down the M11 and around the M25 Ros told herself to remain calm, to drive within the limit, but her stomach was churning and her foot was heavy on the accelerator. It was 3.30 when she opened the front door of her house to find Jake sitting in the lounge watching *BBC News 24*. An emergency number for concerned families flashed up on the screen. Jake and Ros took turns calling to see if there was any news from the man they both loved.

The hours passed and there was still no new information. The phone rang all evening. Family and friends were eager for information. Ros's sister-in-law called after dinner to say that Colin's brother, Brian, had decided to go into town to try and find him at one of the London hospitals that were treating the wounded. The early reports said that seven hundred people had been taken to hospital. Colin might be one of them.

Gavin, Ros's eldest son, called from the United States, where he was working, and had a frantic conversation with his mother via Skype. Oliver called from Liverpool to say he was driving up to London. Ros tried to talk him out of it, to encourage him to get a night's rest first, but Oliver ignored her. He was coming home. When he eventually arrived Ros, Oliver and Jake stayed up late, watching twenty-four-hour news on television, and imagining every possible scenario in which Colin could have survived the day's events.

Angela Gardner arrived at the offices of KPMG in Salisbury Square between eight and half past. Not long into her morning, e-mails started circulating. They were warning that the tube was having problems and so they should be mindful of delays if they were expecting co-workers in for meetings. Angela thought it was lucky that the delays hadn't occurred the day before, when the crowds in Trafalgar Square celebrating the announcement that London had won the 2012 Olympic Games would have caused mayhem.

Angela went back to work and didn't give the tube another thought. But then, slowly, the news started to change. There had been an explosion at Aldgate. After a while, more news came in. There had been a number of explosions, as many as eight, including one at King's Cross. Angela sent her husband David an e-mail to see if he had got into work all right. There was no answer. That was unusual. David was always quick to answer his e-mails.

Not long after 10.00 a.m. Angela decided she couldn't wait any longer. She picked up the phone to call her husband's office in High Street Kensington where he was an accountant for Associated Newspapers. David's boss and friend, Barry Hughes, answered the phone and explained that David had yet to arrive. The two of them agreed it was odd. David had only missed one and a half days of work in his entire life. If he wasn't there by then, well over an hour past his usual time of arrival, there must be a reason. Angela and Barry agreed to keep in touch for the rest of the day.

As the minutes passed the news that London had been attacked started to flood into Angela's office. She called David's mother to see if he had called her but he had not. The call worried Angela's mother-in-law and Angela felt bad about causing her anxiety. But she was worried herself; it couldn't be helped.

Just after 11.00 a.m. the mobile network in Angela's area started working again. She picked up her phone to see if there was any voicemail when the text messages started coming through. Most were from friends but there was one that stood out. It was from Dr Nicole Richards at St Mary's Hospital in Paddington. David was injured but he was all right. The message said that Angela should come straight away.

As David Gardner left the bombed train at Edgware Road he thought of Angela. As he was driven to St Mary's Hospital he thought of Angela. Seconds before he was put under by an anaesthetist for emergency surgery on his leg he was thinking of her, too, and so grabbed a doctor, told her Angela's name and mobile number, and made the doctor promise to get word to her.

The minutes after Angela received the text from the doctor were filled with a flurry of calls. Little Matthew had to be picked up at nursery and taken somewhere safe. David's mother had to be called, as did Barry Hughes. And within seconds Angela was on the streets to find that London had become a confused and frightened mass of pedestrians; there was not a bus or a taxi in sight.

Knowing she was just over four miles away from St Mary's, Angela decided to walk. She knew the general direction to the hospital by Paddington station but not how to negotiate the labyrinth of London streets needed to get there. As she battled the maze her heart raced. Quicker than she thought possible, she reached St Mary's where she could see crowds gathering outside the hospital doors. Cameras and reporters were everywhere.

Angela found the entrance to casualty and pushed her way through the crowd but was prevented from going through the doors into the emergency room by a policeman.

'My husband's in there. I need to go in,' Angela pleaded.

'I'm sorry, I can't let you in,' the policeman said.

'I understand,' Angela said.

As she turned around, the thought of not seeing David was too much and she broke down and started to cry. A reporter came over to her to ask if she was all right. Angela explained her situation and within a few minutes the policeman had changed his mind and let her in through the doors to find her husband.

Donna had been away from her desk making a cup of tea and chatting with a colleague when I tried to call her on both her land line and her mobile. I didn't leave messages.

I wanted to explain myself, voice to voice, rather than leave a load of drivel on her machine. When she got back to her desk her phone rang. It was reception. They said they had an urgent message from Donna's brother, Allan. It was simple and to the point: Peter was okay.

'Of course he is okay,' Donna thought. 'I saw him just two hours ago.'

When I finally made it out of the tunnel and into the Marks & Spencer next to Edgware Road station I was desperate to call Donna and tell her that I had survived. I didn't know how much she knew about what was going on and I didn't want to worry her by leaving her to wonder what might have happened to me. But when I tried my mobile it wouldn't put through any calls.

As news started to break about what was happening across London, people called and sent text messages to friends and family. The number of calls and messages flooding the system was colossal. Vodafone and $O_2$ normally place 30,000 calls every fifteen minutes on a weekday morning. On 7 July, as news of the attack spread, 300,000 calls were being connected every fifteen minutes, ten times the usual number. Other mobile operators were experiencing similar overloads. As a result, some networks were jammed and others were closed to the public by the police so that they could use their own mobiles to coordinate the rescue effort.

After fiddling with my phone for five minutes or so I left Marks & Spencer and started walking in the direction of Marble Arch in the hope that, by putting some distance between myself and Edgware Road, the load on the mobile networks would lighten. After walking for a bit I was still unable to get through so I went into an estate agents, picked up one of their phones and started dialling out. I got some funny looks, wearing a suit with no shirt, my face covered in soot, but when I told them there had been a terrorist attack around the corner they let me be. Donna would not pick up either her mobile or her land line so I called her brother who worked at Oxford Circus.

'Allan. It's me,' I said.

'Peter, what's up, mate?' he replied.

'Look, I have just been in a terrorist attack on the tube,' I said. 'People died, man, right in front of me.'

'Fucking hell, are you okay?' he asked.

'Yes, I wasn't hurt but I have not been able to get hold of Donna. Do you know if she made it into work?' I wanted to know.

'Yes, I got an e-mail from her this morning, mate, she's safe.'

'Could you do me a favour and call her and tell her that I am okay and that I will try to call her later?'

'Yeah, sure, mate.'

'Do that for me right now Allan, will you? Okay?'

'Okay, mate.'

I put the phone down and kept walking in the hope of getting a signal on my mobile. The further away from Edgware Road I got the more normal the world seemed and the more out of place I felt. The sound of sirens disappeared; the police had gone. Still, no matter how far I walked I could not get hold of Donna. I could see from the people around me on the pavement that the mobile networks were still working where I was. People were talking on their phones, laughing, joking, being normal. I wanted to punch every one of them in the face and take their phones from them. I wanted to tell them they were being selfish, chatting away so flippantly while I needed to get through to my wife so desperately. But I didn't. I just kept on walking until my phone eventually rang.

'Hi, darling,' Donna said down the line. 'I got a funny

message from Allan. He said you are okay. Was there some bother on the tube or something?'

I tried to speak, to tell her what had happened, that I loved her, but all that came out was a spluttering of tears and gibberish about what had just happened to me.

'I was in a terrorist attack. I saw dead people. They were all around me,' I cried.

'Where are you?' Donna asked.

'I don't know. I've been walking for ages,' I said.

I could hear Donna starting to cry. For me not to know where I was is more than unusual. I am obsessed with maps, with directions. I always know where I am. Hearing me tell her that I was lost and distraught was frightening and emotional for Donna. Being eight months' pregnant and having your husband nearly killed in a terrorist attack can do that to a woman. I realised I needed to stay composed, to pull myself together for her.

'Slow down, slow down, darling,' I said, looking around and seeing the white stone of Marble Arch across the street. 'I am fine. There is not a thing wrong with me. I am at Marble Arch and I am going to walk to Allan's work.'

Donna and I stayed on the phone for a while and agreed that we would meet at Oxford Circus and travel home to Ealing from there with her brother, who lived around the corner from us. When I arrived at Allan's offices, BBC Online was reporting that as many as eight bombs had struck the city. Seeing me was proof that there had been at least one.

'Donna called, mate,' Allan said. 'She is on her way over in a cab and we'll take it home from here.'

'Cool, Allan. Thanks,' I said. 'Listen, before she gets here I want to get cleaned up and buy a shirt.'

'There is a cheap shirt place on the corner. I'll come with you.'

I went to the toilet and cleaned up before walking outside with Allan. Once in the shop I could see what Allan meant by cheap shirts. There wasn't a shirt over £12 in the place. It was one of those typical Oxford Street bargain shops. Real class. I pointed up to the top shelf at a blue checked number and asked the sales assistant to get it down for me. As I prepared to pay I noticed that she could not stop staring at me. I guess she didn't have too many bare-chested customers in a business suit in her shop.

'What happened to your shirt?' she asked.

I explained briefly what I had been up to that morning and watched as her face turned grey. She hadn't heard yet. It had been over two hours since the bomb went off and she still had no idea.

'How much is it?' I said.

'Oh, don't worry about that,' she replied. 'Here, have it.'

'No, don't be silly. I want to pay. Tell me how much.'

'Here, you take it. I can't charge you. You are an American. You aren't even British and you come here, to our country, and this is what happens to you. No, the shirt is for you.'

'Actually, I am Canadian,' I replied. 'And just for that, I *will* take it for free.'

I asked her to remove the packaging so that I could put the shirt on straight away. It *was* cheap. I could feel the abrasive synthetic fibres itching before I had even done it up. Still, tawdry though it was, it had French cuffs. I reached into my pocket for my Toronto Maple Leaf cufflinks, the Christmas present from Donna's mother Anne, and slid them through the buttonholes. Looking at them, I half-chuckled. To think that I had been about to throw them away.

Heather and Phil Duckworth were staying with Heather's brother, Jim, and his wife in St Albans on the morning of

7 July. They were waiting for a new house they had bought to be ready for them. Bunking in with family made things a bit crowded but they were a close bunch. Phil and Jim had been friends at university. That was how Phil had met, and later married, his best mate's sister.

After Heather saw Phil off to work she prepared her fourteen-month-old son, Robert, for a trip to Sainsbury's with her sister-in-law and her twenty-month-old daughter. They were planning a big shop for the weekend ahead. On the way back from the supermarket Heather could hear a news report on the car radio saying there had been a number of power surges on the London Underground. She wondered if Phil had been caught up in them long enough to make him late for work.

When they got back to her brother's house they found Jim watching *BBC News 24*. Jim was working from home that day because he was planning to fly to Ireland on business later that evening. Flashing across the screen were pictures of a bus that had been bombed while stuck in traffic in Tavistock Square next to the British Medical Association. When Heather saw what her brother was watching she knew the reports she had heard on the radio about power surges were about to be revised.

Heather put the groceries away and then went upstairs to e-mail Phil. She had no reason, at that moment, to assume he had been killed or injured so she sent a message that was calm but curious.

'Chaos in London. Hope you're ok?'

Half an hour after sending the message there was still no response from Phil. It was strange. Phil, like David Gardner, always replied to e-mails straightaway. Heather tried his mobile but the network was down. The City of London Police had, by that time, shut down public access to the mobile phone networks around Aldgate station. She decided to call Phil at work. Phil's team leader, Susan, picked up the phone.

'Oh, Heather, hi. Have you heard from Phil?' Susan asked.

'No,' Heather replied, crying upon hearing that her husband appeared to be missing.

'Don't panic just yet,' Susan said. 'We've been told not to leave the building. There's chaos on the streets. Phil is probably caught up in it all and is trying to make his way to a land line to call you.'

After putting down the phone Heather decided to send another e-mail, this time to friends and family who might have heard from Phil. She was worried, anxious, but she didn't want to sound that way so she sent a message that disguised her concern: 'Typical that I can't get a hold of my husband. Has anyone heard from Phil?'

By six o'clock that evening there had still been no news. Heather and her sister-in-law bathed their children, and put them to bed before returning to the lounge to watch the news in the hope of catching a glimpse of someone on the screen who looked like Phil.

Heather had spent much of the day fighting back tears. Despite her worry, logic told her to reserve judgement. In 1996, while she was working as a holiday rep in Spain, there had been an ETA bombing. In the ensuing confusion it took Heather and her work colleagues twenty-four hours to find and account for everyone in her tour group, and that was with the aid of a manifest listing the names of everyone they needed to find.

Heather's parents arrived from Cambridgeshire shortly after eight in the evening. When Heather's mother walked in the door she took one look at her daughter and said: 'I don't know how we are to get through this but we are.' The idea that Phil wasn't coming home now seemed more likely than his being a phone call away.

I was standing on the street outside Allan's office when Donna pulled up in a taxi. She stumbled out of the door and threw her arms around me. We both cried and were still choked up as we bundled ourselves into the back of the black cab. We had to hurry. The driver thought he was only taking us to Allan's office at Oxford Circus but we managed to convince him to drive across town to Ealing by playing up on Donna's pregnancy and my experiences of the day. The driver wasn't happy at all – he had to pick up his teenage daughter at King's Cross – but he didn't turn us down.

Once we were home safe the only place I wanted to be was at the bottom of a bottle of Scotch at our local pub. I had spoken to the news desk at work and they were almost drunk on the excitement of having a reporter so close to the action. They wanted me to start writing as soon as possible. I had other plans. I knew the next day would be spent at my computer reliving the details of that morning and so for now all I wanted was to get as drunk as possible as quickly as possible. The evening of 7 July was for forgetting.

Allan and I spent the evening in the Duke of Kent just off Pitshanger Lane drinking double shots of Glenmorangie and pints of Guinness in between emotional breakdowns during which we hugged each other and cried and cried. Donna wanted to hug me tight and never let me go but her bump wouldn't let her get a decent hold on the man she had come so close to losing. It frustrated her.

Midway through the evening Allan's wife, Yvonne, came in with her five-week-old son, Morgan, wrapped in a blanket. I had held my little nephew when he was only hours old and Yvonne was putting him in my arms again as I sat there unable to drink fast enough to forget the day. I looked down at him and cried again. He was so tiny, so innocent, so different from me now.

There was no family reunion or night of drinking away the day's events for Heather Duckworth. There had been no news of Phil to calm her fears. As the hours passed Heather knew she was going to have to be strong for her son. He was all she had now, and so she decided to get some rest by turning in just after ten o'clock.

Try as she might, Heather could not sleep. She lay in her bed wide awake until 3.00 a.m. when she went down to the kitchen and made herself a cup of tea. Heather's sister-in-law heard the noise and got up as well. For the next hour the two of them would cuddle on the settee in tears in front of *BBC News 24* until Heather finally fell asleep.

The next morning Heather's brother, and Phil's friend, Jim, decided that he could not stand being around the house waiting for news of his mate any longer. He had to go and find him, dead or alive; the family needed to know. Armed with pictures of Phil and his passport, he travelled into the city and started making his way around London's hospitals with thousands of other worried families who were also carrying photographs and hopes.

Jim scoured the city with no clue of Phil's whereabouts until late into the evening of 8 July when he finally had a break. There was an unidentified male at the Royal London Hospital. The man's identity remained a mystery because all his clothes and personal identification had been blown from his body when he was sent crashing through the doors of a train 100 metres away from the platform at Aldgate station.

Jim rushed over to the Royal London Hospital and asked to speak to the nurse on the mystery man's ward. Phil had no scars or tattoos that would help but he did have a discoloured tooth and an unusual platinum wedding band. Jim told the nurse about both and then sat in the family waiting room for word. A few minutes later the nurse returned and told Jim he was in luck.

When he was led into Phil's room Jim only needed one look to see that his brother-in-law had survived. It was Phil. He was badly burned. His legs had been horribly injured by the bomb and he had lost an eye, but he had survived. Jim rushed to the phone to contact his sister.

'Heather?' Jim said. 'Yes, it is him. We've found him but he is badly injured. He has massive tissue damage to his lower legs. He has also lost an eye and is in critical but stable condition. They have him sedated for now.'

'It doesn't matter,' Heather said. 'At least he's got a chance.'

On Sunday morning, three days after the bombings had ravaged London, David Gardner woke in his bed at St Mary's, Paddington, to find his wife Angela sitting by his side holding his hand.

When Angela made it to the hospital she was told to wait with the families of others who had suffered injuries in the attacks until she could be assigned a family liaison officer from the Metropolitan Police. When the officer finally came into the room Angela was led down a series of corridors where she met the young doctor who had just finished operating on David.

'We have had to amputate David's left leg above the knee,' the doctor said. 'We have also removed his spleen. Your husband is in a stable condition in intensive care. Would you like to see him?'

When Angela walked into intensive care she was directed

to the first bed on the left. There was David. She could not recognise him: he was covered in bandages and burns. 'How can he look like that and still be alive?' Angela wondered.

'Can I touch him?' she asked.

The nurses nodded but made Angela wash her hands thoroughly first. She walked over to his bed, sat down and picked up David's hand. He was cold, but alive. Angela's family would need to be rebuilt, but it was still together.

Brian Morley had spent the night in London looking for his brother Colin. At first he went to King's Cross, hoping Colin was there. Then he started scouring the rest of the bomb sites looking for answers. The next morning Brian started hitting the hospitals desperate for news but everywhere he looked he came to a dead end. He somehow knew that his brother had died.

Ros, however, refused to give up hope. She had been calling the police since Thursday evening and by Friday afternoon two officers from Scotland Yard arrived to take a detailed description of Colin and to collect some DNA samples from the family home. Ros handed over Colin's toothbrush and told herself that everything was going to be fine.

All the signs were that Colin had died but Ros did not want to believe the worst. Colin was a good man. He had dedicated his life not only to improving himself, his mind and body, but to bringing about a better world. He was one of the founders of Be the Change, a movement which encourages people and organisations to advance themselves ethically, socially, environmentally and personally. He had to survive.

Ros maintained this hope until the Tuesday evening after the bombings when the two police officers from Scotland

Yard returned to her home with Colin's wallet, one of his book tokens and the security card he used to gain entrance to his offices in Milton Keynes. The police said that the family should not give up hope, that finding Colin's personal effects was no definitive proof he had died, but Ros had no such optimism. Her hope had collapsed.

The next evening the same officers returned to the Morley home for a third time, this time to confirm what Ros had already come to accept: Colin had been killed in the explosion at Edgware Road. He had apparently been standing very close to the bomber and had taken what the police told Ros was a 'major impact' to the face and chest.

Ros knew that her husband understood the risks of taking the tube in a time when Islamic terrorists were threatening to blow up the world around them. But she also knew that her husband believed deeply that life was for living, and not for being afraid. When the police officers left, and Ros was again alone with her three sons – Gavin had arrived from America the previous day – the four of them stayed in, ate together, and talked of the man they loved who had been so cruelly taken from them.

## Postscript

Two weeks later I was sitting in the sunshine by the water at Canary Wharf. It was just after 1.00 p.m. I was having lunch with three fellow reporters from the *Sunday Telegraph*. One of them was my friend Daniel Foggo, the man who'd sent me to the Family Records Centre near Farringdon two weeks earlier. It was that trip to pull documents for a story about a crooked policeman which had put me on the Circle Line on the morning of 7 July, but I didn't hold that against him.

We ordered our food but it had yet to come, so we chatted among ourselves. In the middle of our conversation Daniel's phone rang. It was the news desk. There had been a number of 'incidents' on the tube network at Warren Street, the Oval and Shepherd's Bush. A fourth was on a bus at Hackney Road. London, it was thought, was under attack again. The news editor wanted us to scramble to the four relevant locations as soon as possible. I was sent to Shepherd's Bush in west London.

'Are you all right to go?' Daniel asked.

'Yes of course I am, mate,' I said. 'I'm still a reporter.'

I might have sounded brave but I didn't feel it. Inside I was shaking. After the attacks I had come to believe 7 July was a one-off, a freak event, like 9/11. I guess it made me feel safer to think that way. If I didn't, if I thought there was going to be another set of bombs just two weeks later,

I don't know how I could have convinced myself to get back on the tube again, and I had to go back to work. I had a baby on the way and a family to support. So, two weeks later, on 21 July, I jumped into the back of a black cab and told the driver to take me across town.

As we left Canary Wharf in east London I put in a call to Donna, mindful that the mobile networks might go down again.

'Hi, darling,' I said. 'I am on my way to Shepherd's Bush. It looks like there has been another lot of bombings. They want me to cover it for the paper.'

Silence.

'Hello . . . Donna?'

I listened closely and could hear that she had started cry.

'What's wrong, darling? Are you okay?'

'What do you mean, am I okay?' she said. 'Two weeks ago you were almost killed and now you are going back for more. Of course I am not okay.'

'I am not going anywhere near the tunnel, even if there is no bomb,' I said. 'I am going to stand outside the station with the rest of the press pack and do the best I can from the other side of the police tape. There is nothing to worry about. The police won't be letting anyone near the stations.'

'Do whatever you want,' Donna said. 'I am going to my midwife's appointment for 3.00 p.m. I will talk to you later.'

'I love you,' I said.

'Yeah,' Donna replied.

I could understand why she was worried. A year before the bombings I had been given the chance to go to Iraq with the British Army to cover the war for the *Ottawa Citizen*, my old paper in Canada, for which I still occasionally string from London. I was excited. Iraq was the story of the moment. But when I told Donna she started crying straightaway, as if I had just turned a switch that let her tears flow free. The trip was eventually cancelled because of an administrative cock-up, but the reaction I got from Donna back then was exactly the same as when I told her I was off to Shepherd's Bush. I felt bad about upsetting her, especially as she was so heavily pregnant, but I needed to go back to work; not only because my job depended on it but because I was a journalist and that is what journalists did.

The journey across London was strange. There was traffic on the roads but no one was honking their horns. Everyone was just waiting patiently. The tube had been evacuated again and the pavements were chockful of pedestrians standing around in a daze. Normally the pavements in central London are a river of fast-flowing people, all pushing to get one step ahead of the person next to them. But on 21 July, people were just standing still, as if they were waiting for the end of the world.

When I got to Shepherd's Bush my assumptions about what I would find were proved right. Everything was cordoned off by yellow police tape. No one was getting anywhere near the station. I spent the next hour and a half walking back and forth trying to find someone who had been on the train but I wasn't having any luck.

It quickly became obvious that 21 July was no 7 July. Two weeks before, the injured were flooding up to street level by this time, covered in soot and blood, screaming at the horror they'd endured. But at Shepherd's Bush two weeks later everyone who emerged from the tunnels appeared to be unharmed. No ambulances were rushing off to hospital. London had been spared.

Four men did in fact try to blow up three trains and a bus that lunchtime but the bombs they used, although similar to those used two weeks before, for some reason failed to explode. No one had died. No one would die. The nightmare was not to be repeated. As this became obvious to those of us outside the station I began to feel relieved. Then I got a phone call that changed everything.

'Donna, hi. I tried to call you but you didn't pick up,' I said.

'I am in hospital,' Donna said. 'My blood pressure is really high and they are going to induce me.'

'Really?' I said.

'Yes, you need to come right away.'

I put the phone down and called the news desk to tell them I was leaving. They wished me luck and I walked away from the scene of the attempted bombing, excited and confused. Two weeks before I had witnessed death for the first time. Now I was about to witness the beginning of a new life. It was a strange juxtaposition of emotional states: desolation and delight.

Two days later, just after 6.00 p.m. on Saturday 23 July, Anja Olivia Zimonjic was, finally, born, a very healthy little girl.

I was a father. Donna was a mother. We were a family.

The midwife put Anja on the scales and told me how much she weighed in kilos.

'What's that in pounds?' I asked.

'Let's see,' she said. 'That is seven pounds, seven ounces.'

'Seven seven?' I asked.

'Yes, seven seven,' she replied.

## Acknowledgements

The day after the 7 July attacks I wrote an account of the London bombings for the *Sunday Telegraph*. A passenger, Andrew Ferguson, recognised himself from my story and contacted the paper. We met up for a beer and had a good chat. It was easy to talk not because of what we said but because of what we didn't have to say. Neither of us had to try and explain to one another, as we had been trying to explain to our families for days on end, just what it was like. We began from the point of knowing what it was to be in the darkness that day and moved forward from there.

After our meeting I decided it would be good if other people could have the same chance to share a drink with someone they may have crossed paths with on the day. Because the tube is such a public place, however, this presented a problem; no one knew one another. To bridge this gap I started a website called London Recovers. It was not meant to be group therapy online; there were no meetings, no membership cards. It was just a networking site intended to help fellow survivors put a human face back into what was a very inhuman day.

By November of 2005 I had given out passwords for the secure forums on London Recovers to over 200 people. Whenever someone wrote to me to ask for access to the site they would invariably include a long and vivid description of the day. Mostly though, people wanted to know if I could put them in touch with someone they met, someone who held their hand, shared an embrace or a comforting word with them in the darkness of the tunnels. More than half of the people writing to me were too timid to post their experiences on the forums and simply asked me to let them know if I found anyone they were looking for. I did my best, but it was big job.

Trawling through the e-mails one day it occurred to me that if these stories were cross-referenced and compared to official reports on the bombings I might be somewhere near a definitive account of the day. At first I thought it would make a good series of articles for either the *Sunday Telegraph* or the *Ottawa Citizen* but my friend and colleague at the *Sunday Telegraph*, Daniel Foggo, convinced me to pursue this idea as a book. It wouldn't be perfect, there were too many people involved for me to ever write a story that would please everyone, but it would go some way towards answering the questions posed by the survivors who wrote to me. I also hoped that writing this book would preserve, for everyone who was affected by the bombings, the human side of an event that has since become heavily politicised.

Many of the users of London Recovers agreed to be interviewed for this book, many did not. Through the network of survivors that started building in the year after the attacks word spread of what I was doing and people started coming forward with offers to help. Other people I had to search for and convince, over a long period of careful negotiation, to agree to be interviewed. This book was only possible because a great number of those people were brave enough to share the worst day of their lives with a total stranger. Asking someone to relive, in intense detail, the day they lost their husband or sister or even their mental health is never easy. I am grateful for the trust that people had in me and this project, especially as the events of the day, and the scars they left behind were, in many cases, still very fresh. I will be eternally grateful for the bravery shown by the victims of these bombings during the interviews I conducted for this book.

Many of the people I interviewed agreed to be named but a significant number of others, while they were happy to tell me their stories in the context of research for my book, wished to remain nameless and I have respected those wishes. The following is a list of the passengers and family members of the victims who did agree to be named in the book and whom I would like to thank publicly for their contribution:

Lizzie Kenworthy, Terry Hiscock, Lesley Watson, Trevor Rodgers, Fiona Crosbie, Mel Finn, Emma Brown, Ian Webb, Robert Webb, Gary Fitzgerald, Alan Dell, Ben Cotton, Kathy Lazenbatt, Jason Rennie, Jacqui Putnam, Rachel North, Michael Henning, Sarah Pellatt, Loyita Worley, Jonathan Fairclough, Carrie-Ann Rhodes, Laura Morris, Paul Bardwell, Judy Mallinson, Dave Taurus, Clair Hearn, Andy Barr, Ray Whitehurst, Natalie Murray, Rhian Jones, Andrew Ferguson, John Nabdoo, Danny Biddle, Tim Coulson, Charles Meaden, Steve Huckelsby, Susanna Pell, John Parkinson, David Gardner, Angela Gardner, Joanne Gittins, Ros Morley, Andrea Calvitti, Ben Thwaites, Chris Stones, Steve Goszka, Peter Tollington, Paul Coote, Alan King, Simon Cook, Phil Duckworth, Heather Duckworth, Tope Teniola, Lesley Ratcliff, Bob Cleary, Celia Harrison, Steve Eldridge, Elizabeth Owen, Roger Matthews, Paul Mitchell, Natalie Whitney, Samantha Lott.

I would also like to thank Allan Ramsay from London Underground. He is living proof to any working journalist that press officers can be helpful, insightful and willing to work with a reporter with a genuine story to tell. Without Allan I would not have had the unprecedented access to London Underground's control rooms, stations, trains, documents and staff that made this book what it is.

Aside from passengers and London Underground staff I spoke with a number of members of the security and police services who provided me with off the record clarifications and information under the condition they remained unidentified. While I can't name them I would still like to thank them for speaking to me despite the inherent career risks our conversations entailed.

It would be unfair to thank so many people without mentioning Christian Wolmar who I would like to thank for helping me work through the more technical parts of this manuscript. His book *The Subterranean Railway* is a brilliant history of the London Underground that is interesting, well researched and surprisingly gripping considering the subject matter. Anyone who wants to challenge their ideas about the tube should read this book.

I would also like to thank David Godwin for believing in me from the start and for convincing Jason Arthur and Rachel Cugnoni at Vintage to do the same. I would like to thank my editor Beth Coates for seeing this book through to the end despite all my rambling questions and demanding requests. I would also like to thank Richard Collins for helping to eliminate embarrassing errors during the editing process. Any which remain are mine.

And finally I would like to thank my family, beginning with my wife Donna who was and is my first editor. Donna was my muse and my conscience throughout. Had it not been for the careful instructions of her big red pen I would have produced a far lesser work. And while they can't quite read yet, I would like to thank my daughter Anja and son Jakob for unknowingly reminding me of what's truly important in the wake of such a terrible day. No man is poor who has family.

## A Note on Sources

There were a number of government reports produced in the wake of the 7 July bombings. Some were better than others but I found the best by far was the London Assembly Report. While it could have been broader it remained the closest thing to a definitive document detailing everything from the human tragedy to the technical challenges of managing the rescue effort of such an attack.

Most of the interviews for this book were conducted face to face and often took several sittings to complete. It is my practice to hand-write my notes which meant my interviews took longer than they should. I have only the patience of my subjects to thank for allowing me to operate as a journalist in the way I feel most comfortable.

Because there were so many people involved in the London bombings it would be impossible to represent the events of the day as they were experienced by everyone who was there. As such I have, in all but a few cases, tried to only include events and speech in this book that could be verified by two or more sources. There were inherent challenges to this. Because it was impossible to communicate by radio or telephone between the tunnels and the surface there were no phone records, text messages, radio transcripts or phone messages to help guide my research. People's state of mind during the attacks was also a consideration that had to be balanced against the facts. Whenever there was any doubt about the veracity of a given detail it was eliminated to ensure overall accuracy.

Peter Zimonjic, London 2007

www.vintage-books.co.uk